D1039492

ENERGY
SECRETS

Alla Svirinskaya

ENERGY SECRETS

THE ULTIMATE
WELL-BEING PLAN

Dedication

To my parents, Galina and Roman,
with my deepest love and admiration.

First published and distributed in the United Kingdom by:
Hay House UK Ltd, 292B Kensal Rd, London W10 5BE. Tel.: (44) 20 8962
1230; Fax: (44) 20 8962 1239. www.hayhouse.co.uk

Published and distributed in the United States of America by:
Hay House, Inc., PO Box 5100, Carlsbad, CA 92018-5100. Tel.: (1) 760 431
7695 or (800) 654 5126; Fax: (1) 760 431 6948 or (800) 650 5115.
www.hayhouse.com

Published and distributed in Australia by:
Hay House Australia Ltd, 18/36 Ralph St, Alexandria NSW 2015. Tel.: (61) 2
9669 4299; Fax: (61) 2 9669 4144. www.hayhouse.com.au

Published and distributed in the Republic of South Africa by:
Hay House SA (Pty), Ltd, PO Box 990, Witkoppen 2068. Tel./Fax: (27) 11
467 8904. www.hayhouse.co.za

Published and distributed in India by:
Hay House Publishers India, Muskaan Complex, Plot No.3, B-2, Vasant Kunj,
New Delhi – 110 070. Tel.: (91) 11 4176 1620; Fax: (91) 11 4176 1630.
www.hayhouse.co.in

Distributed in Canada by:
Raincoast, 9050 Shaughnessy St, Vancouver, BC V6P 6E5. Tel.: (1) 604 323
7100; Fax: (1) 604 323 2600

A catalogue record for this book is available from the British Library.

ISBN 978-1-8485-0206-2

Printed and bound in Great Britain by TJ International, Padstow, Cornwall.

Contents

Foreword

I offered to write this foreword to Alla Svirinskaya's book because I would like to support her exceptional healing work. I hope to draw attention to both her knowledge and the extraordinary Russian heritage of healing into which she was born.

I believe that Alla was one of the first people to make these traditions available to the West. I hope that her ideas and techniques will be very useful to all those people who are seeking better health and a greater sense of well-being.

Alla has been a tremendous help in guiding me in all aspects of my physical and emotional well-being. Whenever I go to see her, she recharges my energy and enables me to cope with the many challenges and demands of my busy life. She offers me sound practical advice that I'm sure would make sense to anyone who is struggling to find time to focus on their health in the midst of a hectic lifestyle.

I have always found Alla to be a very positive and inspiring person. I hope that this book will be helpful for all those people who might not have the opportunity to work with her directly.

I have no doubt that Alla is a remarkable practitioner and I consider myself very fortunate to know her.

Sarah,

Sarah, Duchess of York

Acknowledgements

To my dear mum: I am blessed to have you in my life. It is an honour to be your daughter and your student. Everything I am is thanks to you. Your hands and heart are extraordinary in their readiness to help and channel love to all around you.

To my dear dad: thank you for our special bond. The humour and the laughter we share are my life's healer. I admire you for always keeping true to yourself and never compromising your integrity.

To my lovely sister Ritochka: thank you simply for just being you. You are my little lovely ray of sunshine.

And of course, to my sweet angel, my daughter Raphaela: thank you for being so patient and quiet, while I was writing this book. I hope that one day you will share my passion for healing. I love you more than I thought it possible to love someone. You made me a better person and a better healer. Thank you for coming into my world.

Also a huge thank you to each member of my family and my relatives: you have all brought so much light into my soul.

I am very fortunate to have met some special people in my life, who I also would like to acknowledge and send them all my love.

To my dear friend, Sarah, a big thank you for your support and encouragement. I am grateful and honoured.

To my lovely Russian friends, Nina Koroleva, Lena Ayzenberg and Irina Rudneva, for our friendship, fun and great memories. I miss you, girls! To Kati Stclair for always being there for me, for your uniqueness, wisdom and love. To Andrew Wilson for being a very special person in my life. To Rita Roberts for your care and warmth. I will always be grateful to all the people who believed in me, gave me support and showed me great kindness at the beginning of my western journey. I remember all of you.

A huge thank you to my agent Jonny Pegg for your generosity with your time, support and for being on the same wavelength with me.

To everybody at Hay House, thank you for being my book's guardian angels. I am so impressed with your style of work and your unique blend of spirituality, integrity and pragmatism.

To Dennis Engel and his team for their wonderful creative energy and for setting up my website.

To Jane Alexander for all your input.

To Olivia Lichtenstein, I can't thank you enough for helping me to bring this book into the world. I greatly value your constant support of my healing practice.

I also would like to express my gratitude and respect to the generations of Russian healers whose techniques I am proud to include in my book. I am sorry if some of your names were not handed down to me together with your teachings, but I am sure they live in a different form through your work. I am humbled to be able to carry and pass on your knowledge.

And finally, a big thank you to Life for lining up such an interesting journey for me!

My Story

I was born and raised in the 1970s in Moscow during the time of communist Russia. So I grew up in a country that was very pro-materialistic and anti-religion, in fact anti-anything remotely metaphysical.

My family is a curious mix of the scientific and the alternative. My mother used to be a chemotherapist, working with cancer patients, but she is also a healer. Before his retirement, my father was a scientist, with a PhD in engineering. I have a sister who is eleven years older than me, who is also a healer – she lives in Serbia.

Healing has been a part of my family for many generations, at least five generations that we can count. It always seems to come through the female side and, over the generations, we have used different variations of healing. I didn't know my grandmother but she apparently used a lot of herbs and also the special kind of Russian chanting we call *zagovor*. My mother's healing is different, relying on an awareness of the aura, the chakras and so forth. Everything I learned was passed on to me by my mother and by my older sister.

At the time I was growing up, the idea of practising healing openly was quite inconceivable. My mother would have loved to have been able to come out openly and work at her clinic as a healer but it was totally impossible. However, in a strange way, this worked to my benefit. Patients my mother met in the clinic who were interested in alternatives would have to come to our home for their healing. So, as a very little girl, I had the chance to observe all that was happening. I watched the way my mother treated, the way she interacted with the patients – healing was around me at all the time.

From a very young age I started asking questions. "Mama, why do I have these sensations in my hands?" "Mama, why am I sensing things this way?" My mother knew, of course, but she didn't want to push me into healing. She wanted to watch for my natural talent, she wanted to see it tested in some way and she wanted to guide me. So she started by letting me watch and experience the way she worked. She explained about auras and chakras and I learned about them along with my alphabet!

Then, as I grew, she would invite me to feel energy in her patients. She would show me how different frequencies would indicate the way a person's energy was flowing. So healthy organs would resonate at certain frequencies, while illness would change the wavelength of the vibrations. As a little girl I had to memorise all those frequencies and how they felt in the body. My mother would be working with a patient and she would say, "Alla, come here and go above this stomach with your hand. Remember these sensations in your hand. This is what a healthy stomach should feel like." Then she would call me into another patient who would have a tumour or some other problem and ask me what I sensed in my hand. She would then say: "You must remember this. This is what a disease feels like." I read the vibrations of the body with my fingers, just as a blind person reads in Braille. It's literally just like a code. Because I was trained like that, I can recognise those frequency signatures on my own patients.

I was also taught from a very early age about how you have to look after yourself. How, if you want to stay a pure channel for energy, you have to look after your physical health. My mother and sister both regularly fasted. They taught me early on how to look after my colon, how to look after my liver and kidneys. I learned how to look after myself on all levels.

I grew up in a very open house. It was impossible at that time for people to meet and talk about healing or spiritual matters in public. So a lot of amazing healers and parapsychologists would come to our house. Our kitchen would be full of people drinking tea, eating, and talking. They would share their ideas and their experiences. It was so precious to me to be in middle of it, such an honour to meet these people and to absorb their knowledge. We had no chance to read spiritual books because they were banned, so information was passed around secretly, on pieces of paper. It was good for my development as a spiritual person to be surrounded by people like that. I think in a way it gave me a lot of strength; it taught me how to stay true to your path, even when it is difficult.

At that time spiritual teaching was against the law in Russia. Everything was kept hush-hush and passed down quietly. So my training as a healer and my learning about esoteric knowledge had to be secret, undercover if you like.

I followed my mother into medicine and went to medical school in Moscow. It was during the time of *perestroika*, yet at first there was still huge resistance to the concept of healing and any form of alternative or complementary medicine. However, it did slowly start to change. People were so disillusioned with communism. Suddenly all their idols had vanished. People become lost and so started to turn to God and their more spiritual side to find comfort. At last the old Russian tradition of healing re-emerged. That allowed me to study more openly, at other schools of healing, and I travelled a lot while I was doing my medical degree. As part of this I was able to go to the Open University for Complementary Medicine, based in Sri Lanka, to study acupuncture. I combined this alternative training with my orthodox studies. In my heart I always knew I would follow my healing path.

The fall of the communist party made it possible for my mother and myself to practise healing openly for the first time. So my mother left the clinic she had worked in and, alongside other healer colleagues, set up one of the first centres for healing in Moscow. It was around that time that I decided to terminate my medical training.

However, my years at medical school were incredibly useful as they gave me a good background in traditional orthodox medicine, its understanding of the body and also what is available from orthodox medicine to treat illnesses. I think it gives me a more balanced outlook on people's problems.

I do send my patients to orthodox doctors when I think this would be the most appropriate solution. I also often refer patients to other practitioners of complementary medicine if I feel that would be helpful. It's a holistic approach. I believe in teamwork between all kinds of medicine – be it orthodox, nutritional, psychotherapy or healing.

I first came to Britain in the early 1990s. It was very difficult at that time to build a practice as a healer in the United Kingdom. Even though other forms of natural therapy, such as osteopathy, were becoming accepted, everybody was far more doubtful about healing. People would make sceptical comments about my abilities as a healer or about "energy" in general. The only way I could respond was to suggest they should learn about my subject first, and then form an opinion. It seems wrong to me to reject something purely on the basis of preconceived ideas.

The first centre that opened its doors to me was The Life Centre. Its founder (and former owner) Louise White had initially been cautious about employing a healer; however, her vision and open-mindedness allowed me to introduce her to the power of healing. She was able to see the huge benefits of energy balancing and, ten years on, she still regularly pops in to see me. I am also pleased to say that soon she will be a fellow healer too, as she is currently training with the National Federation of Spiritual Healers.

Although, in the United Kingdom, people were allowed to study esoteric things legally, they were still conditioned not to accept it. So, even though healing was allowed in a political sense, they were unwilling to open up their minds because of their preconceptions about healing. For me it was a familiar situation. Again, I think my early experiences helped me. I was inspired and encouraged by all those people in Russia who had kept their beliefs in spite of such opposition. They helped me to stay strong.

When I started out, people would come to me in secret; they wouldn't even tell their partners. Journalists who wanted to write about my healing work found their editors were scared about what their advertisers would say and about the thought of floods of sceptical letters. I already had a busy practice, due to word of mouth recommendation, when the first media recognition came from *Harpers & Queen* magazine, which decided to run a story about my work, inspired by the impact my healing had had on people. They gave me the first public support. I asked their editor Fiona Macpherson if she was not concerned about negative outbursts but she simply replied: "Healing is real and the results are very tangible. People must know about it." I always will be grateful to her and also to the lovely journalist Kate Bernard for standing by my side and for helping me to change people's perceptions of myself and my healing work. Now I run my own healing practice in London. I prefer to work on my own, in a quiet low-key way.

I am aware that I have been blessed with a wonderful gift. I also have a very pragmatic side, which I get from my father. He's a very down-to-earth man but at the same time he honours and supports our healing gifts. My family are not religious. Nowadays, in Russia the majority of healing practices are linked to religion so you have to pray, you have to be baptised, you have to be confirmed. We have never been like that. But, although we are not religious, we are very much spiritual people. My healing, however, does not come from any religious belief.

How do I heal? I channel pure, received energy. I don't treat people with my own energy. That is really important to understand. It's not *my* energy. If you use your own energy not only are you killing yourself to help others (by losing your own vital energy) but also you run the risk of giving them your "stuff" along with the healing. You're not really helping them, as it simply isn't pure energy. My training taught me how to connect with a higher source of energy and channel it through me.

My style of healing now is very different from the way I healed in the early 1990s. It is something that constantly evolves. As you develop as a healer you develop your own signature. When I started out I was like my mother in the way I worked. But now, although my healing is still based on the foundation of what I learned from my mother and sister, it is very much my own style. We have all developed our own techniques but we share our successes. My sister will write or call to tell me about something that worked wonderfully for her, and my mother still gives me advice. It's an exciting process.

When I heal my patients it's not a purely passive process. They have to play a part too; they have to take responsibility for themselves, their bodies, and their emotions. Healing is also learning about boundaries, about protection: not just how to protect yourself (although that is vital) but also how to respect other people's space. This is what I teach to my patients. I also make it clear that the key for healing is to be aware of moderation in all things: how you eat, how you communicate with people, how you spend your energy, how you spend your time. You mustn't overdo it. I teach people to recognise their own limitations and those of other people.

My mother taught me that there is no end to how much you can master yourself. Through her, I learned that life is very much a creative process: you should never stop learning; you should constantly be doing new things. It's about being in control and having a constant desire to master yourself still further. That is when you feel like a true creator.

The idea for this book came when I was pregnant with my child. I took one year's leave from my practice because the kind of healing I use is incompatible with pregnancy. I used some of my extra time to give talks, explaining about energy and the way it affects us. People kept asking if I had written, or was going to write, a book. They wanted to know more about my culture, our traditions and our healing. Also, I became aware there is so little known in the West about the Russian tradition of healing. You can go to Western bookshops and find hundreds of books on yoga and ayurveda, yet there is none on the Eastern European tradition of healing. I felt very strongly that that was a pity and it should be corrected. In Russia we have amazing healers who are so well known for their techniques at home, who help to change the lives of thousands of Russians, and yet their guidance is not known to the wider world.

So in this book I have made an attempt to share some of their techniques, to help Western people.

The second reason was that, while I was not practising, there were still many of my patients who needed guidance. I devised programmes for them to follow on their own, at home. Based on my experience as a healer I knew exactly which recipes would work and which wouldn't. The results, I'm pleased to say, were wonderful. I have a very straight-forward approach, even when I deal with energy and meta-physical matters and people responded very well to my down-to-earth methods.

My aim with this book is to share with you my knowledge, my secrets and insights. In the past this was available only to my patients; now I would like to make this knowledge more widely known and used in the hope it will touch as many people as possible. Think of it as a form of distant healing.

Introduction

My deepest, most passionate wish is to see all human beings making the most of their lives. As a fifth generation healer I have inherited a knowledge of profound techniques that can help people bring their bodies, minds and emotions to optimum balance. Yet I have only so many hours in the day, so many patients I can humanly see. I wrote this book because I wanted to make these powerful energy secrets available to everyone; I wanted to share my programme for total health. The techniques in this book are the ones I teach my patients. They are incredibly powerful and they have superb results – if you follow them carefully.

I use the word "secrets" purposefully, as I think it's safe to say that many of the techniques in this book have not before been released in the West. On the other hand, you may well find that other concepts, such as auras and chakras, will be familiar to you from other cultures.

The Russian approach to knowledge: absorb and adapt

I would like to explain a little about the mental attitude of the Russian people so you can understand the way I work. Every country, every region has a different way of thinking, different cultures and different traditions. Every nation has, if you like, a collective consciousness – a way of looking at life, a way of sensing life.

In Russia, we generally have an eclectic, holistic, collective philosophy and way of thinking.

In the West, people have tended (in the past) to live where they were born, to explore a small part of their native land, to create stability and firm traditions. Russians are different. Our people have always been a transient people. We Russians are always packing our bags and going somewhere else: historically we have a transient culture. It's always been like that. Because our land was so vast, Russians would constantly move from one area to another. Almost every new generation started somewhere new; we were always on the move. New land, new political climate; always change, always going to the crossroads.

The road is a potent symbol of Russian life. In Russian folklore all things happen on the road. So we have no problem with accepting and integrating ideas and concepts from other lands, such as India and China – it comes naturally to us to take knowledge and integrate it, usually adapting it for our own use. It's also important to mention that at the beginning of the thirteenth century, we were invaded by the Mongols and the Tartars and lived under them. Inevitably we were exposed to their doctrines and learned from them.

So the Russian soul acquired a polycultural perspective and consolidated its ability to accept, absorb, transform and then to teach this new transformed information. We take things from everywhere around us. The *matryoshka* doll, for example, came originally from Japan! The Russian churches and temples that seem so archetypically Russian with their domed basilicas actually come from old Byzantium.

So a great many of the concepts I talk about in my work come from the East, as well as from Russia. Sometimes the two are intermingled. For example, the Slavic people used the word *yar* to describe their life force.

It is the same concept as the Chinese *qi* or the Indian *prana*. Although in the Russian tradition we did not have specific words for the chakras, we accepted that certain emotions were linked with different parts of our bodies. It's a universal thing.

What is good health?

Good health is one of the most important treasures in our lives. Yet how many of us truly appreciate our health? Very few, unless, of course, we lose it or have problems with it. It never ceases to amaze me just how cavalier we humans are with regard to our bodies. Humans created electricity, the aeroplane and satellites. We have discovered the secrets of the atom and unravelled the genetic code. The creativity of the human mind seemingly knows no limits. It appears we have managed to change everything – except ourselves! Despite all our knowledge, all our civilisation and technology, we people still do not know how to control our own selves. Equally we seem incapable of working out how to live peacefully in harmony with one another, with nature, with the world around us. We simply do not know how to be healthy.

Our civilisation has concentrated solely on mastering our external environment, on subduing nature. The result has led to a huge increase in ecological problems. Our toxic load is now huge, and increasing all the time. We are polluting, not only the world, but also our own bodies. Technical progress has brought us not only enormous comfort but also at the same time ecological illnesses. It has slowed down the spiritual development of our personalities, numbed our intuition and dulled the sharpness of our senses. We humans have pushed ourselves away from nature and we have ignored the laws of harmonious development. Now we are paying the price. Many of our modern diseases are the result of the balance being broken between our external environment and ourselves. We are out of touch with our world, out of touch with other people, out of touch with our own intrinsic selves. True healthy evolution should start from personal strength and a strong belief in one's unlimited possibilities and resources. I have to agree with the famous author Leo Tolstoy, who is renowned in Russia, not just as a great author, but also for his wisdom. He cautioned humankind with these words:

"It is amusing that people will smoke, drink, overeat, be lazy and turn night into day, yet still expect the doctor to keep them healthy."

The truth of these words is especially important now that we are in an era of ecological and spiritual crisis. We have become lazy. We expect doctors or healers to "fix" us, without any effort on our part. But the very best doctor, the most talented healer cannot cure unless you, the patient, choose to take part in your healing. You have to decide to become actively involved in discovering your own spiritual resources. This isn't always simple. It can even be quite difficult or challenging, particularly because it often involves rethinking your entire way of life, making deep changes to your habits and lifestyle. Many people nowadays live to excess: we all need to eat, drink and sleep but what is vitally important is to learn moderation, not to indulge anything to excess.

We live in a culture in which we believe there will be a pill for every illness. We have pills to dampen every symptom our bodies throw up. We have pills to dull every negative emotion that begs us to pay attention. Yes, pills can help stave off illness and sometimes cure it.

However, true therapy, true healing is preventative medicine – it should be our way of life. What we do not understand is that our healing lies within. We are so totally converted into the belief of medical power that we do not understand that, in so many cases, our own intuition can do much more. Programming our minds, our intrinsic selves can empower us to become our own healers, our own doctors, our own creators. You can achieve this only by activating and honouring your own inner healing powers.

On the other hand, we are equally capable, if we are not careful, to programme ourselves into helplessness, into sickness, into disempowerment. A famous Russian doctor, Dr Nikolay M. Amosov, once said:

> *"There are people who are cultivating their own illnesses, enjoying and nurturing them. They pull their friends and relatives into their world of suffering. That's their way of life: always complaining about their destiny and not to live, but only surviving. But we must live. We need to find for ourselves our own way of life and style of life. Should people remain slaves to their piteous bodies and their temptations?"*

In Russia, the word for "cure" is *'iscelenie'*, which has the same root as the word for "whole". The old Russian healers, like those from the ancient cultures of India and China, put their faith in the pure genius of their intuition, coupled with thousands of years of inherited experience. Like them, I think that the purpose of life is a discovery of the correct and harmonious attitude towards life and nature. Happiness comes when people find their place in life and resonate harmoniously with their outside world. Sadly, so many people are running after a ghost life. They live in fear and anger, propelled, as Dr Amosov says, by their own temptations.

Spiritual evolution – the new age?

There is, at present, a hoard of literature that talks about spiritual evolution. The whole new age movement calls on us to take on a more spiritual way of life. Yet it is impossible to talk about spiritual evolution until we have cleansed ourselves inside out, and also liberated ourselves from the unbalanced style of our lives. Think about it. How could a musician, even a true genius, ever expect to express him or herself fully on a badly tuned instrument? Our bodies are exactly the same. Until we bring the body into order, it cannot be the instrument of our spirit.

A healing system, in my opinion, can only heal the body and maintain it in good form when the therapy affects us, both on a physical and on an energetic level. The two are entwined – together they make a unity that cannot break. This is why it is essential for any healing process to combine the physical, emotional and mental essences of our being.

In fact, you have to go one step even further. To be truly healthy you have to heal your soul.

So, while we should not glibly talk about spiritual evolution, we do need to work towards our spiritual development. Good heath is not merely the final result; it is a vital part of the process. It's very difficult to cure an illness of the body without changing your attitude to life for the positive. In the course of this book you will learn why it is so important to gain control over your negative emotions of anger, jealousy, hatred and envy. Not everyone is psychologically ready to accept a complex attitude towards his or her health, but I suspect that – if you have been drawn to this book – then you probably *are* ready. There is a saying: "When the student is ready, the teacher appears." In a similar way I believe we are given information only when we are psychically ready to receive it. My aim in this book is to offer my approach towards complete physical, psychological and spiritual health.

A state of inner harmony is a fragile thing and one that is very much affected by internal and external influences. One needs to identify what these influences might be and learn how to control and master them. In the modern world, it's hard for us to accept new ways of being – we are so conditioned by the society in which we live and, particularly in the past hundred years, to achieving our economic goals. There are many pressures on us to sacrifice self-development at the altar of material success. In these conditions jobs, houses and the acquisition of material benefits can claim an unhealthy dominance over our lives.

Perhaps governments have found it easier to control and direct a world driven by materialism rather than encouraging individuals to become self-realised and in tune with their real needs and desires. Ultimately, more and more of us are concluding that holding a purely materialistic view of the world is a dead end. We all crave a richer and more fulfilling experience of life but we don't recognise the energy essence of it. As a result, we are in a prison of our own making and, as we seek for control over our lives, we scuttle from cell to cell in a false bid for freedom. Unless we recognise the importance of energy in ourselves and in the world, we will fail to find the door to real freedom, let alone open it.

The purpose of this book is to enable you to create a different life for yourself and to understand and be aware of all the forces that can influence you. History books the world over are full of tales of miraculous healing. As I have already shared with you, I come from a family of healers. We have helped people for generations and I "read" the energy of my patients and enable them to channel it more healthily.

This book will give you a complete programme, a total manual to help you become master of your own health and well-being. This will involve finding balance on the physical, mental and emotional levels. It will also address matters such as harmony with our environment, our families, our homes and our friends.

Unlike many books on health and healing, I do not start with cleansing the physical body. I start by explaining to you the importance of your energetic body – in fact, the many many subtle layers of energy that surround your body and run through it. At first this may seem very strange and possibly even unsettling. But I would ask you to bear with me, to keep an open mind, and trust that the techniques I show you will have a huge effect on your life.

How to use this book

As I have already said, I am a very pragmatic person. I test out every technique thoroughly and I use those that work, consistently, time after time. Every technique, every ritual, every meditation, every recipe in this book has been included because it works.

If you want to get the best results, if you truly want to heal yourself, and change your life, you will need to commit to the process. You have to have 100 per cent commitment. Otherwise, quite simply, it does not work. I am a hands-on practitioner. I haven't just read a few books and run a few courses. I use these techniques each and every day and I know what works and what doesn't. When you don't have 100 per cent input, you just don't have the same results. It just won't work. It's like when people try to get fit – and they are so proud of themselves because they go once a week to the gym. It's not good enough. They can kid themselves but to get the benefit, it will take them forever because they are not doing the proper programme. It's the same here. It's not a case of half-measures.

It is also impossible to build up a healthy spirit, to have a light emotional and mental energy, if your physical body is toxic. Equally you cannot embark on a new start for your life or a new plan for your well-being if your home and your environment are polluted and heavy.

I recognise that I am expecting a great deal from you: there is a great deal of information in this book. I would advise you to start at the beginning and work carefully through. Don't be tempted to glide over the exercises or to miss out certain sections. This is an entire programme – it simply won't have the same affect if you pick and choose what you fancy doing. You really do need to commit. I realise that the majority of readers are busy people and so I have given plenty of alternatives, some much easier than others. Practise the exercises with an open mind. In fact, if you find yourself baulking at an exercise or thinking "no way", then be especially aware. We often shy away from those things that we most need and it could well be that this is exactly the exercise you need. However, as I am always trying to coax you into a better understanding of your own intuition, I would like you to pay attention to any "gut" feelings you get. If something feels uncomfortable, check with yourself: it may be that you need to work through the uncomfortable feeling, or equally your intuition could be telling you that this isn't right for you at this moment.

Please don't be tempted to skip the early "theory" sections of the book either. It's important to understand how energy works. Also, tempting though it is to head straight for the physical detox, please do practise the house clearing first and, above all, follow the preparation for cleansing week – or you will overload your body. These are very powerful, stringent cleansings and you need to follow the preparatory exercises before tackling them. Once you have completed the house clearing and physical detox, I will be less strict and prescriptive – I promise! This is because, by then, your intuition will be working in better order and I can trust that you will be able to choose wisely and well.

! I would advise you to check with your doctor or physician before undergoing this programme or any of the elements in it. If you are in good health, you should be fine but it's always best to be quite sure. If you have any health concerns or are taking any medication, it's absolutely essential you check with your doctor or specialist. Some of the recipes, techniques and therapies

need caution (or to be avoided) if you have particular health challenges – where possible, I have included alternatives. But, if you are in any doubt, ask your doctor.

Pregnant women and people under 18 years of age should not undergo the programme.

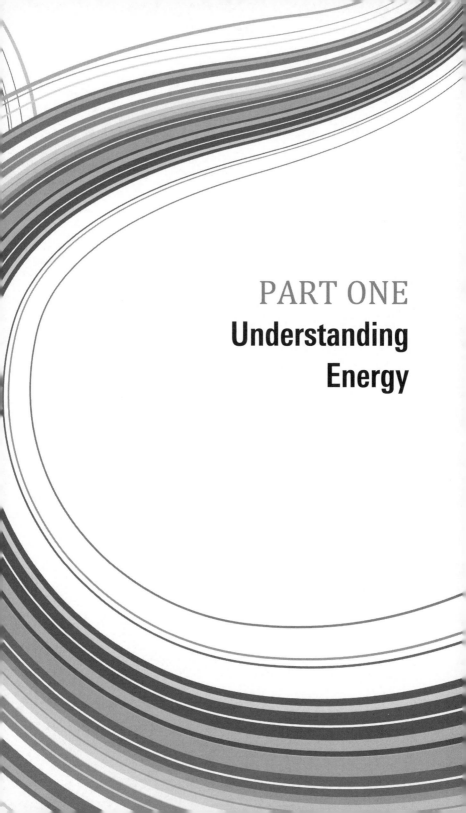

PART ONE
Understanding Energy

CHAPTER ONE

The Importance of Energy

An understanding of energy and how it relates to us is vital for the healing we are going to undertake in this book. You probably know a little about energy in everyday life. Most of us are aware (from all the endless diet books and magazine features) that we take in energy in the form of calories and expend energy by living, breathing, exercising. You might have come across the idea of chi, vital energy, in a vague way through *feng shui* or acupuncture. Yet, for our purposes, we need a much more sophisticated understanding of energy.

Einstein described matter as a form of energy. Everything is made up of molecules and molecules consist of atoms that are in a permanent state of flux. Their movement gives off energy. Hence everything – a human, a dog, a tree, a table, a stone – is giving off energy. Everything in our world is vibrating with energy.

So, if even static objects are giving off energy, imagine the energy given off by all living things. Think about the energy given off by us human beings. Energy is the be all and end all of life, the key to existence. Imagine, for a moment, that your body were a taxi. If you want it to take you somewhere, or to do or achieve something, you have to tell the driver where to go. Now imagine that the driver is your energy. If you talk to the car, you won't get anywhere; you need to address the driver directly.

So the reason we keep failing to achieve either health or fulfilment in life (or both!) is because the vast majority of us aren't talking to the right part of ourselves. We simply haven't worked out who's the boss!

The idea of yourself as an energy being might be tough to take and you might already be puzzled, thinking that you have certainly never experienced your energy field. You're not alone. Most of us simply don't have the tools to recognise our energy field. We simply haven't been taught to recognise it and understand it. Our culture is very materialistic – it recognises the physical and not much else, certainly not energy. It's just not how we live our lives. We have been conditioned not to understand and the power of conditioning is much greater than many of us realise. Let me give you an example to make it clear. Picture the following experiment – it's rather unpleasant but it does demonstrate the point quite clearly.

Two cats were placed from birth in an environment in which they were able to see only vertical lines. When they were released into a normal environment, they were physically incapable of recognising horizontal lines and kept banging against anything that was on the horizontal.

Like these cats, it may be that the reality we currently recognise is one without horizontal lines. We could be missing half the picture and so are constantly surprised as we lick our wounds, having tripped over the latest bout of illness or misfortune.

So, don't feel bad if this is all news to you. Equally it's fine if you have been *aware* of energy but simply haven't been able to figure out where it is or how it affects you. In my book I will show you how, step by step, to discover and work with energy. If you can learn how to find and communicate with your own energy, with that of other people and with that of the world around you, you can start to take back control of your life. You become in control of your own destiny, rather than being buffeted here and there.

Some of my ideas may seem far-fetched, even absurd. But I ask you to try them for size as you might a new hat. You just might find it's the hat you've been searching for all your life! We've all heard of the children of the jungle, real-life Mowglis or Tarzans. Scientists who studied them concluded that if a child spent the first eight to ten years of his or her life with a particular animal, he or she would mimic all the patterns of behaviour of that animal. We are all products of our particular society and behave according to the rules of that society. We take on board the illusions of that world and believe certain things to be critical to our existence. But we should not be satisfied merely to exist as two-legged beings while allowing our energy and soul to rot. We are capable of a much richer existence.

I'm willing to bet that you do already have a sense of your own intuition, that you have felt energy at work. How many times in your life have you responded in a certain way to something and put it down to sixth sense? How often do you come across people who either seem to drain you or uplift you? What do we mean when we say "There was chemistry between us"? What is going on when we walk into a room and say "You could cut the air with a knife"? This is precisely the energy I am talking about. This is the energy that you need to learn: first, to recognise, and second, to master.

Why is it so important? Well, the very first principle of good health is healthy energy. If your energy is healthy, not only will your body be healthy but your life will be too. You will know who and what you are, what you want from life and the right way for you, personally, to get it. We are all unique and it may well be that your way will be different from that of someone else.

The orthodox approach

Orthodox medicine is a science of illness and the way to heal illness. It is not about well-being or health. If you talk to your doctor about illness he or she will tell you all about it and the ways to cure it. But if you ask about your health, and the way to maintain it, it's most likely you will not get much guidance. Orthodox medicine treats with tablets, injections and surgery – often treating the symptoms, rarely the cause. Orthodox medicine does not approach patients individually: the patient almost gets lost in the general diagnosis – you are no longer "Susan Jones" or whoever, you become "a migraine" or "a rheumatism case". But holistic medicine has a different approach, recognising that our personality, our individuality has to come first, and our condition second. Holistic medicine helps people who are sick not to define themselves by their illness and this is an essential part of recovery. On the other hand, the arena of orthodox medicine is that of the physical body and the physical body alone. If you can learn to work with energy often you can stop illness at the energetic level, before it manifests itself on the physical level. You can prevent illness and ill ease.

Obviously orthodox medicine helps many people. But sometimes you won't even have any symptoms of illness. This doesn't necessarily mean you are healthy. We get so used to feeling just "OK" without realising that we could feel so much better. Don't just survive your life: learn to live it to the full. My belief is that we can all be our own healers, to a large degree. Don't get me wrong – I am not against doctors in the slightest and obviously I would not suggest you ditch your doctor. Far from it. In fact I frequently send my patients to see doctors, specialists and consultants, so we can work in tandem.

And finally ...

Let's get to work. The easiest way to understand the principles of the energy that fuels our lives and our beings is, I believe, to adopt and adapt some of the basic tenets of Eastern philosophy. This claims that human beings consist of a physical body and seven fine (or subtle) energy bodies. Our physical body is soaked in our seven fine bodies much as a foetus is soaked in amniotic fluid. Like the foetus, we are fed and nourished by these seven fine bodies and can develop and grow. You might well be familiar with the concept of an aura – if so, that's great, a good starting point. However, what you might not know is that the aura is not one spiritual body but actually the combined seven bodies. Each of these bodies is different and distinct and each has clearly defined functions. They are interconnected and dependent on each other and our good health relies on the good health of each and every one of them.

We'll look at them in the next chapter.

CHAPTER TWO

Our Many Bodies: The Anatomy and Contents of the Aura

I expect you were surprised when I told you that you have not just one body, but seven! By focusing on just the one body, we miss the major part of our existence. Let's redress the balance.

The first and most recognisable body we have is our physical body. Any study of anatomy tells you exactly what it is made of: flesh, muscle, bone and so on. It's easy to see, touch and feel. It's nourished by food. But no one tells us about the complex structure of a human being, the energy centres and pathways that run through it. Nobody tell us about the invisible but vital layers that surround the physical body. Their presence has been recorded by Kirlian photography, an ultra-high speed form of photography that captures auras, the lively energy surrounding everything, as shown right. The aura is also tangible

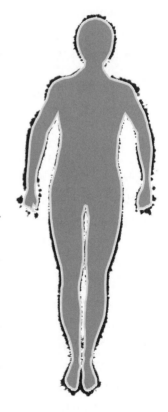

to the trained person and this is what I work with when I treat my patients. I'd like to make it very clear that I do not look at the aura when I work with someone.

I don't focus on seeing the aura. Rather I tap into the frequency of its energy. It comes naturally to me, because of my early training. However, don't worry. It is not necessary to be able to "read" energy frequencies the way a healer does. I will be teaching you how to tell where there are problems in your aura later on, and how to heal these breaches in our non-physical, energetic bodies.

Most of us understand the structure of our physical body, which is essential for taking care of it. But we tend to be very ignorant about our aura. This is a huge mistake as the various layers of the aura play a very important part in our general well-being. In order to take care of ourselves properly, we need to be aware of the anatomy of the aura as well as the anatomy of the physical body.

Illness in the physical body is a manifestation of failure or breakdown in one of the layers of the aura.

This is a vital point that you need to grasp and it's how the seemingly magical effect of healing takes place. If a doctor or healer is able to remove the disease from the aura, then the illness will disappear from the physical body too.

If you work only with the physical body when the root of the problem lies in your energy, the "cure" will be only temporary. The definition of a healthy person is someone who is healthy both in his or her physical body and also in his or her aura. Even if just one layer of the aura is damaged, the damage can manifest itself on different levels of our being. For example, if you are sick on the physical level, it will often affect the energy vibrations on an emotional level, and vice versa. Therefore a healthy, undamaged aura is crucial for our health.

Our aura does not exist independently from nature: it is brought into being by the collision of two energy fields. One energy field travels up from the ground while the other bears down on us from the universe. These opposing magnetic forces, channelled through our physical body, bring the aura into being.

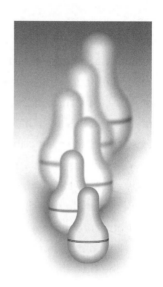

Our aura has a very specific structure and is made up of seven layers. Imagine the famous Russian *matryoshka* doll: the aura is like this. Our physical body is the smallest doll, around that are the layers of our aura, each larger than the other. However, unlike the doll, each body intersects the others.

We will start by looking in detail at the first three bodies, those that lie closest to our physical body. These are the bodies that we will be seeking to heal and balance throughout my programme.

The etheric body

The etheric body is an exact copy of the physical body. It permeates right through your physical body and follows the same contours as your physical body, but it's bigger, extending 3–5 cm beyond it. It is made from the colourless volatile liquid, ether.

The etheric body acts as a link between the physical world and the more sensitive non-physical types of matter. This is the energy that is captured by Kirlian photography and was identified back in the 1950s. If you place a living thing in an electromagnetic field and take a photo, it can capture the etheric body in the form of a fuzzy-coloured outline. People's etheric bodies come in different colours. A sensitive person's etheric body will be blueish in colour;

that of an athletic person, greyish. The darker, heavier colours tend to indicate sickness or heavy emotions.

The etheric body is the energy matrix of the physical body: each organ, each structure, has its counterpart in the etheric body. It is precisely at this level that the energy pathways, known as meridians, exist. One of the main principles of acupuncture is working with these energy streams, the meridians. So this etheric body is your physical body's energy twin – that's why it's such a reliable indicator of your physical health. Any changes in your physical body are reflected in your etheric body and vice versa.

For hundreds of years in Russia, there was a practice, after someone's death, of gathering together not only after the funeral, but also on the ninth day following the actual death of the person. At this gathering it was customary to remember the good things about the person, to celebrate their life and give the person's soul the energy to depart. Interestingly, recent Russian research using Kirlian photography to photograph a dead body confirms that our etheric twin disperses on the ninth day following death.

The astral body: the body of emotions

This second body extends beyond the physical body by 5–10 cm and has a clearly defined edge that mirrors the physical body. However, inside it is in constant motion. You could think of the astral body as rather like a lava lamp, with different clusters of matter flowing in and out of each other, now joining, and now separating. In an emotionally healthy person, this flow is effortless and light. However, in a person experiencing a burst of negative emotions or aggression, there will be a clotting of energy at this level.

The colour of this energy changes too. If you are healthy, it should be light in colour. If you are not, the colours will be brownish grey and dark. If you find it difficult to let go of your negative emotions, your energy will stagnate, clot and obstruct you – ultimately it will turn into a permanent state. Be warned: negative emotions can easily become habits! Emotions like envy, aggression, desperation, anger, resentment and inharmonious relationships with those around you, and with yourself, can promote stagnation, clots or blockages in this emotional energy. Blockages in themselves further create a negative effect on our health. We use expressions like "sick with worry"; "mad with rage"; "bitter and twisted". Be careful, as they are much more than mere figures of speech.

Why are we drawn to some people and not to others? It is their astral body that is either attracting or repelling us. The more in tune we are, and the more we learn to understand our emotions and what triggers stagnation in this energy, the more accurate our intuition will be.

The mental body

This is the third layer of the aura. It is the body of thought, knowledge and experience. This body is highly developed in those who engage their intellect on a regular basis and less evolved in those who do not. It extends 10–20 cm beyond the physical body and, once again, mimics its contours. This body is a very bright yellow and flows from the top of the head downwards. When people are engaged in intense mental activity, this energy has a tendency to expand and its colour to brighten. We talk of clever people being "bright". There are also clusters of energy at this level that can stagnate. An open mind allows energy to flow and is receptive to new thoughts and ideas. A closed and negative mind prevents energy from flowing and leads to stagnation. All our thoughts and ideas and memories carry a certain amount of energy that constitutes this body.

Some memories have a very strong connection with your emotional energy (on the astral level). For example, if you were abused as a child, memories of your abuser will have a very strong emotional colouring. The memory of an insignificant event in your life, by contrast, will lose its emotional colouring quite quickly. It might still affect you on a mental level, but it will not have the same impact as a memory that combines your astral and mental energies. A mental energy coupled with a negative astral energy can be a drain on your overall energy for years and affect your physical well-being.

I'd like you to start to realise that any experience you have leaves a footprint in your energy path. Your attitude towards events and your ability to let go of bad experiences indicate the general health and well-being of your mental energy. We all go through different, sometimes difficult, challenging or unpleasant experiences in life. You have to take care not to allow them to leave dirty footprints in your mental energy. Your attitude is all-important here.

The mental body and the two we have already discussed (the etheric and astral bodies) are born with you and die with you. The other four energy bodies are more esoteric and we will not be working with them directly during the course of this book. However, as you will probably be curious to know what they are, I'm going to explain a little about them.

The karmic body

This is the immortal body – the one that is believed to transfer from life to life. This body comprises the energy that you receive for all the actions you take, or simply propose to take. Most people will have heard of the concept of karma – that what goes around, comes around; that what you give is what you get. Karma forms the basis of the Hindu philosophy of reincarnation.

Psychics claim to be able to see this body as a sort of cloud extending 20–30 cm from the physical body. It is the colour of rose quartz. Because of its position, so close to our astral and mental bodies, it has a very strong influence on our belief systems, our thoughts and emotions and, indeed, our actions. This body doesn't die with us: it leaves the physical body and is reborn with another body. Obviously this is a contentious area and very open to discussion. I find it useful and see the fruits of it in my work. If this is tough for you, maybe for now, just keep your mind open.

The intuitive body

This is like a container for all the previous bodies and it defines the shape from the outside in. It is like a dark blue oval, 50–60 cm outside the physical body. Inside the oval is a space that defines the contours of the other bodies. At this level, the aura becomes far more abstract. This level is considered to be a template for our uniqueness, our inner identity. It is also the level on which we can create through our words and thoughts.

The divine body

This looks like the sun with heat emanating from its circumference and resembles a child's drawing of the sun. Highly spiritual people, or those adept at meditation, access energy on this level and feel ecstasy. It looks like heat or a glow. The haloes on icons of saints or pictures of Christ and angels are a pictorial representation of this energy. This is the level of unconditional love – our emotions set onto a spiritual level.

The Kether body

Some psychics call this the soul or causal body. This is the aura's outer "skin", which contains all the other layers within it. It has a protective film of some 1–2 cm. Although it is the finest of our auric layers, it is also the strongest and most resilient. It needs to be dense, resistant and elastic so that it can stretch but not break. It protects the aura from contamination from external forces and influences, and has a connection to a higher force. To use a computer metaphor, this is the hard drive for your life. It's our spiritual template and through it we meld and become one with spirit.

CHAPTER THREE

The Chakras and Meridians: Energy Centres and Pathways of the Aura

We're going to carry on, this time looking more closely at our aura and how it works. I know this seems like a lot of theory but it really is important. If you want to take control of your health and well-being it is essential to understand your own energy system. Look on this part of the book as the instruction manual for your car or your computer.

The human aura has areas that serve as energy depots. These areas store our energy and transmit it to our organs. In Sanskrit they are known as chakras and, as this term is pretty well known now, I'll use it throughout the book. However, it is important to note that the concept of energy centres is not limited to Indian philosophy. In translation, the Sanskrit word *chakra* means wheel and psychics see them spinning just like wheels or, to my mind, more like tornados.

As I described earlier, our aura is the result of the interaction of two force fields – the cosmic (coming down) and the terrestrial (rising up). These forces cross as they travel through our bodies and their central crossing points are where we find the chakras.

The chakras

The purpose of the chakras is to transform the energy they receive from these two forces and the energy of our environment (diet, relationships, etc.) into forms of energy that the body can utilise. Each chakra in our aura is strongly connected to the physical body, and governs certain physiological processes. That's why, when one of our chakras is damaged, suffering can be immediately detected in a related organ.

Our health is dependent on the proper functioning of our chakras. When a chakra is functioning healthily, it is comparable to a miniature shining tornado. If the chakra is damaged, it begins to grow dull and wilt. Everyone has seven major chakras and they are based along the spine in specific places. Remember they exist on a subtle level – no dissection has yet discovered a chakra!

As each of these "tornado" energy spirals turn, in a clockwise direction, they exert and influence us through the etheric, astral, emotional and mental bodies. Each chakra creates a vibration, the frequency of which correlates with a specific colour and sound. Now I would like to explain a little bit more about what colour really is.

Colour affects our bodies in very specific ways. Colour is the expression of the vital generative life force of light, the force that sustains us. What we perceive as a particular colour is actually wavelengths of active moving energy. Each wavelength has its unique signature and characteristics that impact on us in a specific way. The colours around us are in constant interaction with our bodies as well as with our feelings and emotions.

Colour affects us on a vibrational level just as music does, and I think it's safe to say we all recognise that various kinds of music can affect us in different ways. Think about when you're in the gym. You've been plodding away on the treadmill when a solid pulsing rock track comes on the sound system and suddenly you pick up speed and energy and are able to go the extra mile. The same applies to colour. Each chakra in our body will draw in the energy of a specific ray or colour. When a chakra is underenergised, there is a shortage of its corresponding colour; when it is overenergised there is too much – for example, too much red in the aura will lead to excessive anger. Either makes it hard for us to integrate the positive aspects of that colour. When we come to the detox programmes, I will be giving you energy exercises which balance each colour in the chakras – and hence in the body.

The base chakra (*muladhara*): the coccyx centre

This is the lowest chakra, located in the base of the spine and positioned between the anus and the genitals. Some ancient sources described its location in women as being on the back wall of the uterus and in men, in the prostrate. This chakra is considered to be our core, our base centre and crucial to our survival. Its function is to give us energy and stability in our lives.

If our life is not going well, if our welfare is at stake, then this chakra is activated. It is also one of the main reservoirs for energy. On the physical level, it is related to the reproductive organs, the anus and the legs. When this chakra is unbalanced we are likely to suffer from complaints like haemorrhoids, inflammation of the prostrate and ovaries, and circulatory problems in the legs.

This first chakra feeds our physiological ability to survive, to be confident and stable – all the things we feel necessary to be a "grounded" human being. It is a direct channel for the energy that we absorb from the ground, the Earth.

It is reddish in colour and is represented by the musical note "Doh" (C), a low bass grounding note.

The navel chakra (*svadhisthana*)

This is based in the centre of the lower part of the abdomen, between the pubic area and the navel. In ancient philosophy it

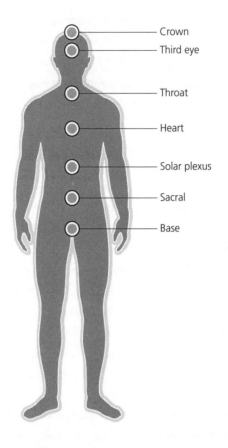

Crown
Third eye
Throat
Heart
Solar plexus
Sacral
Base

governed inner vitality. The function of this chakra is to absorb and store vital energy (known as *qi* or *prana*), from food. It is connected to our sexual function and our creative potential. In India they say that the awakening of this chakra gives us health and long life. It is also an important centre for the body's defence system. In martial arts, huge attention is paid to this chakra. For example, this is the source of the energy needed to chop wood with a bare hand. The energy from this centre controls our adrenal glands, kidneys and bladder and is connected with the ovaries in women.

When this chakra is imbalanced, we can suffer from impotence, frigidity and hypersexuality, illnesses of the kidneys and bladder, and infertility. If this chakra works well, it feeds energies like patience and endurance. When it is imbalanced, it leads to anxiety, frustration and fear. This is the centre of possession, attachment, non-attachment, the centre for keeping things under your control. If you want to master yourself, you need to learn how to keep this chakra under control. This chakra is also related to giving birth, whether to a child or an idea, poetry or some other creative endeavour. Sex and creativity utilise energy from this chakra.

The colour of this chakra is orange and it is represented by the musical note "Re" (D).

The solar plexus chakra (*manipura*)

This chakra is located in the solar plexus region, above the navel but below the ribs. It is responsible for our vitality. This is one of the most important chakras as it governs our visible energy, our ability to act in an energetic fashion and to do things. We connect with the outside world through this chakra and when we are uncertain of ourselves we intuitively fold our arms to protect this chakra. In the past people believed that the awakening of this chakra would provide us with supernatural powers and the ability to endure extreme temperatures of hot or cold.

When this chakra is balanced, a person is full of energy. This chakra feeds the liver, spleen and the digestive system. Imbalance can lead to ulcers, gallstones and poor digestion. It is responsible for characteristics like decisiveness, independent thought and action, personal energy, willpower and colourful individuality. When imbalanced, you can become irritable, lacking in confidence, greedy and full of guilt.

The colour of this chakra is yellow and its musical note is "Me" (E).

The heart chakra (*anahata*)

This is positioned in the centre of the chest, equidistant from your nipples. It is the body's emotional and spiritual centre. This is the chakra you use to relate to your loved ones and it is connected very strongly to your parents. Many cultures believe that the soul lives here and, in fact, when we talk about our soul we tend to place our hand over this chakra. Expressions like "it breaks my heart" are related to this chakra. In India and Tibet they believe that the essence of self, of one's individuality, is located in the fourth chakra.

That's why in many religions, spiritual practice and meditation about higher love are connected to this chakra. They also believe that this chakra awakens our inner beauty, makes our body attractive and activates our ability for extrasensory perception.

The fourth chakra regulates and sustains our biorhythms. It's connected to the heart, lungs and respiratory system. When it is not functioning properly, it leads to heart disease, hypertension and respiratory illnesses. When it works well, it relates to qualities like love, compassion, kindness and efficiency. When imbalanced, people become unfeeling, emotionally shut-down and passive. They feel flat and miserable.

This chakra is green in colour and the musical note is "Fah" (F).

The throat chakra (*vishuddha*)

The fifth chakra confers the ability to access the past and the future. In ancient Japan they thought this chakra governed a person's dreams. It is the centre of aesthetics. This chakra is very sensitive to any changes in a person's emotions, for example in responding to art. This chakra spins when you talk about beauty, aesthetics and ethics. It is the world of the appreciation of beauty. When you watch ballet and connect to the beauty of it, you are looking through the prism of this chakra. Sometimes when you are moved by beauty, say listening to a wonderful piece of music, you feel warmth and joy spreading through your body until it feels as if it takes you by the throat. A nervous cough before an important presentation is our attempt to activate this chakra and free the energy in this area. People for whom this chakra is dominant tend to be artists or working in the creative world. Or people for whom the beauty of life, the soul and the spirit, is of great importance.

This chakra is also the centre for verbal expression and communication with the outside world. The organs connected with this chakra are the thyroid, the neck vertebrae, lower jaw and trachea. Disease of the throat chakra leads to inflammation of the throat, diseases of the thyroid, a tendency towards colds and flu, and discomfort in the neck. When this chakra functions normally, communication and expression flow, your creative potential is increased, as is your inspiration. When it is imbalanced, we tend to be prone to obsessive ideas or behaviours. We become too attached to set behaviour patterns and are much less expressive. This is also the chakra of guilt.

This chakra is light blue in colour and its musical note is "Soh" (G).

The third eye chakra (*ajna*)

This chakra is found in the middle of your forehead, in the spot right between your eyebrows. It is a spot often known as the "third eye".

In China, the sixth chakra is considered to be the centre of wisdom and, as such, considered the most important. It's the chakra of meditation. It's connected to your qualities of will and willpower and paranormal abilities. It's the chakra of intuition and strategy. People who have healthy and active third eye chakras are good tacticians. These people always know how to see the way out of any difficulty. Good leaders use this chakra. In ancient times, the third eye was most active in magicians, shamans and clairvoyants. Everyone has heard of the famous mantra "*Ohm*" – this mantra is related to this chakra.

The sixth chakra is closely linked to the pituitary gland, the brain and the neck. When functioning normally, this chakra activates the intellect, psychological abilities, the imagination and the ability to picture things clearly and vividly. If imbalanced the individual will experience lack of concentration, a stagnant mind and can be prone to schizophrenia. Imbalance leads to headaches and poor connection between the conscious and unconscious mind.

The colour of this chakra is electric blue. Its musical note is "La" (A).

The crown chakra (*sahasrara*)

This chakra is found on the very crown of the head. According to esoteric literature, this chakra exists above the top of your head, not actually on it or in it. It accounts for the connection with the individual's higher self. If this chakra is open, you can enter enlightenment. You know this chakra is activated during those rare wonderful moments when you feel no restrictions of time or space. In the imagination of many ancient cultures, this is the place where the soul leaves the body. In Tibet, when someone dies, they used to remove the hair from the crown of the head to help the soul leave the body. In many religions nowadays it is still considered important to keep the head covered, to protect the part of you that is in communication with God.

This centre is activated when we discuss problems, and switches off when we start discussing tactics. When you start thinking about how to solve the problem, the sixth chakra comes out to play. The seventh chakra selects what is important and what is of secondary or lesser importance. It responds very well to the chanting of mantras.

In India a well-developed seventh chakra is connected to enlightenment, cosmic/higher love and an ability to accept the energy of the universe. This is when you feel in tune with the world, when you feel protected, at one with the universe. When this chakra is unbalanced, you feel shut off from the world, your mind races and you may feel your head is full of bees swarming in a hive. Hallucinogenic drugs like ecstasy and LSD affect this chakra and destroy the balance, leading to mania, panic attacks and psychosis. When it is not working well, it can also lead to high intercranial blood pressure and brain tumours.

This chakra is violet in colour and corresponds to the musical note "Te" (B).

The *nadis* (meridians)

Energy in the body flows through channels known as *nadis* in the ayurvedic tradition and meridians in Chinese medicine. When acupuncturists and ayurvedic practitioners work, they use these energy pathways. The three most important energy channels are known as the Divine, or Magic, meridians/*nadis*. Let's look at them briefly.

☆ *Ida* is the left channel, the channel of the past. It runs from the coccyx, from the left side of the spine to the right side of the brain and intersects the third eye. Energy in this channel is associated with feminine energy and carries maternal impulses. People who always live in the past – the kind who tend to say "It was better in the old days" – mainly utilise the energy from this channel. It is strongly connected to the moon and is often also known as the moon channel. If this channel is dominant in you, you will tend to breathe more through your left nostril – you will have the left passage of the nose more open than the right.

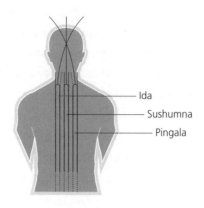

The nadis

☆ **Pingala** is the right channel, the channel of the future. This travels from the navel, intersects the third eye and travels to the left side of the brain. People who have a disposition to use the energy from this channel often talk about the future and escape into it. This channel is associated with male energy, connected with the sun – it's the sun channel. If this channel is dominant in you, you will tend to breathe more through your right nostril.

Many people tend to accept energy from predominantly one or other of these channels. If you do this, unfortunately, you will easily become separated from reality, from what is actually happening in the present. We all know people who live in the past, dwelling on what has been, caught in nostalgia. Equally there are those who are always projecting their energy into the future, hoping for better things, almost wishing their lives away.

☆ **Sushumna** is the third channel. This starts at the solar plexus and travels in a straight line through the third eye and the crown chakras. This is the most balanced channel. People who use its energy live in the present, in the here and now. People who predominantly use this channel breathe evenly, using both nostrils equally. It goes without saying that this is a healthier happier way of living.

All these channels can become polluted. They are affected very much by the energy of our emotions, thoughts and food.

I hope by now that you can see just what complex, multilayered (literally!) creatures we humans are. This book will help you balance, not only your physical body but also all these other bodies. We will find ways to ensure that your chakras are all spinning healthily, promoting a wonderful sense of vitality, peace and well-being throughout your body. We will look at how to ensure your energy channels run free, sending healing energy to every part of your body, mind and emotions. We will work on bringing your attention into the present, so you are no longer dependent on the past or wishing your life away into the future.

PART TWO
Home Energy Secrets

CHAPTER FOUR

Physical Cleansing of the Home

By now I hope I have convinced you of the existence and huge impor-tance of vital energy. Soon we will start working on clearing our own energy and our own bodies. However, before we start that process, we need to ensure we are working in a clear environment. As I am sure you will now be starting to understand, we don't live in some kind of splendid isolation: we are affected by the people and the world around us and, in particular, by our own homes.

Before you start any cleansing programme, it's essential you cleanse the space in which you are living. It is impossible to look after your internal energy when the energies around you are stagnant and toxic.

From my experience as a healer, I know that sometimes just changing the energy of the environment around you can be enough to accelerate a very deep healing process. So, before we focus on the energy within us, I strongly recommend that, first and foremost, you clear the energy of your house. We need to feel safe in our homes, and be surrounded by good or, at the very least neutral, vibrations in order to allow us to open up on a deep personal level.

Over the years we bring so many different energies to our homes. Let us hope that we bring a lot of good energy, the kind of energy that is created when we enjoy happy times, when we share love, when we bring a deep sense of peace through meditation. However, inevitably, we also often bring the energy of our conflicts, remnants of bad moods, the spiteful, angry energy of arguments.

In addition to this, the energy of our homes will also carry remnants of the previous owners' energy. When you move into a house you inherit their energetic imprint – information (in an energetic form) about all the events that took place while they inhabited the house. Almost inevitably, and unfortunately, those events will not always have been positive. So few people are aware of the way energy sticks to a house that hardly anyone thinks about cleansing their home before they pass it on to someone else. So we often move into places that are energetically filthy. If you find yourself feeling not easy in your home, anxious, stuck or wound-up, most likely you are reacting to the old energies of the house.

You can't only blame other people. Because most people in the West have little or no knowledge of space cleansing, it's common for most homes to be cluttered with their owners' own stagnant energy from the past. If your home is full of old energy, it will keep pulling you back into old states of being. You may have forgotten an argument, yet the energetic imprint of it will remain and can affect you days, months, even years afterwards.

Physical clutter also affects houses. If you have a home jam-packed with stuff, it's almost impossible not to be dragged down emotionally and energetically. Hoarding the past (which most clutter is) prevents you from enjoying life in the present.

However lacking in psychic ability you may think you are, most of us are actually very attuned to the energetic imprint of houses. How many of you have walked into a place and just felt uncomfortable, for no real reason? Equally we all know the feeling we experience when we walk into a home with balanced energies. Such places we, in Russia, would call "native". There is no exact translation – it's that feeling of "ah", that sense of coming home. I would like the energy of your home always to stay "native" to you. I would like the energy of your home actively to assist you in your spiritual evolution.

Decluttering

Of course, before we start cleansing the energy of the home, we must first get busy and clear it physically. It is impossible to create positive and healthy energy in a house full of clutter, dirt and dust. Clutter negatively affects our psyche and drains human life energy. You must walk around your house and figure out which things you still need and which you no longer require and can part with. Be as brutal as you can with removing all kinds of clutter. Get rid of things you no longer need; give generously to charity shops or generate some extra money with car boot sales. Make a list of things that need to be repaired and get them fixed. Sometimes it can be hard to get rid of things – I do understand. But remind yourself that you are loosening the energy of the past, making room for new things, fresh experiences, and lively new energy in your life.

A thorough decluttering session can leave your house in need of rearranging. Have a good tidy-up, ready for the next step of our process.

Cleaning

After you have completed tidying up, you must give your house a good physical cleansing. Floors should be first worked over with a vacuum cleaner and then followed (where possible) with a wet wash.

Prepare the water you will use to wash your floors in a certain manner, in order to discharge any negative energy in your home.

☆   Add a quarter teaspoon of ammonia and a tablespoon of coarse crystalline sea salt to a bucket of water. Alternatively, you could add a few drops of juniper, sage, sandalwood or peppermint essential oil into the water. These oils also have the power to cleanse energy – and smell gorgeous too.

☆   Open windows to allow negative energy to leave.

☆   Clean thoroughly. Pay particular attention to corners – stagnant energy accumulates here – as well as dust!

☆   Always discard the used water by flushing down the toilet.

If possible, clean your walls with this mixture too. Certainly give all your paintwork a thorough wash. Make sure you clean windows so they allow maximum light into your home. As the last touch, you need to go around and clean all the mirrors in the house. When cleaning both windows and mirrors make sure you always use a clockwise motion, to stimulate positive energy.

CHAPTER FIVE

Energy Cleansing of the Home

Once your home is physically clean, it's time for directly cleansing the energy of the house. I always recommend you carry out your energy space cleansing during the period between the full moon and the new moon. Make sure you allow yourself plenty of time – this isn't something to be hurried. You should also choose a time to carry out space cleansing when you are feeling well. If you're a woman, you should not space cleanse during your period or if you are pregnant – your energy is focused elsewhere. Switch off the telephones so you won't be disturbed. Arrange to have any children looked after by somebody else – children are very sensitive to energy changes and shifts. Make sure that all food and drink in the house is put away in cupboards or in sealed containers. Space clearing stirs up stagnant energy and you don't want your food to absorb any negativity. Switch off any fans or air-conditioning system as these disturb energy and make it harder to cleanse.

If you have animals, it is well worth watching where they like to sit or sleep prior to your energy clearing. In Russia, nobody will enter a new house before the cat does. This is because cats have a unique ability to sense negative energy and to feed from it. Russians will watch carefully to see where the cat will lie down first and would never think of placing their bed or sofa on those spots. Dogs, on the other hand, are drawn to areas with a cluster of positive energy. So your dog's favourite spot could be a good place for a bed, favourite chair or desk – anywhere you will spend a lot of time. Check out "cat-spots" when you space cleanse and pay them particular attention.

Prepare yourself for space cleansing by taking an energy shower.

Energy shower

Salt helps to absorb and neutralise any negative energy you might be carrying in your aura that day.

☆ Prepare a salt rub. You need to add a little sweet almond oil to a handful of sea salt – just enough to make a thick paste. Add two or three drops of either sandalwood, sage or juniper essential oil.

! Avoid sage oil during pregnancy.

☆ Standing in the shower, smear the mixture all over your body (you can avoid your head and face if you wish).
☆ Shower (you can pick your choice of water temperature). While you shower, sincerely and confidently ask the water to wash away anything negative that you may have accumulated during the day. It is important, as the shower rinses the salt off your body, that the water runs over the top of your head.

Preparing for cleansing

After this shower, you should feel much lighter and more readily able to connect with the energy of your house. Dress in fresh, clean, comfortable clothes. Remove all jewellery and your watch. Ideally you should work with bare feet.

Start from the front door of the house. Always work from the bottom of the house to the top. Remember to leave at least one window open to release any negative energy released.

In Russia, we use several methods for house cleansing. Feel free to choose whichever most appeals. Or try them all and discover which you like the best – most likely one will automatically feel more natural to you.

Cleansing with candles

In Russia we commonly use fire energy for cleansing. The simplest way of using the power of the flame is with candles.

The human energy field is magnetic in its nature. Fire energy can very easily enter into contact with our own electromagnetic field and cleanse it. It is also impossible for any energy entities to survive in fire. Don't worry too much about this now; I will be discussing this aspect in detail later in the book.

In Russian Orthodox churches there are always banks of candles in front of the icons. People visit the church with all their misfortunes and tragedies. By lighting the candles they help lighten their mood because the candles absorb their negative energy. It is also believed that the fire energy from the candles can help any earthbound spirits to gain enough energy to return to the light.

Use only beeswax candles for your cleansing. Throw the candles away after you have finished cleansing.

! Always make sure candles are placed where they pose no risk.

In Russia, we use several methods of cleansing with candles. I will now share them with you.

Methods for cleansing with candles

The first method is simplicity itself. All you do is light candles in every room. To maximise the effect, try to make sure that you can always see the last candle, as you light the next. This won't always be possible, depending on the layout of your home, but try your best to create an unbroken string of light.

In the second method you walk about the room, holding a candle. Take the candle in your right hand and then, with your left shoulder facing slightly forwards, walk around the perimeters of the room in a clockwise direction. Always start cleansing the room from the doorframe and make sure you finish at the point at which you began. See the illustration below for the candle movement directions.

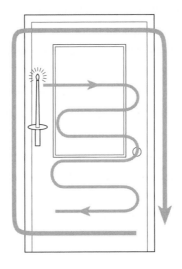

Another ancient Russian traditional method uses a combination of candles and mirrors. Traditional Russian healers believed that all forms of negative energy would be pulled inside the corridor created by two mirrors and so disappear forever. This method will clear the negative energy from a single room. You will need to repeat it in each room that needs clearing.

☆ Take two mirrors and place them so they are facing each other, about 2 feet apart.

☆ Place a burning candle in between the two mirrors. The candle will be reflected in each of the mirrors, giving the illusion that there is a corridor of candles.

☆ Leave for an hour. Make sure the candle is firmly fixed.

☆ After this procedure, thoroughly wash the mirrors with water.

Cleansing with bells

In the old times, it was common knowledge that bell chimes influenced the energy of the environment and could help to purify it. Bell chimes were commonly rung in tragic periods of Russian history. For instance, they were rung during the time of mass epidemics – on the one hand as a practical measure to warn people of danger, and on the other as an esoteric procedure to try to disperse the energy of the disease.

Neighbouring provinces, hearing the bell chimes, would ring their own bells, even before they were affected by the illness. The bells would be rung non-stop. Amazingly, in some cases, the epidemic would pass them by.

In Moscow alone, there were 6500 bell towers in the seventeenth century. There were thirty-two bells just in the Kremlin at the time of Ivan the Great. Some of them were unbelievably huge. One of the most famous bells is called the Tsar Bell. This monumental bell, in the Kremlin, weighs 200 tons. Why such large bells? Well, Russia is a large country and such vast territories need big resonate bells. One of the first things the communists did was to strip the churches and monasteries of their bells – they took away the country's most potent form of energy cleansing. Now, as Russia is in the process of returning to its roots and traditions, bell chimes are, once more, becoming an integral part of Russian life.

Music lovers may be interested to know that Russian composers such as Mussorgsky, Rimsky-Korsakov, Rachmaninov and Scriabin all incorporated the mystical fusion of bell chimes in their musical creations.

How can bells cleanse the environment, whether in our homes, or in the wider community? Well, sound is an energy vibration. During the bell chime, the energy of the environment actually changes. Sound purifies all the molecules of the space around; it acts as a detoxifier. It is the nature of strongly powerful rhythmic vibrations to entrain less powerful rhythmic vibrations (in other words, the more powerful vibrations will bring the weaker vibrations into synchronisation with their own, powerful, vibration.) So with the help of sound, you can cleanse the energy of any building, whether your home or workplace.

You do have to observe certain rules when you cleanse with bell chimes. Your intention, while creating the sound, is very important. The combination of your intent and the sound creates an individual result. No one pattern works for everyone – you will have to experiment to find the best, most healing, sounds for you.

At the end of this book, in the Resources section, I list places you can buy Russian bells (see page 315). However, it is not essential to use Russian bells. Many other cultures use bells and you may well find yourself being drawn to Indian bells, or Tibetan, Mongolian or Balinese bells, for example. It's worth trying various bells out and allowing your intuition to choose those that are most resonant and pleasing.

Method for cleansing with bells

For this method of cleansing, you will need two bells – one with a deeper tone and one with a lighter tone.

☆ Begin by using the bell with the deepest tone. The larger your room, the deeper the tone of bell you will need.
☆ Starting inside the front entrance, ring the bell once and listen. How does it sound? Clear, or dull?
☆ Now walk around the perimeter of the room, near to the wall

(but not so near that when you swing your bell it bangs against the wall). Hold your bell at the level of your heart centre (centre of your chest).

☆   Keep ringing the bell as you walk slowly. The sound should be continuous – before one chime fades, ring your bell again so you create a continuous circle of sound.

☆   Listen all the time for any change in sound. If the sound changes, and in particular if it becomes duller, repeat the chimes in that area until it becomes clear in tone.

☆   When you come back to the point at which you began, draw a figure of eight in the air using the bell, still ringing the bell. This transmits the energy of the sound you created around the room so it flows continuously. It makes the effect much more long lasting.

☆   Once you are happy that you have a clear tone all around the room, repeat this procedure using a lighter toned bell.

If you cannot get hold of bells, there is nothing to stop you using the music from one of the composers I mentioned – or any composer who uses the rhythm of bell chimes in their music. Turn the volume up high and cleanse the room using the music combined with one of the candle methods.

Other cleansing techniques

Cleansing with frankincense

Frankincense has been used for energy cleansing in Russia for many, many centuries. It's hugely popular. You will probably be quite familiar with its sweet heavy scent if you have ever been inside a Russian Orthodox or Catholic church, as it's the major part of the blend used in most churches. Not only is frankincense incredibly cleansing and purifying, but also it is used to enhance spiritual growth. Of course, it is also famous as one of the gifts given to the baby Jesus by the Magi. You can buy frankincense and charcoal burners on which to burn it from most new age shops. Here's how to use it.

☆ Place a charcoal block on a small glass plate.

☆ Light the charcoal by holding it over a candle or a lighter. It will splutter and spark for a while. Wait until the whole block has turned pale grey.

☆ Place a few granules of frankincense on top of the block. Allow it to bubble and burn for a few minutes, letting the smoke swirl around the room. You may need to top up the frankincense from time to time.

☆ Now walk around the room with the plate in your hand (watch out, it may get hot). Use the same method as that described for using a candle. Remember to concentrate on the corners – let the smoke waft into every part of the room.

☆ When you have finished, flush the contents of the plate down the toilet.

Cleansing with sea salt

This is another method that was commonly used by healers in old Russia following a good bout of physical spring-cleaning.

☆ Take some sea salt and place a little in each corner of each room.

☆ Also sprinkle a line of salt over your threshold. Leave it for twenty-four hours.

☆ Then take a broom (in Russia there would be a broom kept especially for this purpose) and start sweeping away all the salt. As you brush, chant this:

*"With this broom, I sweep away all
the dirt and entities from my house."*

☆   Finally discard the salt in the toilet.

Cleansing using meditation

Of course, there is nothing to stop you using purely the power of the mind for your cleansing. This can be very effective – but should not be considered a substitute for a good dose of elbow grease during physical cleaning! Try this deeply cleansing meditation. This is also very useful for places where it would be difficult to use "props" such as candles, bells or salt – in your office, or in a hotel room for example.

The red ball meditation for cleansing

☆   Visualise a red ball (similar to the bright glow of burning charcoal) on the floor, in one corner of your room.

☆   Imagine that the ball is rolling to and fro, gradually lifting off the floor while moving around the perimeter of the room in a clockwise direction.

☆   Each time the ball reaches the point where it began, it rises up a little and then moves around the room again in this elevated position.

☆   When the ball finally reaches the ceiling, imagine the window of the room opening. Once the ball has finished its final circuit, it moves over to the window and flies away. Visualise this very intensely.

Stabilising the energy of your home

After you have purified the energy of your house, in whichever way you have chosen, you will need to stabilise the energy. To "set it", if you like.

For this you will need an atomiser – you can buy them from garden centres where they're sold for spraying houseplants.

☆ Fill your atomiser with pure spring water. Add a few drops of lavender essential oil.

☆ Spray this water around the room. Lavender is used to lighten up the vibrations and stabilise the energy of the room.

Finally cleanse yourself. Once you have finished your space cleansing and have got rid of any waste materials (candles, salt etc.) you need to take either a shower or a bath. Use sea salt in the bath or on your shower mitt to get rid of any negative energy that might have stuck to you. Don't forget to wash your hair too.

CHAPTER SIX

Electromagnetic Fields in Your Home

There is another type of pollution which affects a huge number of homes and which is harmful to your energy. This is the artificial electromagnetic field (EMF) generated by electrical equipment. Electrical equipment ranges from huge power lines and overhead cables right through to common home and office equipment such as televisions and computers, and even mobile phones, microwaves and personal radios. We are awash with EMFs. All these cause a huge amount of stress for our energy fields. Research shows that human bodies radiate electromagnetic vibrations at a frequency of up to 300 MHz. We are constantly surrounded by appliances that radiate across a very wide spectrum of the wave frequency. This creates very strong electromagnetic stress, which influences our energy and health in a very negative way.

These appliances have become a huge part of our everyday lives, and it is not practical (or desirable) to live without them. So we have to learn how to minimise their harmful effects. I would strongly advise you get into the habit of unplugging appliances from the wall when they are not being used. Any equipment that is used to heat or cool, in particular, generates strong EMFs around it.

How to check your home and office for EMFs

This is very easy to do, using a small portable radio. It allows you to check your space and make sure you are not working, sleeping or meditating in a place polluted by EMFs.

☆ Set the receiver to the AM waveband but do not tune it to a broadcasting station. You will hear a low-level static sound.
☆ Turn up the volume.
☆ Move close to an electrical appliance such as an answerphone, television, electrical socket.
☆ An increased buzzing sound indicates an EMF.

How to minimise your exposure to EMFs

Above all, the place where you sleep needs to be as clear as possible from EMFs. Sleep is the time when our cells and aura repair themselves, and heat and radiation can massively affect this vital work. You should follow these golden rules.

☆ Never sleep near an air-conditioning unit, refrigerator or electrical water heater (even if it is on the other side of the wall from you).
☆ If you must use an electric blanket, make sure you switch it off from the mains before going to sleep.
☆ Keep your bed away from radiators. Metal tends to concentrate the effects of the magnetic field.
☆ Avoid electric clocks, clock radios and tea-makers by the bed. We often place these on bedside tables next to our heads, and they emit very powerful EMFs. The head is the most susceptible to electromagnetic stress because it contains the body's most specialised EMF receptors – the retina of the eyes and the pineal gland. Use an old-fashioned wind-up or battery-operated clock.
☆ Resist the temptation to have a TV or computer in your bedroom.

Bedrooms should be for sleeping! If you absolutely must, make sure you unplug it before you sleep.

I would also recommend you take extra precautions from EMFs in the workplace. As far as you possibly can, try to sit away from machines such as photocopiers, fax machines and so forth. If you are working on a computer, make sure you have a protective screen.

You can also buy a clear quartz crystal (from crystal or new age stores), which can be quite effective in protecting your energy from harmful emissions. Once a week, soak your crystal in salty water for twenty-four hours and then rinse under running tap water. Certain plants are also good at soaking up some of the negative effects of EMFs. Cacti really are superb at soaking up EMFs. However, I'm aware that according to *feng shui*, they are considered to send out negative "cutting" chi or energy. Personally I think their EMF busting powers make them worth keeping but you could also try these other plants, which are effective at soaking up EMFs.

☆ Spider plant (*Chlorophytum comosum*)
☆ Mother-in-law's tongue (*Sansevieria trifasciata*)
☆ Golden pothos (*Epipremnum aureum*)
☆ Philodendrons

Of course, it goes without saying (I hope) that you never place your mobile phone next to your head – always use an earpiece.

OK, now let's hope you have a lovely clear home and office environment. I would recommend you keep it like this by cleansing on a regular basis, perhaps at the change of each season. Certainly you should do some cleansing if you have had an argument, shock, illness or any emotional upset.

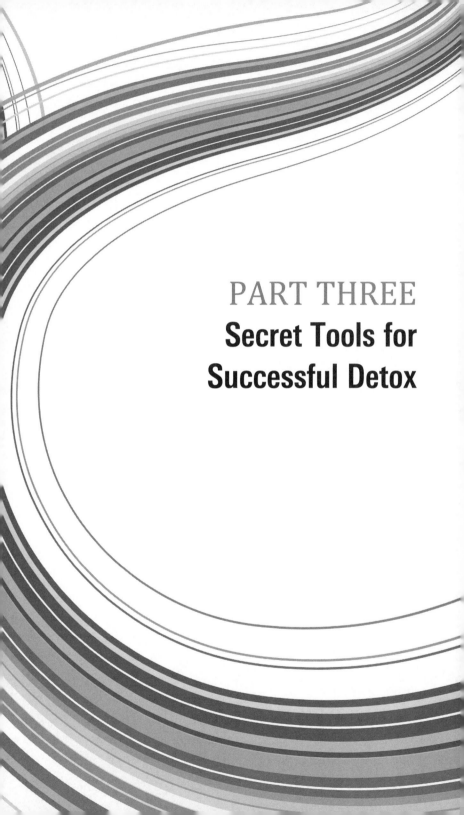

PART THREE
Secret Tools for Successful Detox

CHAPTER SEVEN

Hydrotherapy: The Power of Hot and Cold

Now it's time to start our physical detox programme. It's tough. I make no apologies for that. A weekend detox sounds lovely in theory but it simply is not effective. My four-week cleansing programme works, and works extremely well. It has been tried and tested on many, many people – with wonderful results. But, if you want those wonderful results, it will take discipline and time.

The programme cleanses the body on three levels: the colon, the liver and the kidneys. As we work on cleansing these three vital organs, we will also be cleansing the emotions that are connected with these systems. So this is not in any way merely a physical detox – you are also cleansing your emotions and your mind.

The first week of the programme is a preparation for the deep detoxing that follows. Its primary aim is to loosen mucus. It's a little like going to a beautician – you would not expect her to squeeze out your blackheads before she had opened your pores with steam!

Many detox programmes lose their effectiveness because they skip this vital first stage. Don't make that mistake!

Before we launch into our detox, I want to introduce some of the vital tools we shall be using throughout the programme. Some, such as body brushing, might already be familiar to you; others, such as the use of clay water and the power of chanting, may not.

I think it's important to understand why I am asking you to use these techniques so I want to tell you about their background plus how and why they work.

Let's start with the healing power of water.

Warm hydrotherapy

In Russia we take our health and well-being very seriously. But we also like to enjoy ourselves! An intrinsic part of Russian life is what we call *banya* – our wonderful steam baths. Water (both in its watery state and as steam) has always been used as a therapeutic tool. Modern-day naturopaths still extol the virtues of hydrotherapy and prescribe all manner of water cures for their patients.

I think everyone can benefit from warm hydrotherapy on a regular basis and would urge you to try it – I offer a number of alternatives so there should be a form you can use, even if you don't live close to a sauna or steam baths.

Warm hydrotherapy really comes into its own when we look at detoxing. One of the major problems with detoxification is getting rid of stored mucus in the body. It's hard because mucus in the body tends to solidify into a glue-like jelly. It is impossible to eliminate it from the body without warming it up first. Only then will the mucus loosen up and be ready for elimination. In addition, the ancient Greek healer Galen stated that one of the reasons why our bodies age is poor perspiration of the skin. He invariably recommended steam baths to widen the pores and increase perspiration.

In Russia, the specific form of steam bath known as *banya* has been used for these purposes since ancient times. It's a pleasant and highly effective way of loosening up mucus. Although I know most of you won't be able to find a pure Russian *banya*, I will be offering alternatives. Also I think the history behind it is interesting and so I include it here.

Russian banya

"Medicine is good, but banya *is better"*

– Peter the Great

Banya has been known in Russia since ancient times. The ancient Russian historian Nestor claimed that *banya* was in existence in the first century BCE. In the book *Description of Moscovia*, the seventeenth-century German scholar Adam Olearius tells us that there is no city or village in Russia without *banya*. He says, with great admiration:

"Russians can withstand extraordinary hot steam. They lie down on the benches and request others to whip and rub bodies with warmed-up whips made of oak tree twigs. In winter, they jump into the snow, rub their bodies with it and then again get back into the banya. *Such a dramatic temperature change hardens those bodies."*

From 1877 to 1911 over thirty medical dissertations were published about the healing power of *banya*. Even today the majority of people regard it as a kind of panacea.

Peter the Great swore by *banya*. When he was living in Holland he missed it so much that he built one himself, believing that this was the best way to repair one's health. *Banya* was not only a way of physically cleaning yourself, but also was seen as a form of energetic cleansing. It was the practice in Russia to visit the baths before going to church. Even the tsar was expected to do this.

If you were receiving guests, they would be ushered immediately upon arrival to the *banya*. As the host you would neither talk to your guests nor feed them until they had been cleansed in the bath.

Russians would also go to the baths after having sex. Even the tsar and tsarina weren't exempt and would go to the *banya* after a night of passion. In ancient Russia there was a very strict rule concerning weddings and *banya*. The day before the wedding the groom would always go to the *banya*. The day after the wedding, the newly-weds would go to the *banya* together. Absolutely everyone followed this rule right up until the eighteenth century.

The famous Russian writer Alexander Pushkin described *banya* as "Russians' second mother", since they would go to *banya* for rejuvenation, warmth and a bath.

But why was *banya* so important? The Russian people had a strong belief that *banya* would flush away all their sins. *Banya* always played a very important role in Russian households. It wasn't just an indulgence for the rich either: personal baths would be found, not only in wealthy households, but also in the very poorest households, in the most remote villages. Poor people in towns would go to communal *banya*. *Banya* provided true pleasure for Russians – rest for both body and soul.

There was no one prescribed way of using *banya*, no universal recipe. In every corner of Russia, in every family, there is a personal family technique for the *banya* ceremony. The need for individualism, for tailoring *banya* to your family's needs, was well understood. There is a very old saying that highlights this:

"The best banya is the banya which was prepared according to the nature of the person who was planning to enter it."

The people's belief in the healing properties of *banya* wasn't mere superstition. Their wisdom has been confirmed by research work by scientists all over the world. One of the magical secrets of *banya* is its capability to train our thermal regulation system and to improve secretion from the sweat glands. The Nobel Prize winner, August Crog, whose work was concerned with capillary blood circulation, found that when we expose our capillaries to warmth, we increase the energy balance in our organs.

Other researchers have found that *banya* (when used carefully and under medical supervision) can help to normalise blood pressure, as well as helping those with diabetes and those with kidney and metabolic problems. People with rheumatism respond extremely well.

The *banya*, basically, is a steam bath (using wet heat). It has a stone stove, known as a *kamenka*, and, if you want more steam, you simply put more water onto the *kamenka.*

During the time spent in a *banya*, the human body is subjected to intense heating. Our skin gets heated up first. As more blood flows to the skin, the metabolism accelerates and it is at this time that intense perspiration takes place and toxins are released. One session alone can produce 500–1500 grams of sweat. Russian *banya* also has the ability to regulate movements of liquids in the body, making it most beneficial for our purposes of cleansing, strengthening and restoring the body to balance.

It also has the effect of dramatically decreasing the amount of lactic acid in the body. I heard the famous Bolshoi Ballet dancers built their own *banya* to help them relieve nervous tension after performances and to restore their strength.

Russian *banya* is unusual in that it provides, not just heat (as in Western saunas) but cold water too. You would spend time in the hot steam and then go straight into a pool or shower with cold water. As you go into the cold your blood vessels narrow and blood streams through the internal organs to the heart. From the cold water you go back into the hot *banya*. A new stream of blood rushes from the heart to the peripheral blood vessels. As Igor Boutenko, president of the Russian *Banya* Institute, says: "This is what we call 'gymnastics for the blood vessels'." What differentiates the Russian steam bath from those generally found in the United Kingdom is that in Russia we have several shelves or seats of varying heights so you can adjust the height.

The final element of a *banya* is one that sounds horrible but, truly, is absolutely divine. You are whipped with a whisk made of twigs from either trees (oak, birch, eucalyptus) or herbs (sage, nettle). Not only does this stimulate the skin and the organs, but also the phytochemicals from the trees or herbs penetrate the skin. It's like a massage but even more wonderful!

To gain the best benefits from Russian *banya* you need to adhere to the strict sequence of heat/cold/rest. As it is very difficult to find a true Russian *banya* in the West, I have adapted the principles for use in a sauna or steam room. You will find saunas in most health clubs and spas; local swimming pools often have one too. In the Resources section at the back of the book you will also find links to some Victorian Turkish baths where you can get a good effect from the combination of heat and plunge pools. Many of these will also offer massage – a close second-best to the twig-whisk whipping.

! Steam and saunas are powerful medicine! I advise you to check with your doctor before using these methods. Generally, steam and sauna baths are contra-indicated for pregnancy, blood pressure problems, heart conditions, epilepsy, diabetes and certain skin conditions. However, it may be possible to use warm hydrotherapy under medical supervision.

Take it very easy, until you become used to the heat. While in the United Kingdom it seems as though people try to stay in the sauna or steam room as long as possible, this is not the Russian way. Nor is it necessary or beneficial.

Guidelines for warm hydrotherapy (steam and sauna)

☆   Stick to a vegetarian diet the day you use steams or saunas. Eat breakfast before you go, so you do not feel faint. Ideally go between the hours of 9 am and 11 am.

☆   Before you enter the sauna or steam room, make sure your skin is dry.

☆   Ensure your head is covered with a towel to prevent your blood pressure from dropping. Never use a sauna or steam room with wet hair.

☆   Make sure your feet are warm – the benefits are minimised if your feet are cold.

☆   Once you are inside, sit down and relax. Make sure you breathe through your nose. The air is almost sterile and inhaling it will benefit your respiratory system and will also help to loosen mucus in your sinuses and lungs. If it's allowed, put a little peppermint (or any other mint) essential oil on the coals. If it's not allowed, you can put a drop of peppermint oil under your nose or put a few drops on your towel.

☆   Stay inside for just five minutes – no more. When you start to perspire, you'll know it's time to leave.

☆   Immediately, take a cool (not cold) shower. Do not use soap. Do not wet your head in the shower.

☆   Dry yourself vigorously.

☆   Lie down and rest for about five minutes. The time you spend in the sauna and the time spent outside should be equal.

☆   Return to the sauna or steam room. This time stay for ten minutes (on the high shelf in a sauna).

☆   Repeat steps 7–9 but this time, rest for ten minutes and drink lots of water (tiny sips). In Russia we would drink a lot of mint tea (you could bring some in a thermos). Black radish juice was also used from ancient times to promote a deeper detox in the *banya*. Another good mixture to bring with you is a combination of carrot, black radish and beetroot juice (add a tiny bit of honey). If you can't find black radish, normal radish is fine. This juice is very rich in vitamins and minerals, which are important to reintroduce to the body after excessive sweating. Note: peel the beetroot, cut in half and soak for three or four hours before juicing.

☆ Return for a last time, for ten minutes, and repeat the procedure as before. However this time, have a colder shower and stay in for longer. Even better, if there is one available, jump into a cold plunge pool. This time, wash everywhere, including your head, and use a loofah for your body.

☆ Rest for half an hour. In an ideal world this is the time to have a massage.

Alternatives without sauna

Not everyone has easy access to a sauna. If so, you can still get many of the effects – in particular the loosening of mucus in the body, which is so important in the detox programmes later in the book. When you are preparing for detox you should always receive some form of warm hydrotherapy session on a daily basis. If you cannot get to a sauna, you can alternate between the methods shown below. However, remember before you have any form of warm hydrotherapy, you need to skin brush first.

Skin brushing

Skin brushing is a highly effective technique for stimulating the expulsion of mucus and loosening other toxic matter that clogs the lymphatic system and the lymph nodes. It is a vital part of the programmes but is also a tool for everyday health. Get into a habit of skin brushing regularly – it's not only wonderful for your lymphatic system, but it will improve your skin tone too.

You will need to buy a natural bristle skin brush (available from chemists). Always work on dry skin before you bath or shower.

You should use long sweeping movements. Always brush towards your heart and do not brush breasts, underarms or any sensitive areas. Do not skin brush over broken skin.

☆ First brush the sole of one foot. Then work up the front and back of the same leg and over your buttocks.

☆ Repeat on the other leg.

☆ Work on your hands and arms, starting at your fingertips. Brush the palm and back of your hands, then move up towards the armpits.

☆ Brush across your shoulders and as much of your back as you can reach.

☆ Brush your chest, working down towards your heart. Women should not brush their breasts or nipples.

☆ Brush down your neck.

☆ Now brush your stomach, in a circular motion. Always brush in a clockwise direction, as this helps to stimulate the colon.

☆ Brush until your skin feels warm but don't overdo it. Around five minutes of brushing is ideal but if you're short on time, less will be fine.

☆ After you finish brushing, you can take your warm hydrotherapy bath (or, if you are not on a programme, you can take your usual bath or shower).

☆ Always wash your skin brush in warm soapy water after use.

Towel drying and wet polishing

If you do not have a brush, there are alternatives. You will need a dry terry towel. You simply brush your skin using short sharp vigorous rubbing movements. As with normal skin brushing you always move towards the heart (so, from the fingers to the armpit and from the toes to the groin).

If you choose to use this before your bath or shower, when your skin is dry, you will need to wet your towel. However, the most usual way is to use a dry towel on wet skin, after your bath or shower.

If you would like to follow the advice of the yogis, you could try "wet polishing" instead. This means rubbing your wet skin with the palm of your hand, starting from the stomach area, until your body is warmed and becomes dry.

Salt scrub skin brushing

A salt scrub stimulates the skin and promotes sweating. It is a powerful form of skin brushing – an advanced version if you like.

! Do not use if you are diabetic or have any heart conditions or skin problems.

☆ Put half a cup of coarse sea salt into a large bowl and moisten it with enough water to make a fairly stiff paste.

☆ Stand in the bath or shower. Take a handful of the salt paste and, starting at your feet, briskly rub it into your skin in a circular or up-and-down motion.

☆ Taking more salt paste, as you need it, move up and cover the whole leg. Repeat on the other leg.

☆ Now work on your arms, moving from your hands up to your shoulders.

☆ Next massage as much of your back as you can reach.

☆ Finish with your abdomen and chest. Women should avoid the breasts.

☆ Once you have covered your whole body, rinse the paste off with warm water and towel yourself dry.

Different kinds of warm hydrotherapy

Let's run through some of the options you can use for warm

hydrotherapy if you do not have access to a steam or sauna (or simply if you want to ring the changes).

Epsom salts bath

This encourages the elimination of toxins through the skin. When you are on the detox programmes, I would like you to have this bath twice a week, but never on consecutive days. It is a good bath to have on an occasional basis even when not on the programmes. Take this bath last thing before going to bed – you will sweat during the night but will also sleep very deeply.

! Do not take this kind of bath if you have eczema or high blood pressure. It is also not advisable if you have heart problems, are diabetic or feeling tired or weak.

☆ Pour 225–450 g of Epsom salts and 100 g of sea salt into a hot bath.

☆ Lie in the bath and soak for about twenty minutes, topping up with hot water as needed.

☆ Get out; pat yourself dry and go straight to bed. You may wish to wrap yourself loosely in an old towel to soak up the sweat.

☆ The next morning, rinse your skin and moisturise it well with a natural unscented body lotion.

Aromatherapy bath

Take this at the end of the day, just before bed. You can use this bath as often as you like.

☆ Run your bath (warm not too hot). Then choose your essential oil. In Russia we would usually use olibanum (frankincense) essential oil, which promotes sweating. It is a strongly purifying oil and is also wonderful if you're feeling tense, anxious or stressed.

Alternatively use cedarwood, which also encourages the elimination of toxins through the mucus membranes – it's a hugely popular oil in Russia. Both these oils are generally non-irritant but if you have very sensitive skin it would be worth trying a patch test (dab a drop of oil on your inner arm and wait for an hour to see if you have a reaction).

☆ You can add between five and ten drops directly into the bath (when you have turned off the taps) or you can dissolve a handful of Epsom salts in hot water and add five drops of essential oil before pouring into the bathtub.

☆ Get into the bath and relax for twenty minutes.

Sauna of the yogis

This bath comes from the ayurvedic tradition. You can have it once or twice a week.

! Take extreme care when you get out, as your body will be quite slippery. Use a rubber mat in the bath if possible.

☆ Cover your body in either castor, mustard or olive oil. Gently massage it into your skin. Run a bath – it needs to be quite hot (around 40–45 degrees Celsius).

☆ Now slowly submerge yourself into the bath, gradually allowing your body to adapt to the temperature.

☆ Stay in for ten to fifteen minutes.

☆ Wash or shower using a loofah to rinse off the oil.

CHAPTER EIGHT

The Cleansing Power of Clay

During the detox programmes I will be asking you to use one particularly wonderful tool to help get rid of toxins. In fact, not only does it remove toxins, but also it helps to alkalinise our bodies (more on the importance of alkalinising in Part Eight on Rejuvenation secrets) and generally balances our bodies. What is this super-substance? Clay.

Clay, like us, is part of the earth. Like us, it is connected with the elements of Water, Sun and Air. This connection runs even deeper than it seems. Scientists have proven that the energy of clay and the energy of the human cell produce similar, if not identical, wavelengths.

Imagine you are walking barefoot on the earth. Ten to one you (like me) will be smiling at the thought. That's no accident! When we touch the body of our planet we, in turn, are restoring our ancient connection with it. Incidentally, walking barefoot has been proven to be highly beneficial for our health (but choose your spot with care, away from dog walkers!).

In Russia, we have made earth into a cult – "Mother – Raw Earth". There is a very old custom that when you travel on a long journey, you take a scoop of earth from the place where you live with you. The belief is that it will cure you of any sorrow or nostalgia.

In Russia, clay is used very widely in households. All our kitchenware has traditionally been made from clay, and water is kept in specially made clay containers. Water keeps cold and fresh in these for a very long time, thanks to the anti-bacterial properties of clay. From ancient times, it has been known that herds of cows will choose to drink water mixed with clay, even if there is clean water nearby.

We're not the only ones to have found the marvellous properties of clay. The ancient Egyptians used clay for mummification, which points to the anti-bacterial properties of the clay. The French army, in 1914–1918, added clay to mustard, to help prevent dysentery. Clay was used widely in the First and Second World Wars. Now the wonders of clay are being rediscovered and the use of clay in healing modalities is known as pelotherapy. Scientists are still discovering the wonders of clay and have yet to explain totally its many incredible effects. However, we do know a few for certain.

While antibiotics kill not only pathogens but also good bacteria, clay eliminates only unhealthy microbes and their toxins. In northern parts of Russia where people eat very oily food in the wintertime, they drink clay water to bind the fat and save their arteries; they call it "the earthy cocktail". On an esoteric level, clay has very concentrated magnetisms of Sun, Air and Water energy.

Radium is the main radioactive element found (in miniscule amounts) in clay. It is a very rare element and possesses a great power. The more you keep clay in sunlight, the higher the percentage of radium in it. It prevents the growth of tumours, pushing out everything that is rotten and fermented in our cells. Its natural (and safe) radiation kills all harmful micro-organisms, bacteria and viruses.

Clay is very rich in minerals too. Blue clay has more minerals in it than fruit or vegetables. It regulates the growth and development of the cells in the body, almost attuning it into the right and healthy vibrations. I say almost, because even clay can't do everything on its own – you have to help too.

Clay is alkaline. As we will discuss in greater detail later, if our body shifts too much towards acidity, it can lead to illness. Clay helps to restore the pH balance of the body and some research shows that it stabilises our electromagnetic system. Clay is capable of absorbing and binding toxins and poisons in our digestive system before they can become absorbed into our blood. As clay travels down our body, it acts as a potent purifier, almost like a vacuum cleaner. It not only purifies the body, but also helps to restore our normal energy balance.

The different kinds of clay

There are many different types of clay and you may well come across blue clay, white clay, green clay. You will also come across names such as bentonite, montmorillonite, kaolin. I like blue clay above all, but all these clays are wonderful for helping to cleanse the body.

! Always consult your doctor before taking clay. Although it is usually very safe, in certain cases (such as hypertension or constipation) it should be used only under medical supervision. Also, make sure you never inhale the clay particles.

Clay can be used in many ways – it is wonderful in compresses, poultices or packs for headaches, eczema, acne, bruises, sprains and bacterial infections. You can add clay to baths or use it in massage or face masks for deep cleansing and skin rejuvenation. However, the most potent use is to take clay internally.

Inside the body, clay has the power to do the following:

☆ Detox the digestive system – clay pulls pollution from the body. It can also eliminate unhealthy bacteria and parasites from the digestive tract.

☆ Support the immune system.

☆ Fight free radicals that cause cell damage and ageing.

☆ Support and detox the liver.

☆ Alkalinise the body.

How to prepare and use clay water

Because of its wonderful benefits, clay is an essential part of the cleansing programmes. However, there is nothing to stop you taking it as part of a general healthy eating plan too. I suggest, if you are using it this way, that you take it once a day (before breakfast) for three months, and then take a break.

You can either make up clay water in advance, or prepare it just before drinking – it's totally up to you.

The in-advance method

☆ Pour one litre of cold mineral or spring water into a glass or clay container (don't use metal). Add four tablespoons of clay. Don't stir.

☆ Put the container in a sunny place – a windowsill is ideal – for three to four hours.

☆ Before drinking, stir thoroughly with a plastic spoon (don't use metal). Drink two glasses a day, taking small sips. Keep each sip in your mouth for a few seconds. It doesn't taste unpleasant – though the texture is a little strange. Ideally drink your clay in the morning straight after waking. If this isn't possible, have it before a light meal (either lunch or evening meal).

☆ You can keep this water in a sunny place until you have finished it.

The quick method*

Add one teaspoon of clay to a glass of cold water. You can add a little honey if you like (but not sugar). You can also add the clay to a cold glass of peppermint tea.

! Never heat up clay water, as it will lose its healing properties. Only drink it cold or at room temperature.

* In the first week, I recommend you should follow the in-advance method (i.e. do not stir the water before use).

CHAPTER NINE

Russian Chanting Technique (*Zagovor*)

"For human beings, words act as stimulants, and this is why they can provoke reactions in the body."

– Ivan Petrovich Pavlov

What Pavlov is saying is that words, thoughts, can have profound effects on our physical bodies. If you don't believe me, just imagine you are biting into a lemon. What happens? I'm willing to bet that just from merely thinking about it you will have experienced an increase in the production of saliva in your mouth.

Ancient Slavic healers were known as *bai* which, when translated from ancient Russian, means "to speak". Surprising though it may be, all healing techniques evolved around the power of words. From very ancient times, spells and chants were whispered or sung to accompany herbs or other forms of healing.

A spell is really just a form of psychotherapeutic suggestion, a powerful affirmation of intent put into words. In Russia, this was called *zagovor* (chanting). *Zagovor* has always been pronounced close to the patient, in a rhythmic whisper, which maximised its therapeutic action.

Zagovor has always been performed on a one-to-one basis, quietly, away from other people. This Russian chanting has developed along parallel lines to modern types of scientifically developed psychological formulae – the subliminal suggestions and affirmations used in hypnotherapy. *Zagovor* is effective because it appeals to the dual polarity of the brain – both the left side of the brain, which is responsible for the logical interpretation of information, and the right side of the brain, which is responsible for the imagination and fantasies. So there are two elements to this chanting. First, it builds up images, which engage the right side of the brain. Second, it bombards the left side of the brain with very powerful affirmations. The combination of the two is incredibly effective.

The sound of the voice and intonation is vitally important when using chanting. The voice is low and rhythmical, monotonous like a monk intoning prayers. It has the same effect on the mind as that of the hypnotist's pendulum – it allows the conscious mind to switch off and the person to drift away into a hypnotic state.

Slavic healers used chanting together with ritual. For example, the healer would measure a sick person's body with a length of thread. Then she would slowly knot the thread while chanting. The thread would be placed, together with a sample of either the person's hair or nail, in the centre of a piece of bread (bread is the symbol of life and fertility). In the early morning, the bread would be thrown into a stream or river – the symbol of cleansing.

To give another example, a traditional healer might be called to the house of a woman who was finding it very difficult to give birth. As she entered the room, she would open the door very, very slowly while chanting rhythmically: "Opening, opening, opening, here we go ..." Soon afterwards you would hear the newborn baby cry.

Our brains and thoughts are so chaotic it can be hard to get yourself into the right frame of mind to maximise the benefits of *zagovor*. You may also find it hard to settle your mind in order to meditate. If so, you may find it very helpful to give your mind a jolt out of normal consciousness, to prepare it to enter a different state of consciousness. The easiest way of doing this is to present your brain with two different tasks simultaneously. The method I use with my patients is to have them imagine their hands are cold, very cold, while their feet are hot, very hot. Try it – it does work.

Zagovor works because it affects both our physical and psychological well-being; it recognises that we cannot heal one without the other. It follows the principle that we can all influence our illnesses and misfortunes by correcting our attitudes towards them. It also makes us recognise the power of words.

You are probably familiar with the famous Russian physiologist, Ivan Petrovich Pavlov (of dog fame). What you probably don't know is that through his research, he was able to prove that signals (either as the written word or spoken word) play a large role in the human system. They charge the mental energy so strongly that it has a distinct effect on the body and emotions.

However, the foremost modern master of this technique is someone with whom you might not be familiar, the amazing and talented Russian psychologist G. N. Sytin. Sytin created a series of chantings that could change one's perception of one's illnesses and problems. The history behind these chantings makes a good tale.

Sytin had been interested in psychology since childhood but, as a young man, he became a soldier during the Second World War. A grenade went off near him and he suffered many injuries. His arm was severely damaged, he lost his memory and his co-ordination and he could not move. He had severe shell shock and was considered quite handicapped. As he lay in hospital, bed-ridden, he realised that he could either give in or somehow find the power of will to survive. He chose the latter and psychology became his saviour. He had grown up knowing about *zagovor* and thought he could use their methods to heal himself. So he would chant to himself various different tunings focusing on his recovery. He would repeat them again and again, with amazing results. His memory started to come back and his muscles started to recover. Then, with even more enthusiasm, Sytin moved from choosing the words for his chant intuitively to picking more deliberate components for his verbal formulae. He found that his health rapidly improved as a result of this chanting.

Fascinated by his success, Sytin became inspired to create more tunings, for other pathological states of being. This became the theme of his PhD in psychology.

Sytin collected and studied endless amounts of traditional Russian *zagovor*. These provided the basis of his understanding of the power of chanting. They helped him to understand the underlying structure of effective tunings.

He then created his own linguistic texts that, when chanted, would induce positive emotion and ideas. What was so interesting was that these positive feelings were not only maintained during the actual chanting, but also remained long after the session had finished. Sytin also performed numerous laboratory studies to register and study the effects of his tunings on the human aura. He would measure the effect of each word on our energy system and he would choose the most powerful word or combination of words. His tunings helped a great number of people and their efficacy has been supported by a number of studies. The former Soviet Ministry of Health approved and advocated the use of Sytin's tunings in hospitals. In the Appendix I will describe two tunings that I find most useful to my programme.

PART FOUR

The Detox Secrets:

Deep Cleansing Programmes for Total Health

CHAPTER TEN

Preparation for the Programme

Right, let's start our physical, emotional and mental detox. You should now be familiar with some of the tools we are going to use. I will explain everything else clearly as we go along. The first week of the programme is a preparation. It's absolutely essential so don't be tempted to skip this, as it is vital for the programme and a powerful process in its own right. Before we start, I want to run through a few safety points and general guidelines for detoxing.

When to detox

In an ideal world you would start this programme in spring. It's an ideal time because our bodies and minds are primed to release and let go at this time of year – both on a physical and emotional level. You would be working alongside, rather than against, nature. There is a time to hold on and a time to let go. It makes sense to detox at the easiest time of year. Yet I don't want to be too dogmatic about this. So, if spring isn't possible, it's OK to detox in the summer or, at a push, autumn. However, autumn is not the best time for liver cleansing as the liver is at its weakest at this time. Please, please don't even think about detoxing in winter. It just isn't appropriate and puts strain on your body. I cannot believe that so many papers and magazines push detoxing as a New Year measure – quite wrong. The only exception is kidney cleansing: it is possible to detox the kidneys during winter, as it's a far less arduous detox.

Ideally I would like you to detox all your systems in turn – so, preparation week followed by colon cleansing followed by liver cleansing followed by kidney cleansing. However, if you prefer, you can carry out the kidney detox separately (though do the week's preparation first once again).

When not to detox

There are some important contraindications for detoxing. You should not detox if:

- ☆ You have diabetes.
- ☆ You are pregnant or breastfeeding.
- ☆ You are suffering from extreme fatigue.
- ☆ You have a cold or flu.
- ☆ You are suffering from any acute illness.
- ☆ You are having a flare-up of any chronic condition.
- ☆ You are pregnant.

! Always check with your doctor before detoxing. If you are on any medication or have any health issues, you may well be able to detox under medical supervision but you must check with your doctor.

When you follow my plan, I would also not recommend doing more than one of the advanced techniques. For example if you follow the advanced option for colon cleansing, do not follow the advanced option for liver cleansing as well.

Side effects of detox

It's only fair to warn you that any detox programme, including this one, will usually throw up some form of side effects. I say this, not to scare you but, in fact, quite the opposite – so you can be reassured that nothing has gone wrong, it is just your body reacting to the programme. The most common side effects you can expect are:

☆ Headaches: these are usually down to caffeine withdrawal as you give up coffee, tea, sodas and chocolate.
☆ Spots and rashes.
☆ A shift in your bowel movements.
☆ Tiredness and fatigue.
☆ Emotional shifts and changes.

You may be surprised to find that emotional shifts and changes are included. But, remember, we are working, not only on the physical level when we detox, but also on the mental and emotional. Detoxing can often bring up old emotions, toxic memories, as we let go of physical toxins. Plus we are going to be working directly on our emotions, so don't be surprised if you find yourself experiencing shifts. It can be very useful to keep a journal while you are detoxing, writing out your feelings is a powerful way of keeping track.

A healthy person has good instincts and can adapt well to the external environment. To test how healthy you are, just think about how easy (or tough) you find it to adapt to the outside world. If you are well balanced, you will be far less likely to be overwhelmed or put off your stride by things like bad weather, a bad look or a rude shop assistant (for example). You would simply be much less preoccupied with daily aggravations – as the energy around you transforms, you transform with it. Don't worry if you know you don't adapt well. By the time you finish this detox, you should notice a huge difference.

If you've never managed a detox before – or fear you will fail

Some people simply can't envisage the concept of managing a healing programme because they are so stuck in the past that they simply can't see a way forward. Many people also lead their lives trusting in the future, believing that one day, magically, things will change. In the meantime, they just survive from day to day. I believe healing can take place only when your awareness is in the present.

If you know you find this hard, and it's true for a lot of us, there is one technique that would be worth practising before committing yourself to the programme. This is the ancient yogic practice of alternate nostril breathing that instantly connects you to *Sushumna*, the central energy channel of the present.

☆ Wear loose clothing and sit with a straight back, legs uncrossed.

☆ Close your right nostril with your right thumb, and exhale through your left nostril.

☆ Inhale through your left nostril to the count of four.

☆ Close your left nostril with your ring and little fingers, resting your index and middle fingers on the bridge of your nose, both fingers pressing the area between your eyebrows. Hold to the count of sixteen.

☆ Release your right nostril and exhale. Try to empty your lungs completely to the count of four.

☆ Inhale through the right nostril to a count of four, and then close it; and then keep both nostrils closed to the count of sixteen.

☆ Release your left nostril and exhale to the count of eight.

☆ Start again, and repeat the whole sequence at least ten times – breathing to a count of four, holding your breath to the count of sixteen and exhaling to a count of eight.

☆ Stop at any point if you feel dizzy.

Week One: preparation for the programme

There are seven vital elements for the preparation period. Every day for seven days you will need to practise the following:

1   Diet
2   Warm hydrotherapy and skin brushing
3   Clay water
4   Energy exercise: cleansing the energy of fear of the future
5   Clothing
6   The "Inner Smile" exercise
7   Meditation: *Healthy Way of Life* tuning (see Appendix)

Let's look at these in more detail.

Diet

The aim of the diet during the preparation week is to loosen mucus in the body. This diet also contains foods that put no additional toxic stress on the major organs and systems of the body. It is simple to follow and offers plenty of choice. These are the major points:

☆   Eat organic. If it is difficult for you to find an organic supplier, check the guidelines in Part Eight, on Rejuvenation, on how to clear pollution from your food.

☆   Try to get the majority of your protein from grains (especially sprouted grains as they produce much less mucus), nuts, seeds and legumes.

☆   Eat deep-water fish as an additional source of protein. Deep-water fish are less likely to be contaminated with toxic industrial waste and heavy metals. However, avoid herring, mackerel and tuna, which are particularly susceptible to pollution from heavy metals. Farmed salmon are often fed with artificial colours to make their flesh pink, so this should be avoided too – wild salmon is OK.

☆ Eat lots of raw vegetables and fruit.

☆ Eat plenty of fibre. Some of the best forms of fibre are sprouted legumes, cabbage, carrots and millet.

☆ Drink lots of water. If you're drinking bottled water choose a brand that uses glass, rather than plastic, containers, as bacteria multiplies faster in plastic containers. Keep it refrigerated and drink it quickly, preferably on the same day it is opened. Avoid sparkling water as it produces excess gas.

☆ Stick to cold-pressed oils for dressing salads and adding to grains. Only use cold-pressed olive oil for cooking.

☆ Avoid all products with E numbers, especially E249, E250, E251 and E252, which are used in preservation. Try to exclude completely all processed foods, and products with colourings, flavourings and artificial sweeteners.

☆ Avoid mucus-forming foods.

- Daily produce from cows' milk is the most mucus-forming food – so this will include, not only milk itself but also butter, cheese, yoghurt etc. Goats' and sheep's milk produce has much less mucus but keep it to a minimum.
- Red meat, poultry and eggs.
- Soya beans are the most mucus-forming of the plant foods. Many people use soya milk as a substitute to cows' milk to reduce mucus. It is a big mistake. Use oat or rice milk instead.

☆ Avoid eating large amounts of sugar, especially refined sugars. Instead use maple syrup, concentrated apple juice, date syrup and honey. If you have strong sugar cravings, try cleaning your tongue in the morning with a teaspoon, gently scraping the surface, as this will reduce the craving for sweet and sour foods.

☆ Reduce your salt intake. In the far east of Russia there is plenty of algae, which is known as sea cabbage. Eaten dry, this is beneficial for the body, providing a good substitute for salt as well as providing iodine, which is known to stimulate the metabolism. You can also use one of the many Japanese types of seaweed that are readily available in health shops.

☆ Drink no alcohol. No tea or coffee. No stimulants! You can drink herbal teas freely, or try the suggestions in the box below.

☆ Do not eat at night – have your meal at least two to three hours before bed. If you are pondering whether to eat or not, don't!

ALTERNATIVES TO TEA AND COFFEE

Spicy drink

> *four grains of cardamom*
> *four peppercorns*
> *three cloves*
> *fresh ginger (to taste)*
> *cinnamon (to taste)*

Grind all the ingredients. Put in a saucepan, cover with 300 ml of water and simmer for twenty minutes. Before turning off the heat, you can add a pinch of green tea. When drinking, you may add a little honey, if desired.

☆ You can also try soaking dried fruits in warm water. Add honey to taste for a soothing, sweet hot drink.

☆ Make the most of the huge variety of herbal teas now available – made from leaves, fruits and berries. Remember, don't add sugar.

☆ You can also drink the wonderful Russian drink sbitin freely – see page 277.

Cleansing the body of excess mucus using horseradish juice

You will notice I say to avoid foods that are mucus-forming. This is very important. There is also a specific mixture of grated horseradish and lemon juice that can help tremendously in loosening and eliminating mucus from parts of the body where it tends to stagnate (i.e. the digestive tract, sinuses, throat, respiratory system). Also it has a very good diuretic effect. You will be taking this mixture before your morning and evening meals.

☆ Take 150 g of grated horseradish and the juice of three lemons.

☆ Mix the ingredients to the consistency of thick yoghurt (like Greek yoghurt).

☆ Take half a teaspoon twice daily before your morning and evening meal. The leftover mixture should be refrigerated in a closed glass container.

Warm hydrotherapy and skin brushing

As you will remember from Chapter 7, warm hydrotherapy can help to loosen mucus. Therefore it is an essential part of our preparation. Ideally I would like you to have some form of warm hydrotherapy every day. If you live near a sauna or steam room, that's wonderful. If not, use the home alternatives given in Chapter 7. If at all possible, do make the effort to get to a steam room at least once during your preparation week, as it really is wonderfully effective at loosening mucus.

Remember that, before you have warm hydrotherapy, you need to practise five minutes of skin brushing. You can use any of the techniques given in Chapter 7. Don't be tempted to skip this: remember, skin brushing is a highly effective technique for stimulating the expulsion of mucus and loosening other toxic matter that clogs the lymphatic system and the lymph nodes. It is a vital part of the programme.

Clay water

Clay is important for our cleansing programme. As you will recall, it absorbs toxins, stabilises the electromagnetic system and restores the pH balance of our bodies. You will be taking it early in the morning, before breakfast. You can either make up clay water in advance, or prepare it just before drinking – it's entirely up to you. The instructions are on pp. 69–70.

Energy exercise: cleansing the energy of fear of the future

As a practitioner I see the huge benefits of combining physical work with emotional healing. Therefore each week on this detox we will be using a different energy exercise, meditations that help us release toxic emotions. We start with this energy meditation, cleansing the energy of fear of the future.

As you prepare your body to get rid of mucus and physical toxins, you need to prepare yourself, emotionally and mentally, to be more open. You need to be open to the future and what it will bring. It's important to be able to expand your vision, to accept new recipes and new guidelines. If you are afraid of the future, you will tend to get stuck in your old patterns, to become paralysed by anxiety. You will be unable to enjoy life in the now, because all your energy is pushing forwards, panicking about what has not yet happened and may, indeed, never happen.

This meditation frees you from this anxiety and allows you to create space for the new. It primes you for shifting your life into a new pattern. You will recall from our earlier discussion, that colours affect our chakras – too much or too little of a colour can put us out of balance. The energy of fear of the future manifests itself by an excess of the colour blue, which is why we use this colour in the technique.

The visualisation is accompanied by a physical action (the wringing of a towel) because this engages both the left and right sides of the brain, making the exercise more effective. Also, the wringing is a tangible action and I find that this is very helpful for modern people who like action.

You need to practise this exercise every day this week. I don't mind when you do it but make sure you have enough peace and quiet to be able to give it your full attention. Many people find the evening is a good time for this exercise. The room you use for this cleansing exer-cise should be well aired and a window should be left open for at least half an hour before you begin this exercise.

Breathe freely and naturally throughout this exercise – don't strain. You will require a large bowl and a cotton towel.

☆   Wet the towel thoroughly and place in the bowl. Sit on a straight-backed chair with your legs astride, feet shoulder-width apart. Place the bowl between your legs on the floor. Your back should be softly rounded and your stomach pulled in (as if you were drawing your navel back to your spine).

☆   Hold your arms straight out in front of you with the palms of your hands upwards. You should have a gap of about 10 centimetres between your hands. Lay the towel across the fingers of your upturned hands. Imagine that the towel is a deep pure blue.

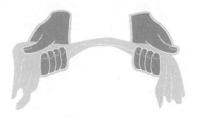

☆   Concentrate on the space between your wrists. Take a deep breath in through the nose and hold it for a few seconds. Then relax, exhale and wring out the towel. As you physically wring the water out of the towel, use your imagination too – imagine that you are wringing out every bit of the blue colour from the towel.

☆ Take another deep breath, hold, exhale and wring yet more blue from the towel.

☆ Now empty the bowl and repeat but, this time, imagine you are wringing a vivid orange from the towel. As you wring out the towel, tone the sound "L-l-l-l" – a smooth, continuous sound. If you are familiar with musical notes this sound should be the same pitch as the note "Sol" (G).

☆ At this moment you should try to feel the sense of release from all fear of future events. Remember this sensation and try to fix it in your memory.

The diet you are following in this preparatory week will also help you to free yourself from anxiety. Certain foods are well known to increase anxiety – in particular coffee, tea and other foods containing caffeine, such as chocolate and many fizzy drinks. Sugar also increases anxiety so it's important to avoid it. Don't forget that sugar is often a hidden ingredient in many (very many) foods. All these foods will lead to a constant feeling of being tired and a deep sense of dissatisfaction with oneself.

Clothing

To support you this week, I recommend you add small quantities of orange to your wardrobe – a scarf, tie, belt, wrap. Orange as a colour helps inspire a whole raft of positive feelings – joy, happiness and inspiration.

The "Inner Smile" exercise

This is a favourite exercise of mine. Possessing this "inner smile", and connecting to it as much as possible, will really help to lighten up your astral body, the body of your emotions. The reasoning behind it is simple. When you laugh or smile (be it externally or internally) you become far less exposed to the forces of negative emotions and energies. When you smile easily and readily, not only do your astral vibrations become lighter but also your aura becomes better protected. Here is a simple meditation exercise that will help you do this. It is a beautiful way to start the day. Perform this exercise as you lie in bed, first thing in the morning.

☆ As you awake, turn so you are lying on your back, arms and legs relaxed and long.

☆ Take a deep breath and gradually exhale, letting out all the stale night air from your body. Repeat three times.

☆ Now move the toes on your right foot a few times – your big toe lifts up slightly while the other toes dip slightly. Repeat with your left foot.

☆ Now move onto your fingers and hands. Take the tip of the thumb on your left hand and lightly shake it. Repeat this with your right thumb.

☆ Smile to yourself – it turns your whole morning and day into a celebration, while you are still in bed!

☆ Take a deep breath, filling your lungs completely, and then allow the breath to go deeper down into your stomach. Hold the breath for a few seconds, and then slowly exhale in the opposite sequence – from your stomach and then your lungs.

☆ Take a small break and then repeat the deep breath again. You should have spent about two minutes on this exercise up to now.

☆ Continue the deep breathing but, in place of holding your breath, smile. So you inhale, pause and smile, then exhale. You should be smiling in such a way that tiny wrinkles appear around your eyes as a result of the gentle movement.

☆ Now make your smile wide and sincere. Your eyes should be relaxed (imagine you are looking at a sky full of stars).

☆ Continue smiling and visualise the colour pink.

☆ Breathe in very deeply so the colour fills your lungs and the whole of your body.

☆ Pink is the energy of love, which takes over all your being. Every cell of your body is radiating the colour pink.

☆ Don't forget to keep that smile! Whilst smiling, clearly say to yourself: "What I have lost I do not regret. The way into the future is free. I am a new liberated person." You need to say this five to ten times, convincingly and energetically.

This is a lovely meditation and the more you do it, the more benefits you will discover. While it is an essential part of this preparation week, you can also use it throughout the entire programme, for even better results.

YOUR DAILY SCHEDULE IN THE PREPARATION WEEK

It may seem as if you have a lot of work to do! But really it is not too arduous. A normal day in the first week would go like this:

☆ Wake up: practise "Inner Smile" in bed, then take clay water

☆ Skin brush before shower or warm hydrotherapy

☆ Breakfast: take horseradish anti-mucus mixture then have breakfast

☆ On way to work: meditation (Healthy Way of Life tuning)

☆ Lunch

☆ Evening meal: take horseradish anti-mucus mixture before eating

☆ Energy exercise

☆ Warm hydrotherapy (if not taken in morning)

Meditation: *Healthy Way of Life* tuning

You need to practise the tuning *Healthy Way of Life* every day. You will find this tuning in the Appendix. I don't mind when you practise this chanting meditation – many people like to do it in the evening, after work. However, if you record it, you can use it any time during the day, on the way to work, in your lunch hour, when in bed.

CHAPTER ELEVEN

Colon Cleansing Programme

This second phase of the programme once again lasts for one week. Having prepared your body and primed your mind and emotions for success, you can move onto this deep cleansing. Do you really need to cleanse your colon? Yes, yes, yes. I cannot think of anyone who wouldn't benefit from this cleanse: in my experience there are precious few people who do not have congested colons.

You cannot expect to be well if the main organ responsible for ridding the body of toxic waste is under-functioning. When the colon becomes irritated by diet, stress, drugs, chemicals and other substances, it tries to protect itself by producing more mucus. This mucus binds with any undigested refined processed foods and builds up on the walls of the bowel into a thick layer of hardened faeces. This not only narrows the passage of the colon but also is an ideal environment in which pathological micro-organisms can breed. Even if your bowel movements are regular it is no guarantee that you have escaped this problem.

Colon cleansing is the first vital step in my programme. I simply cannot imagine that rejuvenation can take place while the colon is toxic and congested.

During the colon cleansing our aim is to regulate the following processes:

☆ Colon cleansing
☆ Regulating peristaltic movements
☆ Restoring healthy gut flora (good bacteria)

This will allow us to eliminate the main source of toxicity in our body and, as a result, to relieve the other purification systems of the body.

Week Two programme: colon cleansing

Once again, there are several elements to your daily routine. The first three are exactly the same as those we used in the first week you have just completed. Let's swiftly recap.

Diet

Continue with the diet you are already following for the preparation week. Tweak your diet if necessary for optimum balance. I will also be giving you some ideal breakfast recipes for this stage of your cleanse. Remember, during your detox, drink no less than 2 litres of water daily. Never take water with food. It's best to drink it half an hour before meals, or two hours after, to prevent interference with the stomach juices.

Clay water

Just as you did in the preparation week, you will be starting each day by drinking clay water.

Warm hydrotherapy and skin brushing

Continue with these as in the preparation week.

The next three are familiar too – energy exercise, clothing and meditation (tuning). However, this week you will be using some variations. Let's take a look.

Energy exercise: cleansing the energy of the past

As with the preparation week, you will be working on your emotions as well as your body. This time we will be working with cleansing the energy of the past. During this week, while you are cleansing your colon, I would like you to practise this exercise every day. In the same way that we are starting to let go of the physical waste matter stuck to our colons, it's also important that we start letting go of negative emotions, which are stuck to our souls.

Many of us spend our lives holding tight onto past hurts and grievances. In my experience people with constipation and colon problems definitely tend to hold onto the past. When we do this, we become strongly bound to the past and totally unable to move on with our lives. In order to begin cleansing the energy of the past, you need to start letting go of past grievances and grudges. Right away! The techniques I suggest here are very effective. They have helped many people so please pay special attention and try them. You will probably be in for a surprise!

If there is someone who disturbs you or has disturbed you, try this:

☆　Start by remembering a person who disturbs you, or used to disturb you in the past. Bring them into your mind's eye in great detail. What did he or she look like? See their face, see their body, notice their body language. Hear his or her voice, its intonations, and its tone.

☆　The moment the image of this person is clear in your mind, imagine (however hard it may be) this person happy and smiling. Something very good has happened to this person; something he or she has been waiting for, or trying to achieve, has happened. This person is truly happy. Try to hold this image for one to two minutes.

☆ In your mind's eye, draw a pink circle, a circle of love, around this person. Now, very slowly and gently, break this circle, dissolving the image of the person with whom you are working. As you do this, you need to try to feel, not only the release from the energy of the past which was binding you to this person, but also happiness from the fact that you have just seen this person filled with joy. Remember these sensations and fix them in your memory.

☆ It may happen that you will find yourself in places where this person lives, or worked, and unpleasant feelings may overtake you. Don't worry. Simply smile and remember the sensations you experienced when you dissolved the pink circle. Say to yourself: "I am not feeling anything. You are forgiven. You are released."

On the other hand, if you know you have offended someone in the past, you must ask for forgiveness – out loud – from the bottom of your heart. Say:

☆ "I am asking (*the name of the person you have upset*) to forgive me for having hurt you."

☆ "I am asking myself to forgive myself for allowing myself to hurt (*the name of the person*). I forgive myself."

☆ "I am asking myself for forgiveness for my behaviour towards (*name of person*) which caused harm to my health."

☆ "I am asking myself to forgive myself for having born grudges and for holding onto the past. I forgive myself."

☆ "I am asking my body to forgive myself for causing it harm by my mindless behaviour."

Clothing

This week, try to introduce splashes of red into your clothing. You don't have to dress head-to-toe in red, just add a scarf, some jewellery, a shawl or tie.

Meditation: *Healthy Spirit* tuning

This week we start using the tuning, *Healthy Spirit* (as described in the Appendix). It's a long tuning but please don't be put off. Sometimes there simply isn't a short, easy solution. Think about it: it's taken all your life to accumulate these unhealthy patterns so it's a little unlikely that they can be wiped out with a sentence. Again, I would suggest the best way to take in this powerful tuning is to tape it and listen to it as it suits you through the day. Remember, you should use a monotonous rhythm. Once again, you may find some of the phrasing strange but give yourself permission to just accept it as it is.

In addition to these familiar elements, we will be introducing some powerful techniques for cleansing the colon. Let's look at these now.

Russian detox recipe

This is another very effective recipe. You should take a tablespoon of this mixture before each meal you eat this week.

☆ Chop up three lemons (with skins left on).

☆ Add to three cloves of finely grated garlic and three tablespoons of honey. Mix altogether with 3 litres of pre-boiled, cooled water.

☆ Infuse the mixture for three days in a glass container with a lid. After this it is ready for use.

Wheat bran breakfast

For breakfast, I recommend wheat bran, which has a powerful cleansing effect on the digestive system. The most important ability of bran fibre is to retain water. One gram of wheat bran can absorb up to five grams of water. The presence of the minute fibres of bran in the digestive system promotes softening and loosening of the stool matter, thus accelerating its transit time in the colon.

Shortly after the Chernobyl nuclear disaster, rescue workers were given 20–30 grams of wheat brain as part of their daily diet and this dramatically reduced absorption of free radicals from the digestive system into the bloodstream. This is another valuable quality of bran – its ability to cleanse the blood and flush out free radicals.

Wheat bran breakfast recipe

☆ Overnight pre-soak two tablespoons of fine wheat bran in enough water to cover it. I recommend you add in dried apricots (unsulphured), prunes, raisins and/or some fine porridge oats.

☆ If desired, you can add in some nuts the following morning. Then eat.

Colon cleansing exercises

I would like you to practise certain exercises daily, before breakfast, to stimulate peristalsis of the colon. Try to keep a good technique when you do these exercises to ensure you do not put strain on your neck or back. Take them slowly and very carefully – this isn't a sit-up competition!

Elbow and knee twist

☆ Lie on your back and lightly support your neck with your thumb and forefinger. Look up at the ceiling to keep a 45-degree angle between your chin and collarbone.

☆ Pull in your stomach, as if your navel were trying to meet your spine. Pull up your pelvic floor muscles and hold them tight.

☆ Inhale. Then exhale as you bend the right knee in towards your chest and reach the upper body over to touch your left elbow to the right knee.

☆ Inhale as you release and return to starting position.

☆ Repeat with opposite knee and elbow.

☆   Continue for at least twelve repetitions.

Double knee twist

☆   Lie on your back and lightly support your neck with thumb and forefinger as before.

☆   Once again, pull your stomach in, navel to spine, and pull up your pelvic floor. Inhale. Exhale and bring both knees up to both elbows. It's a little like an old-fashioned crunch but more slowly and with total control. Remember to keep looking upwards at all times so as not to strain your neck.

☆   Hold for three to six seconds. Inhale as you slowly with control return to your starting position.

☆   Repeat for at least twelve times. Make sure you coordinate your breath with the movements.

Knee-over twist

☆   Lie flat with your arms at your side.

☆   Bring your left knee up to a 90-degree angle as you inhale.

☆   Keeping your shoulders flat, twist at the waist and bring your leg over to the right side as you exhale. Hold for three seconds.

☆   Inhale as you bring the leg back up.

☆   Exhale as you slowly return to your starting position.

☆   Repeat with the other leg.

☆   Continue for about twelve repetitions.

Cycling

Cycling is another good form of exercise because it helps massage the colon as your thighs alternate the pressure on the ascending and descending colon.

Deep colon cleansing

There are two basic ways in which you can gently help your

colon to eliminate caked-on mucus and faecal matter. The first is a traditional Russian recipe that employs several well-known laxatives. The second involves psyllium. Research has found that psyllium binds with, and removes, toxins and mucus that stick to and build up on the colon walls. Psyllium is a powder made from the crushed seed of the herb plantain. This swells when mixed with water or juice to produce bulk and weight. This improves peristalsis without producing too much roughage and dilation of the colon. The husk is more effective than the seed.

Method one: Russian laxative recipe

Every day this week, before you go to bed, take one tablespoon of the following mixture:

- ☆ 100 g each of finely chopped apricots, prunes, raisins
- ☆ 70 g honey (ideally, Manuka honey but any organic honey is fine)
- ☆ 30 g chopped walnuts
- ☆ 100 g dried senna

Mix this with lukewarm water if you prefer. You can store the left-over mixture in a sealed glass container.

Method two: psyllium

Take one teaspoon of psyllium (readily available from health food stores), stir it into a glass of diluted fruit juice and swallow immediately before it thickens. Follow it by a large glass of water. If you don't like taking it in this way, you can buy capsules. Just follow the directions on the jar.

Advanced colon cleansing

Enemas are the most popular way of colon cleansing in Russia. Some people are squeamish about cleansing with enemas, yet they think nothing of storing piles of rotting waste inside their bodies. Nowadays there are many clinics in the West offering colonic hydrotherapy (also known as colonic irrigation), which is a quick and efficient way to loosen impacted faeces and wash away toxins. It is very useful when you are undergoing a stringent detox such as my cleansing programme.

Here's what happens. A sterile plastic tube is inserted into the rectum and filtered water is washed around the colon. An evacuation tube removes the water, taking with it possibly years of accumulated debris and mucus. The process is discreet and not at all painful.

If you choose this method, follow the guidance provided by your practitioner.

You can also perform a modified version of this at home with a water enema kit. This is an effective way of removing toxins, however the water usually reaches only as far as the sigmoid and descending colon – so it is not as intense and far-reaching as colonic irrigation.

Enema kits can be purchased from pharmacies and consist of a two-quart rubber bag, 4-ft piece of tubing with a clamp, a 2.5-inch enema nozzle.

The best time for colon cleansing is either between 5 and 7 am, or 8 and 9 pm, so you can either do this before breakfast or in the evening if you don't have time in the morning.

! This is usually a very safe procedure; however, I would ask you to check with your doctor before taking an enema to ensure you have no conditions that might be contraindicated.

How to use a home enema kit

☆ Close the clamp on the tubing and attach the shorter enema nozzle. Fill the bag with body temperature water. Use only bottled water, as chlorine tends to destroy the good bacteria in the gut.

☆ Thoroughly dissolve one teaspoon of salt and one teaspoon of baking soda in half a cup of warm water. Add this mixture to the bag and stir well.

☆ Open the clamp and let water run through the tubing to remove any air. Then reclamp.

☆ Lubricate the nozzle with olive oil.

☆ Hang the bag on your bathroom door knob.

☆ Lie on your left side on the bathroom floor (or on all fours) and gently insert the lubricated tip into the rectum.

☆ Open the clamp slowly. If at any time you have a feeling of fullness, try closing the clamp, waiting five to ten seconds, and then unclamping. The colon does not like to be rushed, and you may be able to fill it with more water this way.

☆ Although ideally you should be able to take in almost the entire bag of water, the colon may be able to accept only a quarter or half of the bag at this time.

☆ To assist colon cleansing this way, breathe through your nose and as you inhale and exhale make rhythmical pumping movements with your stomach, pulling it in and out.

☆ When you feel full, reclamp, remove the nozzle, gently bring your feet behind your head (optional) and then sit on the toilet to

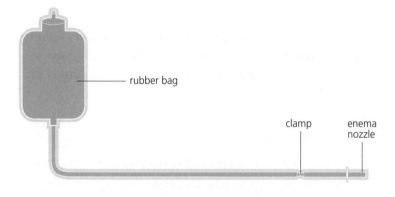

The standard enema kit

expel the water, helping yourself by gently massaging around your navel clockwise.

☆ Empty out any leftover solution, rinse the bag and tubing and reclamp.

Your weekly plan for enema use

☆ Day one: fill enema bag with 0.5 litres of water.

☆ Day two: fill with 1 litre of water.

☆ Day three: rest, no enema.

☆ Day four: fill with 1.5 litres of water.

☆ Day five: rest, no enema.

☆ Day six: rest, no enema.

☆ Day seven: fill with 2 litres of water.

Alternative (for experienced detoxers)

If you have used enemas before, or are returning to this programme for a second or subsequent time, you can use 2 litres of water in the enema bag, which is a more advanced option.

If you are experienced in the use of enemas and if you are also proficient in yoga, you can enhance the process by using yoga *asanas* (postures) while holding the water inside your colon. Start by lying down on your back. Then move into a shoulder stand, followed by the Plough.

! Please do not attempt this unless you already practise yoga on a regular basis.

The salad "broom"

This really does exactly what it says – it acts like a broom sweeping clean your guts. It is a marvellous catalyst for stimulating peristalsis of the colon and helping to get rid of stagnant matter. Ideally you should use organic vegetables for this. During the colon

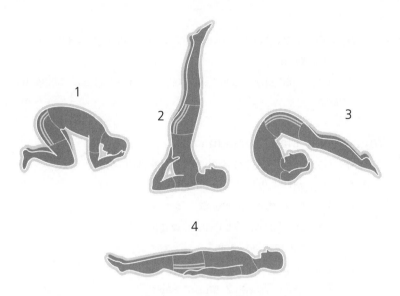

This is the exercise routine you can perform after the enema,
but before expelling the water

and liver cleansing stage of the detox, this will act as your lunch or part of your lunch every day.

☆   Mix fresh grated cabbage, carrot and beetroot in a proportion of 3:1:1.

☆   Squeeze the mixture with your hands to let some juice out.

☆   Add a little lemon juice and dress with linseed oil.

☆   Add four or five prunes that you have previously lightly soaked in water for about two hours.

Balloon exercise to let go of the past

This is a powerful exercise that will help you get rid of old matter – whether physical or metaphysical – from your system. It will help you release deeply seated emotional blockages and also to allow your physical body to let go and open up its passages to release stuck-on matter and toxins. You will need a pack of balloons – any size or colour – and a needle.

☆ Blow up a balloon slowly and carefully. With each exhale, breath out all the unpleasant emotions and memories you have, that you want to get out of your system.

☆ Once the balloon is fully inflated, and full of your old "stuff", tie a knot in it.

☆ Take the balloon in one hand and the needle in the other. Close your eyes, breathe and try to imagine (as vividly as possible) a situation that has caused you pain or which is burdening you. You should find that your emotional response is becoming acute and almost overwhelming. Wait until you feel it is going to take you over completely and, at that point and not before, pop the balloon!

It is important not to premeditate when you're going to pop the balloon. You should let it happen almost of its own accord, in a totally spontaneous way. If you can manage this, you will have a very powerful reaction. The sudden sound will free up the energy and push the blockage out of the aura.

YOUR DAILY SCHEDULE IN THE COLON CLEANSING WEEK

This is how an average day in your second week might look:

☆ On waking:
- "Inner Smile" exercise (optional) (pages 103–5)
- Colon exercises
- Colon cleansing (enema – optional)
- Clay water
- Skin brushing and warm hydrotherapy

☆ Before breakfast: Russian detox recipe (page 111)

☆ Breakfast: wheat bran/oats

☆ On way to work (or any time): meditation (Healthy Spirit tuning)

☆ Before lunch: Russian detox recipe

☆ Lunch: salad "broom"

☆ Before evening meal:
- Colon cleansing (enema) – if not done in the morning
- Russian detox recipe

☆ Evening meal: your choice following guidelines

☆ Evening: energy exercise – cleansing energy of the past

☆ Before bed: if you haven't chosen to use enemas, take either the Russian laxative recipe or psyllium for colon cleansing (page 114).

You can practise the balloon exercise to let go of the past as much as you feel necessary.

CHAPTER TWELVE

Liver Cleansing Programme

Now we move onto the third stage of detoxing. This follows directly after the week of colon cleansing and also lasts for a week.

The liver is our waste disposal unit. When it's working efficiently, it will eliminate environmental toxins and waste products properly. The liver's tasks are the storage and filtration of blood, the secretion of bile and numerous metabolic functions, including the conversion of sugar into glycogen. It plays a vital part in fat metabolism and oxidation of fat to produce energy. It is also the liver's job to make bile, between 1 and 1.5 litres per day, which gets released into the gall bladder. Bile carries with it numerous products that have been deactivated and neutralised by the liver: drugs, hormones and waste products. In its turn the gall bladder expels bile into the intestine. From here it is excreted.

As I've already said, all detoxing works best in spring. It's a particularly suitable time for liver cleansing because, on an energetic level, the liver is strongest in spring. If this isn't possible, try to avoid autumn. The liver is weakest at this time of year and the cleansing process can drain it even further. I will show you various forms of liver cleansing – some gentler then others. If this is your first detox on my programme, I recommend you follow the seven-day gentle liver detox programme.

Week Three programme: gentle liver detox

Once again, there are various elements to your detox.

Diet

Your baseline diet is the same as in the preparation week. However, you need to increase your consumption of vegetables, shifting as far as possible to a vegetarian diet while avoiding mucus-forming foods such as dairy and soya. In particular eat lots of foods that are yellow in colour: dried apricots, Sharon fruit, nuts, lemons, bread with bran etc.

Dandelion tea can and should be drunk freely throughout this week. Dandelion is a very important herb for the liver as it is a gentle liver tonic that helps to increase the secretion of bile.

You can take a milk thistle supplement. Milk thistle (*silymarin*) is another very good herb for the liver. There has been impressive research carried out on milk thistle, proving its liver-protecting qualities as well as enhancing its detoxification processes. It can increase the number of new liver cells replacing old damaged ones. It can be taken as a tincture or in capsule form.

Porridge

For breakfast this week I would ideally like you to eat porridge.

☆ Soak five tablespoons of oats in cold water overnight. Use organic oats. There should be enough water to cover 5 centimetres over the oats.

☆ In the morning, heat but do not boil. Add honey if you wish to sweeten the porridge.

Buckwheat

If you prefer, you can eat buckwheat cooked according to the

Russian oven technique described on page 262. Or you might prefer puffed buckwheat (available from health stores). Remember not to use cow's or soya milk – almond or rice milk is better.

Alternatively, try buckwheat kasha cleansing, which is wonderful at stimulating bile production. Here's the Russian recipe:

☆ Soak one cup of buckwheat in cold water for two to three hours.

☆ Strain and discard the water.

☆ Add three cups of fresh water and bring to the boil. Simmer for ten to fifteen minutes.

☆ Remove the kasha from the heat and allow to rest for a few minutes.

☆ You can add a dash of oil of your choice, but do not add salt.

Liver flush juice

On days four to seven of the programme, you will be taking liver flush juice first thing in the morning, on an empty stomach.

☆ Put 250 ml each of freshly squeezed lemon juice and mineral water into a liquidiser.

☆ Add one fresh garlic clove, one tablespoon of extra virgin olive oil and 1 cm fresh ginger root (sliced). Liquidise for a few moments until it forms a smooth liquid and drink slowly.

☆ If you find it hard to take, try substituting organic apple juice for the lemon and just add a squeeze of lemon juice.

☆ In either case, you can drink some apple juice afterwards to get rid of the after-taste, then fifteen minutes later drink a cup of hot peppermint tea.

Clay water

Continue with clay water as in the previous weeks.

Horseradish anti-mucus mixture

You will also be taking this horseradish juice once more (as in Week One, preparation for cleansing, see pages 99–100) this time to stimulate the liver. Take this before your morning and evening meals except on days four to seven (when you're taking the liver flush juice): on these days just have it before the evening meal.

Salad "broom"

You will also continue with salad "broom" at lunchtime – as described on page 117. However, this week you can take it as just part of your lunch, so you don't get too bored.

Warm hydrotherapy

This week we continue skin brushing and using warm hydrotherapy; however, we will be using coniferous oils in our hydrotherapy. You can continue to take steams or saunas, using pine, cypress or cedar oils (on the coals or on your towel). Alternatively, put a few drops of these oils in your bath.

! Avoid pine if you have allergic skin conditions. Avoid cypress and cedar during pregnancy: remember you should not be detoxing in the first place if you are pregnant!

Energy exercise: cleansing the energy of anger

This week we are going to work on cleansing the energy of anger, an emotion often associated with the liver. Anger usually shows itself by an excess of the colour red in the aura.

I would recommend practising this exercise in the morning. Spend up to fifteen minutes (no more). You don't have to practise this every day unless you know you have an issue with anger. The room in which you work on cleansing the excess red energy must be well aired and a window should be left open for at least half an hour before you start this exercise.

Throughout the exercise breathe freely and naturally. You will require a large bowl and a cotton towel.

☆ Thoroughly wet the towel and place in the bowl. Sit on a chair with your back straight, the bowl on the floor between your feet. Take a few calm, slow breaths through the nose. Now inhale through the nose, hold for two or three seconds, and then exhale, again through the nose. Repeat this for a few minutes until you feel calm and focused.

☆ Take the wet towel from the bowl. Set your legs astride, shoulder-width apart. Your back should be softly rounded, stomach pulled in (as if you were pulling your navel back towards your spine). Hold your arms straight out with the palms of your hands upwards. You need a gap of about 10 centimetres between your hands. Lay the towel across the fingers of your upturned hands.

☆ Now bring your attention to the towel and imagine it has turned a deep red in colour. Take a deep breath in through the nose and hold it. Then squeeze your stomach and begin physically wringing the towel, imagining you are squeezing out all the red colour into the bowl below. Put as much effort as you possibly can into this. As you wring the towel, tone the long, drawn-out sound "oh" through your teeth. If you are familiar with musical notes, this sound is the same pitch as the note "doh" (C).

☆ Repeat the previous step for as long as you feel necessary, until all the red has vanished from the towel and is in the bowl below (in your imagination) and the towel has physically stopped dripping. You should feel a sense of release from all the negative emotions you have experienced in the past. Imagine you are wringing out, not just water, but all the grudges, grievances, misunderstandings, rudeness and insults you have given and received. Remember this sensation; try to fix it in your memory.

☆ When you feel ready, discard the water in the bowl. If you still don't feel calm, wet the towel again and repeat the whole exercise (some of us have a lot of red to release!).

☆ End by sitting quietly and breathing as you did at the start of this exercise. Then get up and have a good stretch.

Keep the towel you used in this exercise and use it to dry your face in the morning. Imagine that it is absorbing all the excess energy of the colour red within you.

Clothing

When you are working with red anger energy, it's a good idea to wear clothes of light grey, with a little green to further balance the energy.

Meditation: *Healthy Spirit* tuning

This week you will continue with the tuning *Healthy Spirit*. If you wish, you can use it with your partner or family – either all say it together or you say it to them. It's beneficial for everyone, whether detoxing or not.

Tougher detox: alternative method (three days)

Once you have completed my programme fully for the first time and are returning, you may like to try this, somewhat more stringent, liver detox. I provide it to give you some variety for when you come back to this detox in future years.

The best time for this cleansing is during the full moon.

! Do not use this detox if you have gallstones, chronic or acute liver or gall bladder problems, in addition to the general contraindications for detox.

YOUR DAILY SCHEDULE IN THE LIVER CLEANSING WEEK

Once again, there seems to be a lot to do. Let's look at how you would plan an average day in the third week.

☆ On waking:
  - "Inner Smile" exercise (optional)
  - Clay water
  - Skin brushing and warm hydrotherapy
  - Liver flush (days four to seven only)

☆ Before breakfast: horseradish anti-mucus mixture (days one to three only)

☆ Breakfast:
  - Porridge or buckwheat kasha
  - Milk thistle supplement

☆ On way to work (or whenever you choose): meditation (positive tuning)

☆ Before lunch: horseradish anti-mucus mixture

☆ Lunch: vegetables/grains plus salad "broom"

☆ Before evening meal: horseradish anti-mucus mixture

☆ Evening meal: vegetables, fruits

☆ Evening: energy exercise – cleansing the energy of anger (as needed)

☆ Bedtime: if you feel your colon is still sluggish you can add in bedtime psyllium or Russian laxative recipe for colon cleansing (page 114).

☆ Throughout day: dandelion tea

This detox lasts for three days only. During that time you should eat only vegetables and fruits. In addition, you drink unlimited amount of the juice and broth that follow.

Beetroot and apple juice

One part of beetroot juice to four or five parts of apple juice (ideally sour varieties of apple only).

Note: always soak the peeled beetroots in water overnight before juicing.

Oat broth

☆ Add three tablespoons of oat grains and oat flakes mixed together to 0.5 litres of water.

☆ Bring to the boil over a slow heat and simmer for two to three minutes.

☆ Sieve it and it is ready to be used (if the consistency of the broth is too thick, you can dilute it with hot boiling water).

This is a fantastic drink as it is excellent for blood purification and for regulating the metabolism.

Variations

You can use salad "broom" on this programme and, if you wish, practise the tunings and energy exercise.

If you choose this method, it is essential you have warm hydrotherapy treatments daily and also enemas. I will now introduce a coffee enema that is used in some of these methods.

Coffee enema

The coffee solution is held in the colon for a short space of time to help detoxification of the liver.

☆ Add three tablespoons of ground coffee (real, not instant) to 250 ml of water.

☆ Boil for three minutes and then simmer for a further twenty minutes.

☆ Strain the coffee and allow to cool to body temperature.

☆ Follow instructions for the enemas given in the colon cleansing programme but, instead of water, use the coffee mixture.

☆ Let the solution run into the colon slowly and gradually – resist the urge to evacuate.

☆ Try if possible to retain the liquid for ten minutes and then expel.

If you prefer, you may substitute this enema with any recipe for gentle colon cleansing from Chapter 11.

Further advanced liver cleansing (seven days)

This is also for experienced detoxers only. Once again, I feel it is useful to have alternatives. This detox is very powerful. It lasts for seven days.

Again, you can use tunings and energy exercises on this programme.

Days one and two

1   During the first two days, eat only vegetables and fruits – mainly sour apples. The malic acid found in apples dissolves and softens gallstones and helps make the liver detox successful. Use only organic apples.

2   Drink plenty of mixed apple and beetroot juice.

3   Have water enemas and warm hydrotherapy.

Day three

1   Start the day with a coffee enema and warm hydrotherapy.

2   Drink mainly apple juice with virtually no food until 7 pm.

3   At 6.30 pm place a hot water bottle on the right side of your body over the liver.

4   After half an hour (7 pm), you will need to start drinking the following mixture: 200 ml of freshly squeezed lemon juice and 200 ml of unrefined cold pressed olive oil.

5   Every fifteen minutes you need to drink three tablespoons of the oil/lemon juice mix. Sip it through a straw. The liquids will separate – this doesn't matter, just alternate between the two, i.e. a sip of oil then a sip of juice. It should take a couple of hours to finish drinking the entire 400 ml of the mixture.

6   About halfway through drinking the mixture (between an hour to an hour and a half after you begin) practise this breathing exercise. The aim of this exercise is to stimulate liver energy. Sit upright, cover your left nostril with cotton wool or hold it with your thumb. Breathe through your right nostril for a few minutes or as long as you feel comfortable. Place your right palm on your liver (under your ribs on your right hand side). If you wish, you can also put a tiny bit of chilli pepper on the tip of your tongue. All this stimulates heat and liver activity.

7   Go to bed with a hot water bottle on your right side.

Day four

1   This morning you will most probably evacuate your bowels with a large amount of tar-like faeces. However, if a natural bowel movement does not occur, you should use a water enema.

2   Have warm hydrotherapy.

3   Make your first meal today, about three or four tablespoons of boiled rice. The rest of the day you should eat a vegetarian diet.

Days five to seven

Continue with a vegetarian diet.

CHAPTER THIRTEEN

Kidney Cleansing Programme

Week four of our detox and you should already be feeling huge benefits. This part of the detox lasts between three and seven days (depending on which time of year you do it) and focuses on cleansing the kidneys. Healthy kidneys expel from our system the end products of metabolism, excess salt, water, alien and toxic elements. The kidneys also regulate blood composition and ensure stability of the internal body environment.

Having cleansed your colon and liver, you will feel much stronger and healthier. Therefore kidney cleansing should go very smoothly. You can cleanse your kidneys at most times of the year (even in winter) but you will need to adapt your cleanse according to the season you choose.

You will probably be pleased to hear that this week is a much simpler detox with far fewer elements about which to worry.

These are the four elements of your daily routine:

1   Diet: this will depend on the season, but whichever method you choose, do not use salt or honey.
2   Warm hydrotherapy.
3   Energy exercise: cleansing from the energy of guilt and grudges.
4   Meditation: *Healthy Spirit* tuning.

Week Four programme: kidney cleansing for spring or summer

I will start with how to cleanse your kidneys in spring or summer, as I hope that you will be cleansing at this optimum time of the year.

Diet for spring or summer

☆ For the first three days you should follow the diet for the preparation week but exclude or reduce your protein consumption.

☆ You should also drink plenty of juice (at least 1 litre a day) – choose from these:

- Carrot, beetroot, cucumber: ten parts carrot to three each of beetroot and cucumber.
- Carrot, celery, parsley: nine parts carrot, five parts celery, two parts parsley.

☆ For the rest of the week you eat plain or toasted rye or wholemeal bread (no butter or spreads) plus watermelons (up to 3 kilos of watermelon a day): cut off the skin and the unripe part next to it to avoid nitrates. Note: if you find the bread and watermelon combination simply too tough, you can add in other vegetables and fruit.

☆ No salt. Throughout the cleansing programmes I have asked you to forgo salt but let me explain why it is absolutely essential that you do not take salt while cleansing the kidneys. Not only does salt make you retain water but also salt is well known to accompany feelings of sadness, sorrow and melancholy. People who overindulge in salt often tend to see the world as a dark place; they often connect themselves to past feelings of guilt. So do try to avoid salt consumption. At the very least, put away your salt mill and don't have it on the table. You can substitute salt with the following herbal mixture.

- Herbal "salt" mix: simply mix together dried dill and parsley, horseradish and garlic. This makes a fantastic substitute for salt and can be sprinkled onto foods where you'd usually use salt.
- If you're cooking, add some lemon juice or apple vinegar instead of salt.
- Celery is also naturally salty in taste so try this too.

☆ No honey. This is because it makes your body retain water, which is not desirable while cleansing the kidneys.

Warm hydrotherapy

Every day take a warm bath at the same time between 5 and 9 pm – at this time of the day kidney energy is at its peak. You can use any of the baths given in the warm hydrotherapy sections. Essential oils that support and tone the kidneys in particular include chamomile, cedarwood and juniper. Any oils with a diuretic action are also useful so you could try combinations of cypress, eucalyptus, fennel, frankincense, geranium and rosemary in addition to the three above. Remember that you will need to practise skin brushing before your bath.

! Cedarwood should not be used during pregnancy. People with epilepsy should not use fennel and rosemary.

Energy exercise: cleansing the energy of guilt and grudges

Guilt is a common emotion in our society. Equally, many of us waste our energy by holding onto grudges. Both these negative emotions show up in our aura as an excess of the colour yellow.

Use this cleansing throughout your kidney cleanse. You can also use it whenever you know (or if you suspect) you have blocks linked to feelings of guilt, sorrow and grievances.

Make sure you carry out this exercise in a well-aired room. Leave the window open for at least half an hour before you begin this exercise.

Throughout this exercise breathe freely and naturally. You will need a large bowl of water and a cotton hand towel.

☆ Wet the towel thoroughly. Sit with your legs astride, feet parallel to your shoulders. Your back should be rounded, your stomach pulled in (as if drawing your navel to your spine). Hold your arms straight out with the palms of your hands upwards. There should be a gap of about 10 centimetres between your hands. The towel should lie across the fingers of your upturned hands. The bowl is placed underneath the towel.

☆ Concentrate on the towel. Imagine the towel has become a deep yellow in colour. Take a deep breath in through the nose and hold it. Then relax, exhale and imagine you are wringing the yellow colour right out of the towel. Wring the towel physically with your hands, imagining drops of yellow falling into the bowl below. As you wring, tone the sound "ah" slowly and steadily (if you're familiar with musical notes, it's the same pitch as the note "fah" (F).) Make the sound really vibrate.

☆ Repeat this step until you feel you have wrung out all the yellow.

☆ During this exercise you should feel a sense of release from all your past grievances and unpleasant memories. Remember this feeling; fix it in your memory.

☆ Imagine now that the bowl is full of yellow water, all the colour you have wrung from the towel. Discard the water and have a good stretch.

In the future, any time you feel sad or guilty about the past, or remember being offended by anyone, immediately summon up your memory of how you felt at the end of this exercise. This simple action will help you get rid of all your past negativity.

Meditation: *Healthy Spirit* tuning

Continue with this tuning throughout your kidney cleanse.

Alternatives for other seasons

It is possible to cleanse your kidneys at any time of year, even winter. This is because it is not such a stringent detox. But you will need to adjust your diet a little. All other elements of the pro-gramme remain the same.

Diet for autumn

During the autumn period a shorter, three-day watermelon cleansing is recommended. This is actually the same as the second part of the spring/summer kidney detox.

☆ Simply eat plain or toasted rye or wholemeal bread plus watermelons (up to 3 kilos of watermelon a day): cut off the skin and the unripe part next to it to avoid nitrates. Note: if you find the bread and watermelon combination simply too tough, you can add in other vegetables and fruit.

Diet for winter

At this time of year you follow a diet of vegetables and fruits (if watermelon is available you can combine this method with that for autumn.) Again, this is a short, three-day cleanse. Make sure you drink plenty of water – at least 2 litres daily.

In addition, you will need to drink the following infusion (Russian recipe) for the first two days.

☆ Infuse one tablespoon of linseeds with a glass of boiled water in a thermos overnight.

☆ In the morning, filter the infusion and discard the seeds, add half a glass of boiled water.

☆ Drink this three times a day. If you find the taste unpleasant, you can add a little lemon juice.

After the detox

Following the detox you should be feeling absolutely wonderful, clearer and lighter in both body and emotions. So don't be tempted to launch straight back into bad habits. By now your intuition should be functioning well, and so it's unlikely you'll find yourself craving fry-ups or wanting to go binge drinking! However, I expect you will welcome a return to a normal routine and a less prescriptive diet. My best advice is to go to the basic guidelines for healthy eating, described in Part Eight on Rejuvenation, enjoying a wide variety of seasonal, fresh, life-enhancing food.

If you wish, you can continue elements of the detox programmes, and your body and mind will be delighted! Skin brushing should now be such a habit that it makes sense to continue: it's five minutes a day well spent in enhancing your immune system. If you can, make warm hydrotherapy a weekly event – or whenever you need a boost.

I would suggest you carry on with the tunings and energy exercises until you feel the full benefits: your intuition will tell you when you've done enough. Then you can use them as and when you need them – as a top-up or to deal with unpleasant emotions if they arise in the future.

Do not continue with the enemas or the detox recipes after you have finished the programme. It's also a good idea to give clay a break.

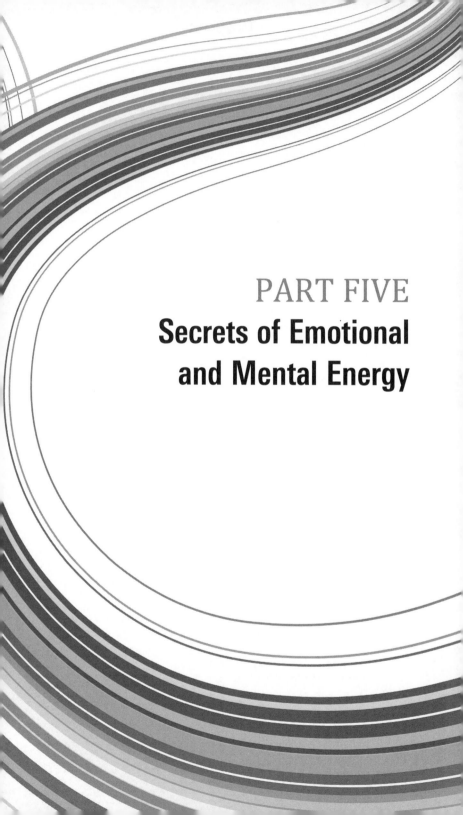

PART FIVE

Secrets of Emotional and Mental Energy

CHAPTER FOURTEEN

Negative Emotions in Our Astral Body

Congratulations on completing the physical cleansing programmes – it's a huge achievement and a wonderful gift to your body. You will also have been doing some valuable groundwork for the next stage of my programme for total health: detoxing emotional and mental energy. As I have already explained, the key to physical healing and emotional equilibrium lies with the seven energy bodies that make up our aura, and also the energy centres (chakras) and channels (*nadis* or meridians) that run through our bodies. I cannot say it often enough: there is no point in patching up your physical symptoms if you are leaving the root cause untouched. The symptoms might be suppressed and disappear for a while but they will almost certainly return. All true healing starts on an energy level.

I hope you will now realise just how complex our energy bodies are. Just as many things can go wrong in our physical bodies, our energy bodies are vulnerable to damage in many, many ways.

You may recall that the astral body is also known as our emotional body. So it's not that surprising that negative emotions such as anger and fear can damage our aura. So too can negative attachments to other people. There are even such things as "energy vampires" but don't panic – they don't have pointy teeth and blood-red eyes! In this part of the book, I will explain how imbalance is caused in our auras and chakras, and show you simple techniques for bringing yourself back into balance.

I give many techniques, mediations and rituals, a huge number. Please don't be alarmed – I don't expect you to practise all of them, all the time. Although I was very firm about the need to follow every part of the physical detox programmes to the letter, you'll probably be relieved to hear that I am not so strict from now on! This is because your own intuition will have been freed following the physical detox and you will be more in touch with your real self. You will find it much easier to know what you need, and what you don't. I would love you to try them all and, where I feel they are essential, I will say so. But trust your own self as to when and how often to practise them.

Negative emotions in our astral (emotional) body

Let's start by looking at a major cause of problems, our own negative emotions. Negative emotions have a very strong disturbing effect on us. Especially unbalancing is the effect of suppressed negative emotions.

You would have to be a saint in order to avoid having the odd negative emotion. It's only human to get cross, to have fears, to feel the occasional pang of envy. I'm certainly not going to suggest you live a totally emotionless life. Emotions, both positive and negative, are part of your normal psychological state. Negative emotions have, in fact, been incredibly important in our evolution and our survival. They help our bodies adjust to external conditions; they allow us quickly to assess uncomfortable and unfavourable conditions. For example, we see something dangerous and we feel fear. Someone threatens us and we feel anger. In the past, we would have felt the emotion and instantly followed it with action (the well-known fight or flight response). This response was essential for our survival as a race, as it was vital to be able to respond swiftly to any potentially dangerous change to the environment. This is why negative emotions are generally accompanied by physiological changes in the body – blood flowing into muscles, heart rate increasing etc. You should not feel afraid of your negative emotions.

It's important to realise that it's not actually the negative emotions, on their own, that cause us damage and danger. In fact negative emotions, if correctly handled, can give us a fabulous nudge into finding imaginative solutions to problems and life issues. What *does* cause the danger, what can create an unbalancing effect in us, is when we suppress them and pretend nothing bad is happening. In other words, when we sit on our emotions.

So, we need to stop demonising our negative emotions and instead focus on our attitudes towards them. The problem is that, ten to one, you probably aren't even aware of your own emotions. We become so used to our moods, our ways of reacting, that they become ingrained and represent a comfort zone. We may think we're being calm but often we're living in what I would call a passively defensive state, which accumulates more and more negative emotions. We never even stop to understand why we create these negative states and we certainly do little about trying to release them.

In almost all systems of healing, you will find teachings about the need to create a condition of inner freedom, a way of interacting harmoniously with the world. Such harmony can only occur and exist when, on the one hand, you do not suppress your emotions or feelings and, on the other hand, you don't allow yourself to become a victim to your desires or passions (with all the ill-thought-out actions and reactions that automatically follow).

Sounds tough? It is, and it is possible to achieve only when we follow one rule:

You must fully understand and consciously be aware of your emotions, and be able to regulate and reattune them.

If, and only if, you can do this will you experience a feeling of inner freedom and enlightenment. When you can access this state, your emotions and feelings serve your intuition. They can give you the energy and power to live a liberated and wise existence, fully enjoying every part of your life.

Most people lack control over their emotional lives. They are wide open to any external influences that happen to come along. Emotions become an untouchable part of their inner life: they simply are not able to interact with them.

Dealing with inner discomfort

Let's look at what usually happens when we feel negative emotions. We feel the emotion and it makes us uncomfortable. Desperate to get rid of this feeling of "disease", generally we use one of three methods to change this state of inner discomfort.

First, we might hurl the emotion right back. In other words, we lose our temper, we kick the door, we burst into tears.

Second, we might deflect our emotions by switching attention to something else (for example, comfort eating, drinking alcohol, watching TV).

Third, we might suppress our emotions in the hopes that "time will heal". In so doing, of course, we let our lives pass by with the emotion unresolved.

We allow external circumstances, however small or large, to rule our emotional response. This causes very deep inner conflict and discomfort. External events can, without a doubt, allow certain emotions to appear but they should never ever rule our response to the situation. I'm not suggesting for a moment we should become zombies, devoid of emotion. We need our emotional connections because, without them, we would live a pretty mechanical life, without any joy or pleasure. However, emotional connections should never be so extreme that they cause imbalance on a personal level.

All emotional problems create colossal inner tension and lead to serious dysfunction in the aura.

Negative emotions that are not released, or reacted to, quite often will cause blockages in our emotional and mental energy. This will make your auric imbalance considerably worse. People often cannot liberate themselves from their past, stressed situations. Instead they replay the past over and over again in their minds. This creates incredible psychological and emotional tension in both the astral and mental bodies. Every time we replay and create a different scenario of our reactions to the past, we drain our aura even further.

Just start to become aware of how often you do this. How often are you replaying the past?

It has a huge knock-on effect on daily life too. Our emotions are directly related to the way we perceive the world, and how comfortable and happy we feel in it. If you're the kind of person who has upbeat positive emotions, the world will seem kind and joyful. However, if you're the sort of person who lives in fear and hatred, the same world will appear dull and dark.

When we do not release negative energies from the body, the energy of these emotions is accumulated in our aura primarily on the astral level where it upsets its vibrations. We already know that the astral body has a deep link to the physical one and, as a result, your emotions will clearly influence your physical body's vibrations and can, eventually, lead to illness.

Seven emotional factors

Chinese medicine teaches that there are seven emotional factors, which can weaken certain organs if they are unbalanced in the body. These are anger, fear, fright, sadness, grief, pensiveness and joy. Some of these overlap and some (such as joy) might sound strange to us. Let me explain.

☆ Anger (also resentment, irritability, frustration): affects the liver. This can result in headaches, dizziness, high blood pressure and stomach/spleen problems.

☆ Fear and fright: affect the kidneys and can also cause problems in the ears.

☆ Sadness and grief: affect the lungs.

☆ Pensiveness (in other words, over-thinking, too much mental effort): affects the spleen. This can lead to worry, fatigue and inability to concentrate.

☆ Joy (an excess of the emotion – in other words agitation or over-excitement): affects the heart. This can result in agitation, insomnia, palpitations.

So I hope you can see why emotional cleansing is equally as important as physical cleansing. Cleansing the emotions can act as a catalyst for cleansing the body. Equally, you may well have found that, when you started physically detoxing, negative emotions arose, demanding attention. If so, that's very good – you will have plenty of material with which to work.

According to the spiritual law of transformation, when we suppress emotions they do not simply disappear without a trace but their energy transforms internally into something negative. We react to negative emotions in several different ways and each of these ways can lead us to very different outcomes. We've already looked in a simplistic way at how we cope with negative emotions. Let's now look in more detail.

Ways of reacting to negative emotions

Let's take the example of the emotion anger and different ways we might react to it.

☆ You feel totally overwhelmed by anger, yet you don't express it. So, you feel the anger, but don't show it – you suppress it. This is the sure way towards illness.

☆ You are really angry yet you pretend (to others and even to yourself) that you're not. So, you make believe everything's fine while on an inner level you're seething. At first sight, this seems better than suffering and bearing the emotion, but it's an illusion as you are only masking the problem. This way will also lead to an illness of the aura.

☆ You feel angry and you express that anger. So, if someone makes you angry, you shout. Someone pushes you, you push back. This is certainly better than suppressing anger but such an intemperate approach will weaken you spiritually.

☆ You feel angry. You recognise the emotion and accept it. You ask yourself why you are feeling angry and decide to work on the cause behind the anger. This way you accept all events in your life, including negative emotions. You view them as god-sent – as a valuable lesson. This way will lead you to better health and towards wisdom.

☆ You observe the emotion, the anger, in a remote, passive way. The exercises on achieving a neutral state that we will look at later in the next chapter can help enormously with this. This is another good energy-friendly way of dealing with negative emotions, as passive observation will cause any negative emotion to diminish or will help you to choose the best way to act on it.

Just as a woodworm will eat through the foundations of wooden buildings, so blocked emotions jeopardise the development and glow of our astral body. Each emotion carries a certain charge of energy, and if this emotion is negative as well as unexpressed, the vibration of these emotional energies will settle in and block our aura. This will, in turn, continue to attract and form similar negative vibrations.

So, I hope you now realise how vital it is that we work at dealing with the negative emotions already stored in our auras, and also learn how to avoid clogging up our aura in the future. In the next few chapters I will show you ways of controlling your emotions and thoughts, and clearing your astral and mental bodies of possibly years of accumulated negative energy.

CHAPTER FIFTEEN

Cleansing Our Astral Body

I am asking you, in this chapter, to learn control over your emotions. It's not really that new a lesson because we learn control all through our lives. As children we are trained to control our bladders and bowels; we start to exercise control over our muscles and learn how to walk, to run, to grip. We gain control over our hands – fine-tuning our reflexes so we can write. Yet somehow we never seem to master our emotions. We do learn however – often quite early – how to suppress them ("don't cry", "don't be angry", "there's nothing to be afraid of", "it's not nice to be jealous"), but nobody teaches us how to express our emotions safely. This is a crying shame (to coin a rather apt phrase) because emotional control is hugely important.

As I mentioned before, all emotions, including the negative ones, are very important for our spiritual health. But when we give excessive meaning to those emotions, they can transform into a very destructive force. Fear can be a valuable signal, forewarning us of danger. But if you give too much energy to fear, it will paralyse you. You simply won't be able to act.

Let's take another example. Anger is a powerful tool for boosting your energy resources but flashes of uncontrolled temper will cause you to lose your mind and will usually provoke you into making bad decisions. Throwing back a sharp response when you're attacked is a short-term way to protect your aura: it certainly puts up your boundaries. However, sulking – in the long run – will lead you to a feeling of hatred and will transform the natural protective energy layer into an immovable shield. You really need to learn more effective ways of protecting yourself and of handling negative emotions.

The answer: the "neutral state"

One powerful way of controlling our emotions is to learn how to induce what is known as the "neutral energetic state".

This state both protects and maintains your energy. It's actually a very respectful lesson to learn as it withdraws your judgement from other people's actions. It is up to each and every one of us to decide how we react energetically with other people and with the outside world. Everyone has the right to engage or not to engage and we must respect this right in each person. This concept is remarkably freeing. Think about it: you can truly be free only if you allow other people their freedom. This freedom has to be unconditional. Yes, sometimes it will mean that people make mistakes, but that is their choice. When you stop judging people and start accepting them the way they are, you will save yourself a huge amount of emotional energy.

To "close down" in the first place is not so difficult. What is much more difficult is to stay "closed" and maintain a neutral stance. Very often we think that we are "closed" but instead we are sending out the energetic equivalent of thorns. We just don't realise we are being passively aggressive towards everyone around us.

There are several effective meditations that will help you achieve a true neutral state. If you're feeling worried about this, I'd like to reassure you that when you enter the neutral state, it does not mean that you switch off and break your connection with reality. You are just becoming less "promiscuous" with your emotional energy. We are exceedingly protective when it comes to our physical body – we wouldn't dream of letting people touch us without permission, and certainly not our private parts! Yet we are quite willing to be over-available with our emotional body.

I would like to describe some methods for meditations that will induce a state of neutrality.

The middle state of attention

You can either sit or stand for this meditation – whichever you find most comfortable. If you wish you can tape the instructions to leave you free to concentrate on the visualisation. Choose a time and place where you will not be disturbed. Spend a few moments getting yourself comfortable and relaxed. Follow your breathing, not trying to alter it but just becoming aware of it. You may well notice it soon starts to slow down quite naturally. Now you are ready to begin.

☆ Imagine there is a little person on top of your head – a little you, yourself. This little you is small enough that it can easily descend into and through your bigger (normal) self. Take your consciousness into this little you.

☆ Slowly and gradually you find yourself descending on a parachute into the big you's head. Inside the head you find yourself floating down through clouds. They can be foggy or cloudy. You may see lots of lightening and hear thunder.

☆ Now imagine rays of sunlight coming through the dark clouds as you move slowly, so slowly, down.

☆ You reach the level of your larger self's throat, your neck, and now you are floating through blue sky, gliding lower and lower slowly through your throat area and down through your shoulders and chest.

☆ At the level of your stomach, you land on the ground, feeling its softness and warmth. The freshness of the green aromatic herbs around you relaxes you. Then you continue downwards.

☆ Just below the level of your navel, you find a beautiful quiet lake with a little boat waiting at the edge. You get into the boat, sit down and it sails off onto the still waters.

☆ You look down into the water and at the lilies floating there, from your boat. Have you ever seen water lilies, the way they float, their petals opening? It is impossible to compare this view with anything else. It deserves your undivided attention a little longer so just observe; don't think about anything else.

☆ Stay inside your internal world. Rest inside the world of yourself. Observe your breath.

☆ You are breathing almost through the top of your head. Through the top of your head, you inhale air from the surrounding environment; the air of higher levels, free from the energy of other people. It is almost as if you have a pillar on top of your head, which is both light in colour and in weight. It allows you to pull down the air from the higher levels of the atmosphere.

☆ Together with the air, you absorb light and then inhale the light inside yourself. Allow that little self that is resting so beautifully inside you, on that blue lake of your inner world, to take this beautiful light as a precious gift.

In such a state you can live, work and interact with people in a comfortable way. People around you will notice a difference (though they might not realise exactly how it has come about): they will find you simply radiate harmony. Deep in their subconscious they will feel safe with you. The beautiful thing about this exercise is that; once you have experienced the feeling of the neutral state, you will find you can enter it easily at will, whenever you need to. The neutral state allows you to protect yourself, rejuvenate yourself and will deflect any psychological pressure under which you may find yourself. I recommend you practise this several times until you find you can go into the neutral state at will.

Periscope

This exercise is also an excellent way of inducing the neutral state. I would suggest you experiment with both exercises and discover which best suits you.

☆   Imagine you are pulling out a periscope from the top of your head (through the crown chakra). Pull it out until it extends about a metre above your head.

☆   From this height, look through the periscope and start to observe your external world. Note how you gain perspective from this height.

☆   Now, every time you are presented with a difficult situation, immediately pull out your "periscope" and observe what's going on through it. You will be able to resolve the situation much easier, in a wise and detached manner.

So, from time to time, pull out your "periscope" and view your life through its thick glass, as if you were viewing a movie from an auditorium. You will find it helps you look at the bigger picture of the situation, rather than seeing it in a narrow-minded and petty manner.

Further cleansing for the emotions

Once you have mastered the neutral state, you should find life much easier! I would now like to show you some other techniques that will help you handle particular situations or troublesome emotions. Do try the techniques – they are very effective.

The ritual of letting go

This ritual is particularly useful when you have a particular emotion that is really tough to deal with. You might find that, however hard you try to keep a neutral state, the emotion just keeps coming back, time and time again. In Russia, we call this the "ritual of letting go" and it really does work.

Here's how to do it. Do be careful while doing this. You will need a fireproof bowl of some type (pyrex, stone, metal) in which to place your burning pieces of paper. Alternatively you could use an open fireplace in which to burn your paper.

☆ Place a charcoal block on a small glass plate.

☆ Light the charcoal by holding it over a candle or a lighter. It will splutter and spark for a while. Wait until the whole block has turned pale grey.

☆ Place a few granules of frankincense on top of the block. Allow it to bubble and burn for a few minutes, letting the smoke swirl around the room. You may need to top up the frankincense from time to time.

☆ Light a plain beeswax candle.

☆ Now sit opposite the candle with some small pieces of white paper.

☆ On each piece of paper, write down an emotion that is preventing you from living freely and happily. For example: "I often feel guilty." "I often get offended." "I cannot forgive." And so on.

☆ Look at the candle flame for a while and, piece by piece, burn each piece of paper with the flame of the candle. You will feel yourself becoming freer and happier after doing this.

☆ When you have finished, flush the ashes and the remains from the incense plate down the toilet.

Aura-combing ritual

In the old times in Russia there was a ritual that was used whenever a person experienced deep negative emotions, or had been badly hurt and was unable to free him or herself from the emotion. The person would take a big wooden comb and brush their hair with it while looking straight into their eyes in a mirror. While brushing their hair, they would fix their attention on the problem or the emotion and, by combing their hair through, they would physically "brush out" the emotions and problems. They would then take the comb to the forest and bury it in the earth, often in front of an aspen tree. In Russian folk traditions, the aspen tree is known to ward off negative energies and spirits. Having performed this ritual, people would often describe a feeling of deep release.

It is a familiar feeling too for us here in the West. When somebody feels disturbed or upset, our natural response is often to stroke their head, almost brushing their hair with our fingers, as if we were trying to brush their worries away.

I would suggest you perform this adaptation of "aura combing" based on the old Russian tradition, on a daily basis or whenever you need to release certain emotions.

☆ Before you start, cleanse your room with essential oils of sandalwood or juniper. Alternatively, place a few drops of these oils on your wrists before you begin.

☆ Sit down. Breathe in and out deeply and relax.

☆ Imagine that your hands and fingers are a comb. If you can, visualise your fingers are a few inches longer than they really are, so they become a more effective "comb".

☆ Comb through your aura, from the outside towards your physical body, starting above your head and sweeping down to your feet. Do not touch your physical body.

☆ Continue with this for a few minutes. As the blockages start to disappear, you should feel much lighter.

☆ After performing this aura combing you should immediately rinse your forearms under running cold water. The tap is fine!

Getting rid of a bad day

If you happen to have a really bad day, or have just had an argument with some-body, there is another technique you can and should use so you don't end up sharing these negative experiences with friends and loved ones.

☆ Go to another room (say the bathroom) and shake your body, as if you were a dog shaking water from its coat. Really shake.

☆ Then brush your fingers over your body as if you were clearing a spider's web from your body – start at the top of your head and work your way down to your feet.

☆ Wash your hands under cold running water (let the water pour down from the elbows to your hands). Now dry them.

☆ Now resume cleansing, this time work more from your head to your feet as if you were peeling off a very tight body stocking, almost as if you were sloughing off all the bad vibes you have accumulated during the day.

If you do this exercise straight after a negative experience, you will notice not only that your attitude towards that situation has changed, but also that you won't have such an urge to vent your frustrations. It will not only save you a huge amount of valuable emotional energy but also spare your family and friends from carrying the outburst of your negative emotions and frustrations – much fairer!

Shaking off impurities

This is another exercise that will help to lighten up the vibrations of your aura and to shake off all the energy impurities.

☆ Lie down on your back.

☆   Lift your arms and legs up so they are both at a 45-degree angle to your body. Simultaneously shake your extremities, as if you were trying to shake off water from them.

You can also release bad emotions with this following exercise. If you are feeling angry, inhale and, as you exhale, clench your fists forcefully so that your hands vibrate from the tension. Hold this tension until you finish exhaling. Do this up to ten times until you feel exhausted. The emotion will be extinguished using this physical tension and vibration. The result? It will disappear.

The "Inner Smile"

This should now be familiar to you, as you practised it regularly throughout the physical cleansing programmes. I'd recommend you practise it regularly, whether or not you're detoxing, because connecting to this "Inner Smile" as much as possible will really help to lighten up your astral body. The reasoning behind it is simple. When you laugh or smile (be it externally or internally) you become far less exposed to the forces of negative emotions and energies. When you smile readily, not only do your astral vibrations become lighter but also your aura becomes better protected.

It only takes a short while and starts your day off in a lovely way. When we come to Part Eight on Rejuvenation, I shall show you how to combine it with another powerful technique to make you look and feel younger!

Using art to boost your emotional energy

If you would really like to nourish your astral body, you can do this by developing your emotional intelligence. Communication with art, either theatre, music, looking at wonderful paintings or reading a beautiful book, increases your emotional energy dramatically. If you like dancing, singing, drawing or playing a musical instrument, you should make it a regular habit: the more you do it, the "happier" your aura will be. Whenever you access your creative energy, you open your astral body to fresh energy from the universe. Human life force and creativity are directly dependent upon each other. Through your creativity you can access your intuition and move closer towards enlightenment. We enter a stream of universal energy and are able to recharge from its divine energy frequency. It is well known that truly talented artists know how to enter an altered state of consciousness, ecstasy, which allows them to channel through that which truly resonates with their nature. But anyone can access this energy – you don't need to be a "good" artist or musician or dancer – skill is not the key issue. It's about engaging with your creative self on whatever level suits you. Free yourself of inhibitions and just let yourself follow your muse.

If you would like to maximise the effect of art on your astral body, you can try the following meditation.

Art meditation

☆ Sit comfortably in front of any artwork: painting, print, drawing, photograph. It does not matter what kind of picture it is — but it should be one you like or which appeals to you.

☆ Relax and calm your mind.

☆ Find the most important details of the picture and then start to unravel the whole painting in space, as if the whole picture were leaving its frame, expanding and coming to life. It can help to focus on one specific point while you do this.

☆ Move your focus from the main images of the picture to the secondary details, without moving your eyes from the picture.

☆ After this, start moving through the contrasting elements: earth/water, up/down, left/right and vice versa.

☆ Then shift your perspective from the close-up details to those in the depths of the picture and vice versa.

☆ With your left eye focus to the left of the picture and with your right focus on the right of the picture while you are squinting at it. This takes some practice but it will help you to create an almost stereoscopical view of the picture.

☆ Close your eyes and try to imagine that you can view the picture through your eyelids, focusing deeper and deeper into the picture.

☆ You may experience slight dizziness with a tendency to tilt forwards into the picture.

☆ You may also have the sensation that you are very light and almost weightless.

☆ You will finally have the feeling that you are almost inside the painting. You will be able to see almost beyond the frame and will have a sensation of space and continuation of the image.

To maximise the effect, you can also add music to your viewing. For example, if you look at a landscape you could choose the music of Debussy. The Russian composer Rimsky-Korsakov is fantastic if you're viewing pictures of the sea. Every time you look at an image you will find you become able almost to tap into its rhythm – so you should feel free to choose music that is most appropriate to its frequency. Use your intuition.

Every time you go to view paintings in museums or exhibitions, or just sit quietly in front of the paintings you have at home, try to do the above meditation and you will enjoy the paintings just that little bit more. It will turn into a whole experience, which will enrich your astral/emotional body.

Fun family exercise to lighten heavy energy

This lovely exercise is really a children's game but I feel it is a great exercise for the whole family to enjoy. It's particularly useful if the energy of the family has become heavy for any reason and especially if you have just resolved a big argument. This laughing meditation not only disperses the heavy dense energy, but also will give you a good time.

It's very simple. Everyone lies on the floor in a circle, each with his or her head on the next person's stomach. One person begins by saying an expulsive "Ha!" three times. The next person quickly follows with his or her own "Ha! Ha! Ha!" and then the next and so on, round and round. As your head bounces on the stomach below you it is only a short time before the "Ha! Ha! Ha!" becomes genuine laughter.

Love meditation with a partner

There is a lovely method for attracting and maintaining love with your partner or children. Or teach your children to do it with each other. It's a beautiful way to nourish their heart chakras and to restore peace within families. This exercise also helps you to balance the vibrations of your astral body.

☆ Sit opposite each other, with a candle between you.

☆ When you both feel relaxed and comfortable, send loving energies to each other (simply think warm, loving feelings about the other person).

☆ Remember that this energy is unconditional love; it is not sexual.

☆ Imagine you can see the energy flowing between you in a figure of eight movement between your heart chakras.

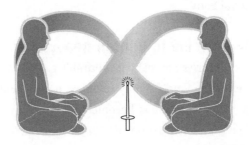

CHAPTER SIXTEEN

Working with the Chakras

Now it's time to take a closer look at our chakras, the seven spinning spheres (or vortices) of bio-energetic energy that run from the base of the spine to above the crown of your head. The chakras are precise monitors of our physical, emotional and mental well-being. Each spins at a different frequency and when they are in balance, you will radiate health and well-being. If one or more fall out of harmony, you will start to notice problems.

Imbalances in the chakras

You don't need to be a psychic to figure out which chakra is under stress or out of balance. Because each chakra is closely linked with various organs and systems in the body, and with different emotions and thought patterns in the psyche, it is usually relatively simple to work out where you have problems. Answer these questions to gauge how your chakras are functioning.

1   Do you feel disconnected to your body, as if you aren't quite in it?
2   Do you feel insecure and unsafe?
3   Do you have low energy levels, often feeling tired, exhausted or weary for no real cause?
4   Are you either very overweight or very underweight?
5   Do you "escape" through alcohol, drugs or food?

6 Did you have a trauma between conception and the age of 5?

7 Do you suffer from disorders of the bowel or intestines; problems with bones or teeth; eating disorders; problems with legs, feet, knees, base of spine and buttocks?

8 Do you fear change?

9 Do you dislike social occasions, feeling ill at ease?

10 Is your sex drive quite low or do you have problems in general with your sex life?

11 Do you tend to fantasise rather than commit to a real relationship?

12 Do you tend to deny yourself pleasures and enjoyment?

13 Did you suffer any trauma or upset between the ages of 5 and 8?

14 Do you suffer from menstrual problems, disorders of the reproductive and urinary systems, loss of appetite; sexual dysfunction, lack of flexibility in the lower back and knees; lack of taste?

15 Are you a bit aggressive and domineering? Maybe rather controlling?

16 Do you have to have the last word?

17 Do you feel frustrated that, no matter how hard you work, you can't achieve your true potential?

18 Do you sometimes feel powerless? Can you be a bit of a victim?

19 Do you either just go along with the crowd, or alternatively go your own way without thinking of how it affects others?

20 Did you have any distress or upset between the ages of 8 and 12?

21 Do you suffer from digestive or eating disorders; ulcers; chronic fatigue; hypertension; stomach, pancreas, gall bladder and liver problems; diabetes and hypoglycaemia?

22 Are you critical – of either yourself or others?

23 Do you often get depressed, pessimistic and/or lonely?

24 Do you have problems with relationships? Possibly being too demanding, clinging, jealous or dependent? Or you could be overly self-sacrificing, always the martyr?

25 Do you find you get too involved in other people's lives?

26 Did you have any trauma or problems between the ages of 12 and 16?

27 Do you suffer from disorders of the heart, lungs, breast, arms; asthma or breathing difficulties; circulation problems; immune system deficiency; pains in the chest; tension between the shoulder blades?

28 Are you frightened of speaking out? Are you shy?

29 Are you scared or nervous of putting your feelings into words?

30 Do you have any problems with your hearing or speech? Are you tone deaf or incapable of following a rhythm?

31 Do you gossip and interrupt a lot? Do you talk rather than listen?

32 Do you feel your creativity is stifled or blocked? Or do you feel you have no creativity at all?

33 Did you have any problems or traumas between the ages of 16 and 21?

34 Do you suffer from tension in your jaw; problems with the throat, ears, voice, neck; thyroid problems?

35 Do you find it hard to remember your dreams, or even think you don't dream? Alternatively, do you have frequent nightmares?

36 Do you have a poor memory?

37 Do you ever feel guilty that you're not happy?

38 Do you feel stuck in your life and crave freedom? Do you find it hard to visualise the future?

39 Do you find it hard to find balance – in your moods, your body temperature, your hormones?

40 Did you suffer any trauma or problems between the ages of 21 and 26?

41 Do you suffer from headaches, migraine or vision problems?

42 Are you cynical?

43 Are you very intellectual, tending to live totally "in your head"?

44 Do you have very rigid belief systems, ridiculing anything that doesn't fit into your pattern?

45 Do you tend to be sceptical about spiritual matters, or completely immersed in the spiritual, at the expense of everyday life?

46 Are you greedy and materialistic?

47 Are you apathetic, confused or "spacey"?

48 Do you suffer from migraines or amnesia?

Now divide up your answers into seven groups, like this:

> *Questions 1–7: base chakra*
> *Questions 8–14: sacral chakra*
> *Questions 15–21: solar plexus chakra*
> *Questions 22–27: heart chakra*
> *Questions 28–34: throat chakra*
> *Questions 35–41: brow chakra*
> *Questions 42–38: crown chakra.*

The more "yes" answers you have in a section, the more likely you are to have an imbalance in that chakra. It is quite common to have imbalance in several chakras so don't be surprised or depressed if you have scored highly. I'll show you plenty of ways of redressing the balance.

Restoring balance in the chakras

Sometimes there are really simple everyday activities that can help to bring a chakra back into balance. Let's look at some of the most effective.

Base chakra

You need to do as much as possible to reconnect with your body. Start with as much physical exercise as possible – choose a sport or activity you enjoy (maybe dance, aerobics, running, swimming). Try massage – find a professional aromatherapist or bodyworker – or ask a friend or partner to give you massage. Yoga would be excellent as it heals and balances all the chakras. Gardening and pottery are also good grounding exercises if you have a deficiency in your base chakra. On a psychological level look at your early relationship with your mother: talk to her about it if you can; if it's painful, talk to a trained therapist or counsellor. On a practical level, organise your drawers. Set the breakfast table for yourself before bed. Pay your bills on time. Investigate and take workshops on self-care. Make peace with your family. Get to know your neighbours. Establish comforting routines. Fragrances that boost this chakra include cedarwood, myrrh and patchouli. Choose scented candles in these fragrances, use the oils in your bath or massage blend, or seek out incense in these fragrances.

Sacral chakra

If this chakra is out of balance, you need to learn to trust and enjoy your senses. Start by feeling the textures around you; listen to new music and sounds; look at nature and at art; taste different foods and drinks. Dance can help to liberate this chakra – so can bodywork. Gently try to get in touch with your emotions (with professional help if necessary) to release any old feelings of hurt, anger and guilt. See more romantic movies. Listen to sensual music. Surround yourself with scented candles. Have a glamorous photo taken of yourself and put it in a beautiful frame. Go to the theatre and dance shows. Get pampering treatments. Wear the best fabric you can. Throw a party for yourself, or have a romantic dinner with the person you love. Buy yourself more sensual underwear. The fragrances that boost this chakra are jasmine, rose and sandalwood.

Solar plexus chakra

If you have a deficiency here you need to learn how to take risks. You also need grounding and emotional warmth. If, on the other hand, you have an excess of energy in this chakra you should look at stress management techniques (meditation, biofeedback, etc.) and deep relaxation. Anyone with problems in this chakra would benefit from doing sit-ups (abdominal crunches) to strengthen that area. Martial arts such as judo or t'ai chi would be excellent. Psychotherapy can help you build up the necessary strength to release or contain anger and strengthen your sense of autonomy. Write a mission statement for your life. Give yourself and others compliments freely. Admire other people rather than holding onto jealousy. Read books on time management and leadership, plus biographies of powerful people you admire. Say your name out loud over and over until you feel you own it. Share your plans only with people who will support you. Do a marathon or walk for charity. Fragrances for this chakra include vetivert, ylang-ylang and bergamot.

Heart chakra

Breathing exercises will help all those with problems in the heart chakra – join a yoga or *qi gong* class that teaches breathing (and practise the breathing exercises I give throughout this book). Start a journal – writing down all your feelings and thoughts honestly. Look at your relationships and try to free yourself from suppressed grief and loss (with professional help if necessary). Start to accept yourself – just as you are. Read poetry or humorous books. Be tactile with the people you love. Write a letter of appreciation to the person who made a positive difference in your life. Have a loving chat with a childhood best friend. Practise forgiveness exercises. Fragrances for this chakra include rose and melissa.

Throat chakra

If your throat chakra is deficient you need to use your voice: singing, chanting, humming, shouting – anything to release the voice. Sound therapy or voice work would be wonderful. If you have excessive energy here, practise the art of silence and concentrate on what the other person is saying. All problems in this chakra would benefit from bodywork or massage to release tension in the neck and shoulders – or try Alexander Technique or Pilates. Write your thoughts and unspoken feelings in a journal; write letters to people with whom you have troublesome relationships (remember they don't have to be sent). Breathe before you speak and while you are listening. Practise saying what you want to say in advance. Write letters to those with whom you want to connect or come to closure. Observe silence for ten minutes every day. Scream into a pillow or sing a song from the bottom of your lungs in a car. For one day, stop criticising yourself and others. Fragrances for this chakra include chamomile and myrrh.

The brow chakra

Try painting and drawing – use whatever materials and colours you like and paint whatever comes to mind (it doesn't have to be artistic). Look at your painting and see what emotions emerge. Start to write down and work with your dreams – you could try painting them, writing about them or imagining what might have happened next. What do the symbols and people in your dreams mean to you? Don't rely on dream dictionaries – dreams speak in very individual, personal ways. Try meditation or autogenic training. Guided visualisations can be useful – so can hypnotherapy (with a qualified expert). Invent a recipe and make it, then serve on your best china. Change your image. Finger-paint with your children (or someone else's) and hang up your creations. Redecorate your living room. Get rid of your old clothes. Visit an art gallery. Visualise succeeding at the things you want to do in life. Fragrances for this chakra include rose geranium and hyacinth.

Crown chakra

If your crown energy is deficient, meditation could be very useful for you. Be open to new ideas and new information – don't dismiss things until you've tried them. Open yourself to the idea of spirituality, allow yourself to drop your cynicism and have an open mind. Examine your attitudes to spirituality and religion. If, on the other hand, you have an excess of crown chakra energy you are probably far too "spacey" and so you need to connect with your body and the earth – try physical exercise, massage, gardening. Recycle. Avoid waste and pollution. Donate to charity. Meditate more. Create a meditation based on a beautiful event in your life and accompany it with music that also has meaning in your life. Be kind to yourself and others as a spiritual practice. Sponsor a child in a developing country. Fragrances for this chakra include lavender, frankincense, and rosewood.

Diet for the chakras

When you are working with your chakras, I would advise you to supplement your work with the right diet. The foods that we eat are pure energy. Energy is not static but resonates at certain frequencies so every type of fruit and vegetable, every protein, carbohydrate or fat, has its own energy character. One of the secrets to keeping your chakras radiant and healthy is to nourish them energetically with the appropriate diet.

I would suggest that you pick the foods you eat by focusing on the colours of the food and their vibrational characteristics. This way you can eat a diet that correlates and corresponds to the chakra with which you are working.

A really great idea would be to work with a different chakra each week or each day. Alternatively you can focus on those chakras that you know to be out of balance.

First chakra

Boost your diet with fruits and vegetables with red skin or flesh, such as tomatoes, red peppers, red apples, cherries, radishes etc. As this chakra is the base, foundation or centre, you should try to eat more protein (meat, poultry and fish as well as pulses, tofu etc.). I also recommend that you eat more cooked food with strong aromas, as the first chakra is also responsible for the sense of smell.

Second chakra

Increase your intake of orange fruits and vegetables such as carrots, satsumas, oranges, sweet potatoes, pumpkin etc. As the energy of this centre is connected with the element of water and with the sense of taste, I would recommend that you have more soups and drink more water. Try to make sure that your food is not bland, indulging your taste buds with different flavours. I would strongly suggest that you reduce the level of salt, as it tends to stagnate water in the body.

Third chakra

Have plenty of yellow foods such as bananas, melon, yellow peppers, grains such as wheat, corn, buckwheat, oats and seeds etc. As this chakra is associated with fire, you need to eat more products that release a lot of energy during the metabolic process, for example, complex carbohydrates such as whole grains. This chakra corresponds with your visual senses, so try to present your food creatively.

Fourth chakra

You should seek out green vegetables and fruits such as broccoli, courgettes, green apples, green peppers, spinach, runner beans, lettuce etc. The energy of vegetables is known to be neutral and carries, in itself, the energy of the Earth and the Sun. This chakra is associated with the sense of touch, so if you want to indulge your fourth chakra, you can buy all the vegetables in the market, touching and feeling the products on the stalls and later, when eating the prepared food, try experimenting by eating with your hands or feeding your partner with your hands.

Fifth chakra

Boost your diet with purple vegetable, and fruits such as aubergines, blueberries, black figs, raisins, plums, prunes, purple kidney beans, purple corn, purple onion, beetroot, sea kale, olives, purple mushrooms, etc. This chakra is associated with the sense of hearing, so at meal times try to play beautiful music.

Sixth and Seventh chakras

Both of these chakras connect you with your intuition, clarity and higher self. These chakras possess very light vibrational qualities so, if you are working at this level, I would recommend that you do not overload your system with food. If you can fast, this is the time you should do so. If you decide to have light meals, make sure that the colours blue and purple predominate. You will also find it helpful to turn your meal times into a form of meditation. Light candles around your dining room, eat in silence and chew for a long time. It would be quite nice to dress your dining table in a blue or purple scheme of colour.

Balancing the chakras

Having looked at specific practical steps you can take to bring a particular chakra or chakras into balance, let's look at more general ways of balancing all the chakras. There are many, many techniques and meditations that can really help. I am going to share with you some of my favourite methods. We will start off with a beautiful and highly effective meditation.

Meditation: journey through the chakras

I particularly like this meditation because it appeals not only to the right side of the brain with its beautiful imagery, but also to the left side of the brain with its strong affirmations. This meditation will balance your astral body perfectly. It will also balance your mental body. The more you practise this meditation, the better the results will be. You don't think twice about showering every day to cleanse your physical body, so think of this as a kind of shower for your energy bodies!

It is best if you record these instructions beforehand so you can play them to yourself and put all your attention into listening. Before you start, find a place to sit or lie where you will be comfortable – but not fall asleep!

Spend a few minutes allowing yourself to focus on your breathing and calm your thoughts. Then begin.

I breathe out any tension in my body and begin to relax, knowing that I can use my energy in other, more interesting ways. I imagine my spine is like a stalk, as if there was an invisible connection from the base of my spine down into the Earth and this keeps me grounded. The other end of my stalk is aligned to a point of bright light above my head.

I take my awareness into my first chakra, the root chakra, which is at the point between my legs known as the perineum.
My root chakra is like a spinning vortex, which opens towards the Earth. I breathe into the root chakra and imagine a vibrant, red flower opening there now. I feel the energy increase in that centre.

I change my focus to my exhaling breath and breathe out any feelings I may have that it is not safe to be here, any feelings of insecurity. I breathe them all out. I say to myself:

"I am part of the living universe. I acknowledge my connection to all living things. I am fully alive and here in my body, I have everything I need."

Now I take my attention to my second chakra, the sacral (or water) sexual centre. This is just below my navel and I breathe in orange, deep orange. As I breathe colour into this chakra, it opens up like a flower. Now I change my focus to my exhaling breath. I breathe out any thoughts about my sexuality that I no longer need. I breathe out any feeling that I am not creative.
I breathe out old pictures and memories of relationships held in this chakra that I no longer need. These thoughts and feelings limit me. I breathe them out. Now I say:

"I have the power to create. I am able to bring something new into this life. I feel confident about my sexuality and my relationship with others."

I take my focus into the third chakra, my solar plexus chakra, my power centre. I breathe yellow into this chakra, beautiful solar yellow. As I breathe yellow into my centre of personal power, I get a sense of the energy of this chakra as it opens up. Now I change the focus of my breathing to the exhalation and I breathe out any feelings that I have to be perfect. I breathe out any feelings of being a victim or being powerless in certain situations, any worries about what anyone else may think, any resentment towards authority. I breathe it all out of my solar plexus and now I say:

"I am in control of my own power.
I am able to make my own decisions.
I respect myself and I respect others.
I am powerful."

Now I take my attention to the fourth chakra, my heart chakra. I breathe beautiful green into the centre of my chest. I become aware of this centre of unconditional love expanding and opening up. I breathe this flower open; this is the centre where the power of love resides. I breathe in green and feel that power. Now I focus on my exhaling breath, and I breathe out any feelings that I will get hurt, feelings about being vulnerable, about restrictive, conditional love. I breathe out all those beliefs about love that limit and contract the heart. I breathe out any beliefs that do not deserve love – that it's wrong to love myself – and then I say:

"I feel compassion for myself and for all living beings. I give and receive love without condition. I am full of love."

I take my attention to the fifth chakra, my throat chakra and I breathe in a beautiful blue, an aquamarine or turquoise blue. I breathe in this colour and get a sense of the flower of my throat chakra expanding. This is my centre of honest communication, of speaking up and speaking out freely and openly. I breathe blue into this centre. I focus on my exhaling breath and breathe out any feelings or memories of situations where I was afraid to say what I felt, when I couldn't speak my mind. I say:

"I express my deepest thoughts and feelings with clarity.
I can speak openly and freely. I trust my soul to speak."

Now I take my awareness to the sixth chakra, my brow or third eye chakra, and I breathe indigo blue, a beautiful dark blue, the colour of the night sky, into this centre of inner vision, insight and intuition.

I breathe this chakra open and, as it opens up, it becomes a gateway for my spiritual awareness. It becomes the eye that sees in all directions, it shows me the way to expand my entire being. I say:

"I am in tune with an infinite source
of guidance. I trust my intuition."

Now I take my point of consciousness to a point just above my head to the seventh chakra, the crown chakra. Here there are the energy colours of white, gold and amethyst. I imagine these colours and breathe them into the space just before above my head. This is the place where my halo exists, my knowledge that there is more than just physical reality. As I focus on this chakra, I move into a place of nothingness that is also everything.

This is the gateway of the soul, there is nothing to say here, because it is a place beyond words, a place where I connect my whole being with the universe. I am the Universe, unlimited and timeless. I hear myself saying:

"I am that I am."

Now I imagine myself radiating all the colours of the spectrum, all the colours of the rainbow. I see them spin and rotate within me, all the colours that make up white. I am a shining white light; I am in a shining white light. I become the whole light. I allow all the cells and atoms in my body to remember the lightness of being. Then, when I feel ready, I gently bring my awareness back into the room, knowing that I am connected to Mother Earth and guided by divine power. I am centred and focused. I take some deep breaths and

gently move my fingers and toes as I open my eyes and come
back into everyday reality.

Chakra balancing with bells (*kolokol*)

Bells (*kolokol*) are very effective tools for cleansing energy. Just as I use bells to cleanse energy in the home (see Part 2), I also like to use bells to cleanse and balance the chakras.

Here's how to cleanse yourself with *kolokol*.

1   Stand upright or sit comfortably on a chair.
2   Pick up the bell with one hand and hold it about six inches away from your body, over the position of your root chakra.
3   Take a deep breath, imagining you are sending the breath right down to your toes. Exhale.
4   Start ringing the bell, moving it upwards along the centre of the body (following the path of the central meridian). Increase the speed of your ringing as you go over the areas of the major chakras: belly button, solar plexus, heart, throat and third eye.
5   Please make sure that your ringing is melodious and flows smoothly – you do not want a broken sound.
6   When you reach the top of your head, the crown chakra, draw an invisible figure of eight with your bell to seal in the energy.
7   Go back down to the base chakra and repeat steps 2 to 6. Do this three times in all. Three is considered a magical number in Russia and we like to repeat our rituals three times. Each time you run through your body, you should notice the sound becoming clearer and clearer as your energy balances.
8   Clean your bells with salty water at the end of your balancing session.

Cleansing the aura with scent

In Chapter 5 on house cleansing, I talked about using oil of frankincense for cleansing the energy of a home. This technique can also be used to cleanse your own aura, or that of someone else. However, it doesn't have to be just frankincense. There are a variety of aromas you can choose – depending on your emotional state. Some are aromatherapy essential oils; some are everyday household scents.

These are the most important scents for self-cleansing:

☆ Clove: to help resolve difficult relationships at work or at home.

☆ Cinnamon: for protection from other people and for calming yourself.

☆ Freshly ground coffee: to help banish continuous nightmares.

☆ Frankincense: for promoting spiritual growth.

☆ Crushed garlic: for liberating yourself from negative thoughts, or when ideas keep disturbing you.

☆ Honey: to soften your temperament.

☆ Cedarwood: to clear anxiety or stress.

☆ Sage: for deep cleansing and purification.

☆ Sandalwood: for grounding and for stability.

Here's what you need to do.

☆ Prepare the burner by placing a tablet of charcoal on a plate and lighting it until it smokes and turns grey. Then place your choice of any of the above on the burning charcoal.

☆ Take a straight-backed chair and place the burner in front of you on the floor.

☆ Taking a white cotton sheet, tie the sheet around your neck, creating a tent-like canvas around the chair and the burner.

☆   Please make sure that the sheet covers all the areas around you and lies loosely on the floor. It will be a little like a steam bath. Be very careful. Take all the precautions you can, ensuring that the sheet is not touching the burning charcoal or in any danger of being set alight. Place the burner inside the "tent" only when the charcoal is smoking and *not* burning.

☆   Allow your body to absorb the aromas for ten to fifteen minutes.

! This method may not be suitable for anyone with asthma or respiratory difficulties.

Chakra balancing using musical instruments

You can also balance your chakras by listening to certain musical instruments. You will need to pick music for each chakra, or any that you feel are particularly out of balance. Find a comfortable place to sit or lie down and play the music quite loudly so it creates gentle vibrations in your body.

These are the instruments that can balance each chakra:

☆   First chakra: responds very well to the deep low notes produced by an organ, drums or the double bass.

☆   Second chakra: responds to music from the viola or the classical guitar.

☆   Third chakra: responds beautifully to the saxophone and brass instruments in general.

☆   Fourth chakra: can be fed with classical violin. Mozart's music has a very balancing effect, in particular.

☆   Fifth chakra: responds well to the flute.

☆   Sixth chakra: responds well to harp music.

☆   Seventh chakra: will respond to the loud ringing of bells or the resonating sound of two crystal glasses being tapped against each other; a sound similar to that of the triangle.

White cord

This is another powerful energy exercise I like very much. It is an excellent exercise to perform whenever you need to feed your "survival centre" in the base chakra. I also recommend it to sportspeople, or anyone who needs that extra energy in order to perform faster and better.

☆ Sit comfortably. Inhale and imagine that there is a bright white cord (its light is similar to that produced by a daylight lamp) moving up your spine from the area of your coccyx.

☆ As it moves up, it reaches the area behind the solar plexus on your back. The light enters your solar plexus and then leaves through your solar plexus at the front of your body.

☆ Now the light moves back downwards, along the centre line of your stomach, before re-entering the area opposite your coccyx, back where it started.

☆ You are producing a shining white energy circle formed by the cord of light (see the illustration overleaf). This will start to spin faster and faster – visualise it like a fast-spinning Hula-Hoop. Continue to visualise this spinning for three to five minutes.

Solenoid

This is another wonderful exercise. It works well in balancing and distributing your vital energy throughout your entire body.

☆ Sit down comfortably and focus on your breathing to help you relax.

☆ Visualise a glowing ball of bright white energy (about the size of a tennis ball) moving up along your spine, starting off at the bottom, at the area of the coccyx.

☆ The ball of energy moves along your spine as water would move through a hosepipe.

☆   When this ball of energy reaches the first vertebra of your neck (the one next to your head), move the ball over towards and out from the right shoulder. The ball can now travel back down to your coccyx, but this time along the outer edge of your body. It's as if you were drawing an invisible wing on your back.

☆   Repeat for the left side of the body, starting with a new ball of light at the base of the spine.

☆   Maintain a firm image of these wings in your mind. Now imagine the two glowing balls of energy spinning along this route. You should visualise two circles spinning as if you had two energy propellers on your back.

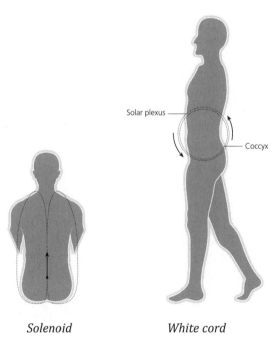

Solar plexus

Coccyx

Solenoid   *White cord*

CHAPTER SEVENTEEN

Cleansing the Mental Body

Having taken steps to cleanse and clear our astral body and our chakras, it's now time to look more closely at the mental body. If you remember, this is the next level out from the astral in our aura. In other words, I'm going to ask you to think about thinking! I will also use this opportunity to teach you more about the magic meridians, the energy channels that run through our bodies. This will help to detox and balance both our emotional and mental bodies.

Thought

A famous Russian physician, M. Sechenov, once said that thought is the equivalent of actions put on hold. A thought expresses the readiness of your body to move into future action. What I mean by that is that you only have to start thinking about creating certain movements and your muscles will start to tighten up in anticipation of the action. Our thoughts have a very powerful physiological effect upon us. Remember how, earlier in the book, I asked you to imagine biting into a lemon? And how you found the mere thought increased saliva production – without your going anywhere near a lemon? I think that demonstrates the point rather nicely.

Thought not only governs physiological processes in the body, but also is a tool of spirit. Thought has a direct effect on your spiritual and energy self. If your thoughts flow in a smooth way, you will feel happy and have a strong sense of vitality. If your thoughts are chaotic or suppressed by the wrong kind of negative thinking, you will feel sick and flat.

Every time you think about some-thing, you produce a thought. This thought affects not only the frequency of the energy in your aura, but also the energy in the auras of people around you. The energy of these thoughts can be either very heavy and dense, or light and loose. If this is hard to believe, just think about what happens if you become depressed. Your thoughts become dark, thick and sluggish and, the more you allow your thoughts to sink, the more depressed you become. Now, think about what happens when you're around someone who is depressed. It becomes very hard to maintain your own optimistic state – if you're not careful you find you're being pulled down yourself.

Many people produce blocks in their mental energy because they attach themselves too much via their thoughts to objects, people, the past or the future. This not only blocks your energy but also overwhelms your mind with too much unnecessary negative energy. These blocks in mental energy also occur when you have rigid or unrealistic expectations of how other people should behave. When people do not act according to your expectations, your thoughts (together with the energy of expectation) create a block in your mind, which leads to internal conflict. There's a simple, very simple, way of avoiding this: drop the expectations! Don't demand or expect particular behaviour or outcomes from other people. This can be hard, but it is very important to teach yourself to accept everyone and everything for what it is, without judgement.

You may also be too attached to things, without realising that you are. Sometimes it is only when you lose something that you realise just how much it has dominated your psyche. You can literally "lose your mind" trying to forget about it, and switch off. If this chimes a bell with you, it would be worth practising the energy exercises we discussed in Chapter 15: the middle state of attention and periscope (see pages 149–51).

Expectations

As for expectations, I want to tell you a joke, which will illustrate my point very clearly. This is a story about a very religious man who lived his whole life obeying the rules set by the church and described in the Bible. One day, his little town was flooded and all the people were told to evacuate. The people called to the man, urging him to leave with them but he refused, insisting that God would save him. The water rose higher and higher, so the people sent a boat to rescue him from his flooded house. Once again, he refused to join the people, saying he would rather rely totally on God. Water continued to rise so that the man was eventually standing on the roof, trying to keep his head above water, gasping for air. A helicopter was sent to rescue him but, once again, he replied that God would appear to save him and he refused to join the people.

He drowned.

Then he appeared before God, in Heaven, and asked: "God, please tell me. I have been so faithful to you and true to your teachings all my life. Why didn't you save me?" God replied: "Silly man. Didn't I send you the boat? Didn't I send you the helicopter?!"

What I am trying to tell you is that you have to try to keep your mind open. Don't create unnecessary limitations in your mental energy, as you never know where your "rescue boat" may come from. I do not want you to lose any opportunities or chances in life just because your "radar" has been mentally pre-tuned to a set station.

In the course of life, we go from one stage to another, accumulating various memories and experiences. All of these invariably enrich our mental energy and evolve our mind. These various stages can be compared to the different sets in a theatre. You wear a particular costume, speak in a particular voice, meet certain people and use various props. As you move into a new chapter in your life, you are presented with a completely new stage design, maybe a new act for your life, possibly a completely new play. This new play teaches you something new and, once again, gives you further opportunities to learn just that little bit more about yourself.

Unfortunately, what many of us do is to carry all the props from one performance into another. The result? An overcrowded new stage. As we move forwards in our life, we end up carrying such a vast burden of props and costumes and decorations that we lose the ability to learn and act out a new performance. As a result, we stop noticing the new set design, only seeing the old scenario over and over again. We even complain that life is dull and boring. Basically we do not allow space for the new energies in our life. This is why I think it is so vital that we all know how to put closure on the past. We need to be able to evolve and attract new energies into our lives, untrammelled by the past.

Balancing mental energy

You may be thinking this is all fine in theory but that it's easier said than done. Well, I will now show you some tried and trusted techniques to clear and balance our mental energy.

The empty room meditation

This energy mental exercise will help you to gain more control over your thoughts and will bring an order to your mental energy.

☆　Imagine that your head is a room filled with various pieces of furniture or objects. Each item is connected to a certain event or person in your life. For example, the sofa might be your work, the chair your partner, the table your parents, the stools your children, and so forth.

☆ Now, step by step, remove all the objects from your room, so that the room is left completely empty.

☆ Then imagine you pick yourself up too and remove yourself from the room as well, closing the door to the room from the outside.

☆ If you think you are putting things back in the room, you can from time to time look into the room through a small window. Throw away the objects (your thoughts) that spontaneously occur.

Breathing exercise

Pranayama yoga also teaches us a rhythmic breathing technique, which is known to help balance the mind, emotions and all the body's functions. It will give you – almost instantly – a sensation of well-being. During the practice of this breathing exercise, your body will experience a very deep rejuvenation, similar to the feeling that follows a deep and well-rested sleep.

You should perform this breathing exercise, either sitting upright or lying down flat on your back. There are four stages:

☆ Inhale
☆ Holding the breath
☆ Exhale
☆ Holding the breath

Depending on how long you spend on each stage of the breath, you will experience different results. For example breathing in for a count of two, holding for a count of one, breathing out for a count of two and holding for a count of one before repeating the cycle ($2 \times 1 \times 2 \times 1$) can help to speed up your respiratory rates.

Let's look at what the different breathing sequences can do for you.

☆ $4 \times 2 \times 4 \times 2$: stimulates your glands and massages your heart.

☆ 6 × 3 × 6 × 3: balances your emotional body and reduces anxiety.

☆ 8 × 4 × 8 × 4: helps you enter a meditative state and balances the frequency of vibration in your body's cells.

☆ 10 × 5 × 10 × 5: very stimulating and invigorating; it speeds up the metabolism.

☆ 12 × 6 × 12 × 6: charges your mental energy, clears the mind and rejuvenates your memory.

☆ 14 × 7 × 14 × 7: induces serenity of mind.

☆ 16 × 8 × 16 × 8: the most advanced breathing sequence – if you can master it, it will significantly boost your overall well-being and help to clarify your karmic path.

Cleansing the magic meridians/*nadis*

I have already described the three energy pathways that run through our aura, and how they directly relate to our past, our present and our future. Now I want you to start getting into the habit, every time you work with a particular emotion or thought, of asking yourself with which time frame the emotion or thought pattern is connected: past, present or future?

One way to do this is simply to ask yourself directly: "Does this come from the past; the present or the future?" Usually your subconscious knows and you'll find the answer popping into your head. Otherwise you can use automatic writing. For this, all you need to do is sit down and relax. Write down the emotion at the top of a page. For example: "I feel angry." Then write down: "Why do I feel angry?" Next, just allow your hand to write whatever comes automatically. You might be surprised at just how much information you can find out this way.

When you establish the answer, you must work with that time frame of your life.

The meridians, like all channels, can be either polluted or purified. They become polluted with negative energies, dense energies, which carry vibrations of evil and unbalance. What pollutes this energy? First, our negative emotions: evil, hatred, dishonesty, fear and sadness. Second, our negative thoughts: aggressive thoughts; egotistical thoughts. Third, even the kind of food we eat can affect this energy: over-processed food, synthetic food, the kind of food that holds information about death (for example overloading your system with meat or overly processed foods).

Fortunately there are simple ways of clearing these essential energy pathways of the body.

Cleansing the three magic meridians/*nadis*

Start by drawing a simple diagram of the three channels – *Ida* (the past), *Pingala* (the future) and *Sushumna* (the present) (see Figure (a) below).

Sit quietly and think about the channels. From which channel do you take the most energy? Try to figure out what percentage of

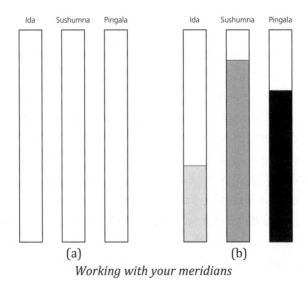

Working with your meridians

each channel manifests itself in your life. For example 60% present, 20% past, 20% future. Rely on your intuition to figure out which channel is the cleanest. Which has manifested itself most in your life? Then colour each bar according to its dominance in your life (see Figure (b)). This will help you to visualise your channel's function.

Now you are ready to practise this meridian-balancing exercise.

This is an ideal exercise to practise regularly, to ascertain whether you are taking energy from the past, present or future. It is also a wonderful idea to combine the visualisation part of this exercise with meditative jogging, which I describe overleaf.

☆　Undress and run a shower (normal temperature).

☆　Before you step under the shower, imagine that rays of sunlight are coming down on you from above.

☆　Now step into the shower. Pure clear water is pouring from the showerhead over you. Adjust the shower so that it comes out in a solid stream, not a spray of water. Let the beam of water run along your spine, from the left side to the right side. You can do this by removing your body from the beam of water and then moving closer to it again.

☆　Imagine that this stream of water is cleansing your three main meridians. Watch how a beam of water sluices through the channels, washing away all the impurities from their internal walls.

☆　Before you finish, stand for a few seconds under the shower so the stream of water touches the top of your head (crown chakra) and place the palm of your right hand on top of your solar plexus, with your left hand on top. Breathe quietly and say to yourself in a calm and strong voice: "I am here and now."

☆　Spend at least three to five minutes on the whole meditation. Keep in your mind the whole time that you are cleansing your channels – make this a strong command. Remind yourself that you have in your heart the knowledge of what you want to achieve and in your solar plexus the deep desire to do this, to complete it. If you like, when you are working with the water, you can also work with colour, imagining that your colour of preference is pouring into your body with the water and is flushing out your body.

The skin pinch test

There is another very easy way to establish which channel works well, and which does not. If the channel works well, the skin above it or along it is very elastic and can be pinched and pulled quite easily. If the channel is blocked or sluggish, the skin will feel stiff and unyielding along it.

Connecting with the energy of the present

You can try a very effective breathing technique to stabilise the work of these channels and to help you to connect more with your central meridian, the pathway of the present. This technique (introduced in Chapter 10) is known as alternate nostril breathing and it is a good idea to practise it regularly. It's also a very calming and balancing exercise so do make time for it.

☆ Wear loose clothing and sit with a straight back, legs uncrossed.

☆ Close your right nostril with your right thumb, and exhale through your left nostril.

☆ Inhale through your left nostril to the count of four.

☆ Close your left nostril with your ring and little finger, resting your index and middle fingers on the bridge of your nose, both fingers pressing the area between your eyebrows. Hold to the count of sixteen.

☆ Release your right nostril and exhale. Try to empty your lungs completely to the count of four.

☆   Inhale through the right nostril on a count of four, close the right nostril and then keep both nostrils closed to a count of sixteen.

☆   Release your left nostril and exhale to the count of eight.

☆   Start again, and repeat the whole sequence at least ten times – breathing to a count of four, holding your breath to the count of sixteen and exhaling to a count of eight.

☆   Stop if you feel dizzy.

Meditative jogging

This may seem like a strange idea, but in Russia meditative jogging has been used for centuries. It started when messengers were used to deliver information. These people were able to walk and run for incredibly long distances. Their purpose was to run in a particular state of consciousness, focusing on one idea. In this state your physical exertion is almost pushed into second place and you find yourself focusing more on the meditation than on the physical act of putting one foot in front of the other. For our purposes I want you to use a very slow pace – this isn't a race! Remember your mind should focus not on your speed but on your meditative practice.

! If you have any health problems, check with your physician before jogging. Start slowly, for short distances, and build up your stamina.

☆   Start running very slowly in as soft and gracious a way as you can. It's almost as if you were running in slow motion, with no strenuous effort.

☆   Allow all thoughts to lift out of your head, and form a colourful stream of fog.

☆   Also release a very colourful fog from your heart – one containing all your senses and emotions.

☆ Visualise the fog dispersing into the surrounding atmosphere, almost like snowflakes melting in the warm air.

☆ Now start visualising golden fountains of energy beaming straight from the ground into your coccyx.

☆ As you run, you can almost feel your bottom bouncing on those endless fountains of energy, almost as if you were riding on top of them.

☆ You should now be feeling more relaxed. Make sure your back is straight and your legs, arms, neck and stomach are calm and relaxed. Check your face – are your facial muscles relaxed? Let any tightness, any tension go. Allow your entire body to loosen up and to feel free.

☆ Now you can move onto the second part of your meditative jogging. This helps to detox your energy. It is very important that you start at the bottom, with your feet, and move upwards in stages.

☆ Start with your feet. Imagine that, every time your feet touch the ground, they are releasing negative energy in the form of black dirt. Visualise this as a black powder or dust. With every step, the soles of your feel push out all the black dirt – all your problems, issues, cluttered paperwork and so on. Run smoothly, observing what is happening. As you do this, your feet will feel much lighter.

☆ Once your feet feel light, you can continue upwards. This time bring your consciousness into your lower legs. Once again, visualise the black dirt leaving this part of your legs by draining through the soles of your feet.

☆ Continue up through the body, one part at a time. Each time you work with a new area of your body, imagine the black powder, dust, sand, black flakes, however you choose to imagine the webs of old stuck energy, being pushed out of your body with every step.

☆ Once you have got rid of all the negative energy (you will have just cleared your head), you can move towards recharging. Imagine that there is a column of white light descending upon you from the centre of the universe. This light enters your body through the crown chakra. Visualise your whole body, your entire being, as being filled with a golden-white glowing light.

☆ You may notice that some parts of your body will fill with the light more quickly than others. If you see black dots resisting the light in any part of your body, stay in those areas until they give way.

☆ If you notice physical problems or sense illness in any part of your body, send just a little more nourishing light to that area or areas.

☆ At the end of your jogging meditation, stand still and straight with your arms by your sides and inhale. As you inhale, lift your arms up above your head and then release your arms back to your sides as you exhale. While doing this, visualise yourself creating a clear bubble of energy all around you.

☆ Keep breathing. With each breath, the bubble will become fuller and you will feel an increased sense of protection.

I strongly recommend that, if you have the chance, you should perform this jogging in nature so you can surround yourself with nature's energy. A park is fine. However, if you do not have this opportunity or, for some reason, you are unable to jog outdoors, you can do this in a gym, jogging on a treadmill.

In the modern world, it is very difficult to find the time to look after all aspects of our being, our subtle bodies in particular. But do try to find the opportunity. What is lovely about meditative jogging is that you can look after both your physical body and your subtle bodies at the same time!

Once you have become accustomed to the practice and it has become almost second nature, you can combine meditative jogging with the cleansing the channels exercise I gave you earlier (page 185). Of course, instead of physical water, you will be using the power of your imagination. The two work beautifully in tandem.

Overcoming negative self-talk

Remember that your thoughts are always forming your life. Don't rush to pile the blame for your mental energy on some outside perpetrator. More often than not, we are the ones who are guilty and responsible for forming the blocks in our mental bodies. Unfortunately we tend to communicate with ourselves in a really destructive manner. For example, we habitually think thoughts like "I am a useless person", "I am ugly", "I am not destined to be happy" and so forth. Sounds familiar?

You may well have heard about positive affirmations. These are positive statements that you repeat over and over to yourself in order to bring about beneficial change in your life. Many psychologists and researchers have found that this sort of self-talk really can affect our health, our success, our whole lives. Unfortunately, negative self-talk can be equally powerful. The more you say something to yourself, the more your subconscious will endeavour to create it in your life. All these negative thoughts will create persistent blocks in our mental energy and have a tendency to rule and form our lives.

We can find internal balance and heal our auras only when we start loving ourselves and stop humiliating or beating ourselves up with our thoughts. We should learn to accept ourselves – just the way we are – and try not to expect perfection. Remember perfection just does not exist in this world. If something appears to be too perfect, I often find it has a shadow, just as there are always two sides to each coin. It is important to accept your imperfections without allowing them to overpower you. Use your positive energy and connections with the Universe to master yourself without cursing your faulty sides. Remember these are also part of the divine you, and have been given to you for a reason. Do not give yourself name tags based on your imperfections and do not allow anyone else to do this either.

Reprogramming the subconscious mind

There is a wonderful exercise that can help if you are constantly running yourself down. It is also very useful in helping to overcome negative experiences from the past.

☆ Lie or sit down so you are comfortable. Focus on your breathing and let yourself relax.

☆ Imagine you are sitting in a cinema. In front of you is a huge screen.

☆ Now, project onto that screen an unpleasant picture. This could be a picture of how you see yourself negatively (i.e. as fat and feeling uncomfortable at a party) or a scene in which you behaved badly (i.e. losing your temper at someone).

☆ Make this picture as bright and clear as you possibly can, as if you were focusing a camera.

☆ Now, in the lower right-hand corner, there is another (small) screen. On this you can see the same scene but this time you're looking or behaving in a positive way. This picture is small and blurred.

☆ Now you need to inhale deeply and with a sudden breath, exhale and say loudly something like "oof!" or "ha!" It needs to be an explosive sound – you push your breath out with the sound. And, at the exact moment that you exhale and shout, you bring up the little picture so it pushes out the big picture. It becomes huge, very clear, very bright, very focused.

☆ Keep breathing, with every exhale (and your sound) the picture becomes more defined, more bright.

☆ Experience the joy and sheer pleasure of seeing this new big picture, which describes you in a new ideal way. Really feel how good it is to be this way. It's vital you experience deep satisfaction and positive emotions when you view this new picture.

Training the mind to register and absorb positive information

We can look at our moods as the base melody of the many interacting melodies of our inner world. The level of satisfaction we have with our life – our expectations, our dreams, our hopes – are all formed and reflected within our moods. Our attitude towards things and our reflections on life are influenced by the tone of music within our soul. This is why one person will be completely knocked out by the smallest problem while another may remain high-spirited, even when they are facing major misfortunes. Each of us to a certain degree wants to be different or to have a different look, or status, or family dynamic. Our dreams are reflected in our thoughts and desires combined: all of this forms our "ego of desire". Our mood is also very dependent on the level of closeness between the ego of desire and the ego of reality (in other words, what we crave and what we can realistically have). We all have to try and learn the right attitude towards the distance between the two; no matter how short or long. Once again, we need to teach ourselves how to appreciate the present and how to train our minds to focus on the positive aspects around us.

In the early days, people used prayer to help then achieve this aim. Prayer gave people faith in their success, encouraging them to rely on God's help. Modern people nowadays tend not to rely on anyone except themselves. This is why we need to find new ways to maintain a positive mental outlook and mood. To achieve this, we really need to train our mind to absorb and record positive information.

Enriching mental energy with positivity

Practise this exercise in a calm environment in the evening (in bed perhaps).

☆   Close your eyes and try to remember, in minute detail, everything that gave you pleasure during the day. It can be as simple as the memory of a beautifully presented meal at lunch or the memory of the scent of a new perfume you tried in a department store, or perhaps the memory of a hug from your child.

☆   Try to sense those feelings once again. The more detailed your recollections are and the more they activate your five senses, the more effective they become.

☆   To begin, you may struggle to find one or two positive beautiful moments in your day, but the more you continue to train your mind, the more you will start to focus on details which eluded you at the beginning. You will also begin to find more beauty and joy in the simple things such as dewdrops in the sunlight or a stranger's smile.

The more you notice the positive in your life, the more it will allow you to fine-tune the melody of your soul towards the lighter and higher vibrations. That music of our inner self is always playing through our eyes. Take a look in the mirror and see what kind of music your eyes are transmitting. To my mind, the key to the secret of youth lies within that music and the ability to feel and go with that rhythm no matter what life throws at you. I always find tremendous joy in meeting elderly people and looking at their faces, especially when they still have young and sparkling eyes. Their young and youthful spirit makes them much more vibrant than many twenty-somethings.

Letting go of unwanted thoughts

Our thoughts are intricately connected with our moods; their energy makes us the way we are. We have to ask ourselves what our thoughts dwell upon? What is our soul tuned into?

Maybe somebody told you something really offensive and, as a result, your mood is far from joyful and you are filled with resentment. This means that your thoughts are controlling you and your mood. It is very important to understand which thoughts are yours and which thoughts belong to someone else – someone whose energy is controlling and managing your destiny. It is easy for somebody else's thoughts to become your own and, even worse, to start to dominate your own thoughts.

Why does this happen? Why do we *allow* this to happen? Basically because we don't know ourselves; we are not able to control our thoughts and we cannot control our destiny. We are not building our destiny consciously; we are not managing our own energy. We are often living, not as intelligent beings (which humans really are!) but more as impulsive animals, which are pulled from one mood to another depending on external energy from the environment around them. When we live like this, we are very open to the waves of external influences, it's as if we were just floating. Most people have had these moments, when suddenly we feel these heavy, dark, sad thoughts coming into our heads. Perhaps it happens in circumstances when an inner disharmony of your subconscious mind tries to push something out, to get rid of inner negativity. There can be many reasons. Whatever the reason, we always should liberate ourselves from any strange and disturbing thoughts or thoughts, which have been imposed on us by somebody else.

Here's a technique to help you let go of unwanted thoughts.

☆ Inhale fully and deeply. As you inhale, push all those unwanted thought into a dense ball-like cluster in your imagination. It might be black, or some other colour. If you cannot manage to cram them all in on one inhale, keep inhaling, as if you were pumping up a balloon. You can imagine this ball of dense energy anywhere in your body: in your stomach, your heart, or in your throat.

☆ When you have created the cluster, exhale sharply: it's like a strong sneeze or blowing your nose. Pump out that unwanted cluster from your body with the exhale, imagining it moving upwards and through the top of your head until it is pushed out into the environment.

☆ If you feel that you haven't entirely got rid of everything, take a normal natural inhale and then exhale again under pressure with a rhythmic pumping breath. Continue until you don't feel those unpleasant sensations, and are sure they have left your body.

☆ Now imagine that the ball-like cluster you exhaled is floating about one or two metres above your head. Take one natural inhale and a very slow exhale. Now start breathing in the forceful pumping breath again, as if you were bombarding the ball with your breath, eventually breaking it up with the force of your breath. Continue the bombardment until in your imagination you see the ball is almost like a firework, exploding and breaking, creating many bright flashes. The flashes are bright, clear, beautifully multi-coloured particles – let them go.

Working on the mind and emotions through the physical body

I'm aware that the exercises in this section of the book have been, on the whole, quite metaphysical. Some of you may feel uneasy or uncomfortable about working so much with visualisation and meditation. If so, there are alternatives. Because the levels are all interconnected, there is nothing to stop you working with emotions and thoughts on a physical level. If you would prefer to do this, I would recommend you try ice cube therapy, described in Part 8 on Rejuvenation. You can also switch to the alkaline diet, again described in the Rejuvenation section.

Clothes as an energy booster

As we are working on improving our moods, I would recommend that you also focus on your clothes and your image. When you are in a good mood, it enhances your desire to be attractive and to dress beautifully and vice versa. When you wear beautiful new clothes and when your image reflects who you are, it also elevates your mood. When we are wearing clothes that we like, not only do we improve our mood but also we correct our posture and the way we walk (often people walk with a light spring in their step conveying their confidence to the outside world).

I recommend that people should not wear old clothes or keep clothes for a very long time because our clothes absorb our energy and, after a while, they will start to carry our moods, both negative and positive, from the past. So it can be as if you are wearing an echo of the energy of old upsets and worries. New clothes have an almost liberating effect on us, encouraging us to let go and move forward. Even snakes shed their skins and birds shed their feathers! Intuitively, during festive seasons, we wear beautiful new clothes almost in an attempt to leave behind the daily worries with our usual clothes. Festivities are often linked to new beginnings, so by wearing new clothes we are subconsciously trying to attract new chapters in our lives.

Equally, by wearing uniforms (at work or school for example), we are helping ourselves to enter an altered state of mood to help us to perform better. We should all take a look at our wardrobes and see if they truly reflect our authentic personality. Do your clothes have a positive mood-enhancing effect on you? Or are they just another uniform to help you through the day?

One other thing: don't wear clothes that are too tight, and try always to find clothes that are made of natural materials. Our aura does not like to be restricted by tight and synthetic clothes. For example, if you look at the spiritual guides of a majority of religions, they are often wearing very loose clothes that allow energy to move freely. A lot of the time when we come home, we like to change into non-restrictive clothing, which gives us a sense of release. So when you are at home, as often as you can, try to wear loose clothes made from natural fibres, as synthetic fibres considerably reduce the flow of energy around us.

PART SIX
**People
Secrets**

CHAPTER EIGHTEEN

Energy Exchange Between People

So far we have looked in some considerable detail at how our own energy works. We have looked at ways of balancing energy and dealing with negative emotions and also negative thoughts. If you have started practising the exercises I have given, you should be noticing a huge change in your energy and well-being already.

However, unfortunately it's not enough just to pay attention to oneself. Our energy is also affected by how we interact with other people. Every single person we meet can affect our energy – from close family and friends, through work colleagues, employees, bosses, right down to vague acquaintances and even the people we sit next to on the bus or the person who serves us in the shop.

The different types of negative energy exchange

There is always an energy exchange between people and it does not always have a positive effect on our health. Good healthy energy exchange usually occurs between, for example, two lovers or between a mother and her child. On the other hand, examples of negative energy exchange would include cases where people are angry with one another, or jealous or afraid. Start noticing how different people make you feel. Allow your intuition to give you information about people and about how your energy reacts to theirs, and vice versa.

I would also like you to become aware of the most common types of negative energy exchanges between people. In my work, I frequently come across energy imbalances, which are often caused by the energy exchange between my patient and other people. It's not that surprising. Think about when you have an argument with someone. It can be hard to shake off the bad feeling, can't it?

Surely negative energy is just negative energy? Far from it. As a healer, I diagnose many different types of negative energy exchange. It's useful for you to be aware of the various levels. It's not that you particularly need to treat them differently, more that I would like you to become aware of how you can be affected. You will probably recognise people and situations in the paragraphs that follow. This is useful because it may well help you to avoid such problems in the future.

Type 1: energy holes in the astral level of the aura

Just as physical material can be torn or split, energy layers can be perforated too. The aura is highly vulnerable to any kind of negative exchange between yourself and other people. One way this happens is when another person directs a string of negative emotional energy at you – for example, during an argument. This can significantly damage the way your energy exchanges with the outside environment. If you are a victim of this kind of exchange, your energy field, your biofield, will develop holes through which your vital energy can leak out. There are usually anywhere up to seven punctures, depending on how many of the chakras are affected.

How does this happen? When someone is being verbally aggressive (such as during an argument) their energy field expands and begins to vibrate at a very fast frequency. It's as if he or she were producing energy thorns or spikes. A person with a weak aura, or whose aura is temporarily below par, can be badly punctured by these invasive fast frequencies.

Unfortunately, it's not only verbally expressed negative energy that can cause damage. Passive energies, those that are not necessarily expressed, can be just as bad. In those cases, people are sending out negatively charged emotional thoughts such as envy and hatred. Let's take the example of a couple getting married. The man's mother is not at all happy with her son's choice of partner. By channelling negative thoughts constantly at her daughter-in-law, it's as if she were almost trying to destroy and weaken her son's new wife.

People can strike your aura both consciously and unconsciously. Many people do not have the remotest idea of how powerful the energy of their negative emotions can be. For example, you can become very run-down by working with, or living with, someone who is disturbed, or over-possessive, for a very long time. Also if you spend time with somebody who has a very strong energy presence around them, but does not resonate on the same frequency as you, you can end up with your aura dented in quite a few places.

We all have our own frequency and that frequency can change throughout our lives. Depending on what you learn in life, your frequency can become finer or denser.

We are naturally drawn to people whose frequencies are harmonious with our own. You will be familiar with the idea of there being "chemistry" between people – well, this is the real reason. It also explains why you can be best friends with someone but then find, months or maybe even years later, that you no longer really "get on". What is happening is that your frequencies are no longer resonating. In fact, they might even be repelling you. I think this is very useful knowledge because so many people feel that they should keep friends for life, or feel guilty that they no longer seem to have anything in common with their oldest, dearest friends. You are very lucky if all your friends evolve at the same pace as you do, so you can maintain the same level of chemistry. You don't need to cut people brutally out of your life, but maybe think about gently distancing yourself from those friends with whom you no longer have much in common.

How to tell if the astral layer of your aura is damaged

These energy holes, as I've already mentioned, can occur in all your chakras and, depending on your symptoms, you can establish (without being in the slightest bit psychic) where you are most likely to have these imbalances.

If you have an energy imbalance, you will notice almost immediately a subtle change in your emotional spectrum. I also find that people who have these types of imbalances often experience a severe lack of energy, irritability, impatience etc.

I will describe to you now the most common emotional changes that take place if you suffer damage caused by negative energy imbalances. Dents or holes in your chakras will correlate to certain changes of emotion. Here are the emotional changes connected to damage in each chakra.

First chakra

Suddenly you start feeling mean and over-calculating. You may start rushing into impulsive actions, taking rash decisions that are not thought through properly. What makes it strange is that most likely you will find yourself thinking how totally absurd these actions are; yet you still feel unable to stop yourself. It feels as if your legs lead you into any "abyss" all of their own accord!

Second chakra

Suddenly you notice that a relationship within your family has started to change. You lose your energy drive, feeling lonely and possibly useless. The leaking of energy from this chakra can often be misdiagnosed as depression. You may also begin to envy other people's success because holes in this chakra can ignite sparks of jealousy and obsessive clinginess. You may notice that it becomes more difficult to tell the truth and you may also want to coerce people to follow your will. In extreme cases, people with this form of energy hole can turn into extremists and even terrorists.

Third chakra

You begin to act like the proverbial ostrich. You hide your head in the sand, afraid of everything and everybody. You shy away from taking any responsibility for your health or work. You become afraid of leaving your house and can feel distrust or even hatred towards other people. In my practice, I often see people in this state being dragged in to see me by their relatives.

Fourth chakra

If your energy is cracked in this chakra, you will notice yourself developing a cruel, dry and cynical personality. You may become restless and anxious. You will find yourself starting useless and empty discussions and arguments. People whose aura becomes very cracked at this level will find it means nothing to betray someone or they may delight in playing cruel jokes.

Fifth chakra

You suddenly begin to change your connection with loved ones. You begin to blame the past for all your misfortunes. People with this imbalance abruptly lose any interest in their achievements and their success. They stop listening to anybody but themselves. They do not even notice how they are ending up in complete isolation from other people.

Sixth chakra

Imbalance in this chakra will lead you to become very scatty and forgetful. You lose your inspiration and your sense of humour. Very often you begin to distance yourself from other people.

Seventh chakra

If this chakra is leaking or torn, you will find it affects your "internal antennae" and you will start attracting the wrong people, often "fake" people. You can no longer be selective and start to feel internal aggression towards people. You may start doing things you have completely rejected before – such as taking drugs, or drinking alcohol to excess. The people you attract into your life push you towards bad, dysfunctional behaviour and actions.

Aura damage caused by violence

It's also worth knowing that we can affect our auras, especially at this astral level, by watching programmes on television or in the cinema that are full of violence and aggression, or by listening to music that has an angry, disturbing sound. Pornography, aggression and violence are all connected with the low chakras so these pursuits can lead to their overload. I think that violent computer games, in particular, are especially dangerous, as they can damage such a vulnerable astral level – particularly in children. In Russia, children's cartoons simply aren't violent – they are always very positive and there are no violent images to harm a child's aura.

While we're talking about children, I would also like to discuss the dents and holes that can occur in a baby's aura due to exposure to negative energy fields. It's important that you're aware that a baby's aura is present and functioning from before birth, when the baby is still in the mother's womb. Parents should be super-conscious of their emotions, as strong outbursts can weaken certain chakras in an unborn baby. Mothers, in particular, should take necessary precautions, isolating themselves from all violence, and unsettling information. In old Russia it was common for a pregnant woman only to look at beautiful peaceful things during her baby's gestation.

Type 2: energy holes on both the mental and astral levels

There is another type of external energy that can affect us and which can rip open our auras – this happens not only on the astral level but also on the mental level.

This is a very serious energy imbalance, which occurs under external forces and is created when somebody consciously and deliberately channels negative emotions at you, accompanied by strong commands (a kind of negative affirmation).

In the first type of energy imbalance we discussed above, the energy only leaks from the chakra. In this imbalance, however, not only is your energy leaking, but also it starts to vibrate at entirely the wrong frequency for your own nature. Your aura starts to resonate according to someone else's command. It's as if you became "de-coded".

This type of energy imbalance is not, as you might think, created by magicians or witches, but can be caused by people who are close to us. It usually happens during very powerful mutual psycho-emotional stress. Let's take the example of a competitive colleague at work who is full of jealousy and envy towards you. At times when you are particularly run-down and stressed, this person can impulsively, from his or her deep core, shout direct, strong affirmations: "You're a loser!" or "You'll never be a good boss." If this type of thing is said to you when you are in a weak energetic state, this outburst of negative energy and affirmations combined together, and channelled directly at you, can turn you into a zombie-type person or even lead to the outcome their evil wish desired.

People's precious free will and the glow of their astral body become suppressed underneath another person's energy and may become totally dependent on it. This type of severe energy imbalance does not necessarily have to be caused by another person. Unfortunately, more often than not, I see people themselves subject their aura to such a destructive attack. We very often become overloaded with the emotions of self-hate and self-denial, speaking in a destructive and careless manner to our own minds so we subconsciously reprogramme ourselves from vibrating on very light frequencies to vibrating on very dark and dense ones.

Type 3: "energy vampires"

When we talk about vampires, we are used to the image of scary creatures with fangs dripping with their victims' blood. It would actually be quite useful if "energy vampires" were as visible and obvious as these creatures! "Energy vampires", however, come in many – often innocuous – guises. They can come in the disguise of your parents, your employees, your boss, or simply in the form of the man or woman who sits next to you on the bus. Even certain animals or plants can have a draining effect on your energy.

There are three types of "energy vampires": conscious, subconscious and temporary. Let's look at these in turn.

Conscious "energy vampires"

These are premeditative and feed consciously from your energy. They do this because they know, from previous experiences, that stealing another person's energy makes them feel better. They almost turn into "energy addicts", emulating behaviour similar to that of a drug addict. These types of people consciously provoke others to experience strong reactions – usually anger – because this kind of energy is directly channelled to them and provides the easiest energy "fix".

The people who precipitate these outbursts are the "vampires" and the method they usually use is belittling or humiliating comments, picking on the smallest and the weakest around them. Sometimes they will begin with long and patronising speeches to provoke the energetic reaction they need. They push people to ignite with white hot rage and shout with anger – and at precisely that moment the energy is released and transferred from the angry donor to the provocative "vampire". You'll often find such vampires in crowds, or on public transport, usually trying to provoke an argument. They can be deeply irritating and will keep pestering you, asking you about something, wanting advice which they do not really need or will not follow.

All bullies are "vampires" as they feed from the energy of despair, fear and submissiveness.

Although I call this kind of imbalance "conscious", it can often be manifested in a very subtle form and is often impulsive rather than premeditative. This sort of "vampire" is often completely unaware of their perverted energy illness. They simply know they feel good when others feel bad, so they seek to do what makes them feel better. When we communicate with this kind of person, we start to feel ill while they, at the same time, feel better. These kinds of "vampires" are aiming to create within others a complex of guilt, fear and anxiety. They torture others by being over-mysterious, secretive or using incomplete sentences. They love to moan and complain.

Subconscious "energy vampires"

As a healer, I often come across damage done to my patients by subconscious "vampires". Unfortunately, more often than not, they tend to be mothers. You may find this surprising, so let me explain. We are connected to our mothers by an invisible energy cord, similar to the umbilical cord. Up until the age of 5 or 6, we remain connected to our mother through our second chakra, sharing the same auric egg or cocoon as her. After the 6th year, our energy "cord" begins to disappear and we obtain our own complete, individual, autonomic energy bubble.

In cases where the mother experiences a strong need for the presence of her child, often due to divorce or another kind of emotional struggle, she will use her child's energy to stay emotionally afloat. She subconsciously pulls and feeds through the cord, preventing the separation. Often with such interactions, the mother's energy turns into either suffocating love or very turbulent love–hate relationships. The energy of the mother, in such cases, will never allow the child to stand on his or her own two feet. They will live their entire life in a symbiotic pattern. If you feel this applies in your life, it would be worth practicing the exercise "Cutting energy cords" that I will describe on pages 224–5. Plus keep working with your undeveloped first chakra.

Temporary "energy vampires"

The most common type of "energy vampire" is the temporary type. We can all do this, from time to time, if we are not careful. In moments when we feel ill, feel the desire to complain or a shoulder to cry on, we can act as energy "drinkers". Elderly people often need energy feeding in particular.

These types of people are not particularly dangerous to our energy and it will do no harm to share your energy temporarily with another person. Your aura will quickly replenish all the shared energy and, who knows, maybe one day those people will share their own energy with you. Do not be afraid to give to someone who really needs it. But again, be aware not to over-drain yourself, keep grounding yourself and practise energy exercises to stabilise your own energy field. You have to be strong, first of all for yourself and then for others.

I think that, if you give yourself a moment to think about it, you will know exactly who your own "energy vampires" are. They're the people whose phone-call you dread because you just know you'll come away feeling low and depressed. They're the people who drain you every time you see them.

Mutual energy abuse has become a real epidemic for our time. We constantly live in such a tense time, both emotionally and physically, that when we interact with other people, we tend to imbalance and upset each other's tunings.

In my practice, I sometimes come across "energy vampires" who do not really want to be healed. What they really want to do is to feed off my emotional energy. These types of people are very draining as they try to take my personal reserves of energy, instead of using the free energy I channel for healing.

Energy cords in our chakras

As we have already discussed, we have a space around our physical body filled with our bioenergy – the aura. We often refer to this space as our "personal space". In order to feel balanced, not only should our physical space not be invaded, but equally our auric space should not be invaded.

We have already looked at some severe energy imbalances and punctures that occur under the force of other people's will and emotions. Now it's time to look at other types of imbalance that can occur when we attach ourselves too much to other people or when other people attach themselves to us. What happens is that your energy fields can cross, creating an energy cord. The energy of the weaker person becomes directly co-dependent on the stronger one – we have a master and servant situation. These cords can be created through the energy of different chakras and can depend very much on where the energy cord has been connected. I'm going to describe to you the effects that can occur, according to which chakra is affected.

First chakra

This chakra is the centre of survival in our aura. If you have an energy cord stretched from this chakra to another person, it is almost as if you were saying: "I need your energy." This cord can naturally occur between parents and children, when one sincerely cares about the other and tries to help them survive. In more negative circumstances, this energy cord can occur when people, for example at work, use your ideas and input in order to push forward their own work.

Second chakra

This is the chakra of sexual and emotional intimacy. The knot in this chakra can occur between you and the kind of person who is interested in you only in a sexual way, rather than as a whole person. It can also exist between people who rely heavily upon your emotional support.

Third chakra

This chakra is like the energy generating station of our body. If you are connected through this chakra to another person's energy, it is almost as if one of you has a strong desire to feed from the other person's energy. This sounds similar to the first chakra but it's more about wanting to share in your image, your persona.

Fourth chakra

This is the chakra of love. When you feel love or have deep sincere feelings towards another person or vice versa, you will create a very strong energy bond through this centre. If you connect to somebody through this cord, you have to take responsibility for the positive effect this connection can have on the other person. This can be a very spiritual and enlightening experience for both of you. Normally this connection will occur with mutual intent; however – in the case of unrequited love, for instance – it can be forced by one person.

Fifth chakra

This is the chakra for aesthetics and communication. A link here means, "I want to communicate with you." Sometimes this bundle of energy can even give you a sore throat – for example when your boss imposes their desire for communication upon you when you do not desire it.

Sixth chakra

This is the chakra of intuition and clairvoyance. If somebody is constantly thinking about you or you are unable to get somebody out of your head, you establish a very strong energy bond with each other. It also occurs between two people, when one of you always wants to know what is going on in the other person's mind.

Seventh chakra

This is the chakra of true knowledge. If somebody wants to control you, or push you into following their way, they impose this particular energy cord upon you. It has been known, in some occult schools for instance, that teachers would especially create this energy connection with their pupils in order to keep them close by their sides and obedient. Another example is the way politicians may try to brainwash you in order to control you and your thought processes. This also creates energy bundles between yourself and the powerful energy of the political system.

The hands

You can also connect with people through the bundles of energy in your hands. This is a centre of creative energy. It is like having someone shout at you: "Do this for me!" or "Be like I am!" It's a highly prescriptive, controlling form of energy. If there is a connection here, people always feel as if their hands are tied, and that they are dropping everything from their hands.

The soles of the feet

These auric centres connect you very strongly with the earth. When you have blockages through bundles in this chakra, you lose your sense of reality and you almost start floating through the sky. You become unreasonable and ungrounded.

Ritual walnut bath

Here is a ritual bath, which is designed to help you get rid of these energy connections. Walnut has the power to sever ties, to help you start afresh. It facilitates new beginnings.

☆ To prepare your walnut bath, take six walnuts (still in their shells) and soak them overnight.

☆ Boil them for an hour in about 1.5 litres of water. You can use any type of pan, except an aluminium one. As the walnuts boil, add more water if necessary.

☆ You will be left with a black liquid. Allow this to cool.

☆ Run a bath (whatever temperature you prefer). Add the walnut mixture to the bathwater and get in the bath. You should take this bath for eight minutes. If you can, try to submerge yourself completely under the water, seven times. Each time ask the universal energies to help you cut the cords.

The question of "entities", ghosts and earthbound spirits

I need to talk briefly about what I call "entities". This is an issue that is much misunderstood so I would like to clear it up. As a healer I work with energy on a day-to-day basis. People come to me and want me to work with their energy. As I have just explained, if people do not know how to protect themselves, to keep their aura healthy, they will have a very low energy field, a very vulnerable, porous protective layer of the auric egg. On the other hand, when we are healthy, we have a very strong protection around us; it's almost like rubber. A strong aura will repel negativity easily. So if, for example, you become angry and you start saying aggressive things to me, you are releasing energy with a horrible frequency towards me. But, as my aura is strong and firm, that energy will just bounce off. It's this negative energy that I call "entities". It's usually someone's unpleasant energy that sticks to you, or penetrates through your aura and eats your own energy. Entities can be the presence of somebody else's emotional energy, or mental energy or an intentional blast of negative energy through their will, as we have already discussed.

Yes, there *are* discarnate entities, earthbound spirits, but I have to say they are rarely the cause of our problems. I receive so many phone calls from people saying, "Dr Alla, I have been psychically attacked", that I can't count them. I would say that 99 per cent of the time, the problem is not external; it's not "out there". Yes, people do feel as if there is something inside them, something alien, but it's actually they that are doing it to their bodies.

It happens usually when people are not in control of their emotions and/or allow other people to overrule them. That's why I think it's essential that people learn how to have the right attitude towards their emotions. It's also why I have insisted you should not be scared by your emotions, whether negative or positive. You have to look at emotions as a process of life, rather than fearing them. Maybe you have experienced something traumatic in your life and if you didn't truly possess it, and process it, it can be very unsettling.

In maybe 1 per cent of the cases the entity is something else, something outside of yourself, what you might call a ghost or spirit. Usually it is a remnant of the energy of someone who died while too attached to his or her earthly problem, say someone who drank too much, or someone who committed suicide. The energy of these people is very dense, it doesn't have enough light, so it floats around us, looking to attach itself to our energy.

Mass healing and mediums

I also strongly advise against mass healing sessions. Healing has to be very intimate, one-to-one and in a safe, neutral environment. At mass healings, energy just gets shifted from one person to another; you could end up with someone else's baggage, with their old negative energy! I don't even like it when people have healing at shows and festivals: the chairs are all lined up next to each other and everyone is invading everyone else's auric space. You just can't heal like that. All you do is absorb other people's stuff.

If you wish to consult a medium, you should remember that even if the medium does work with evolved spirits of the light, less evolved entities will often accompany them (just as moths are drawn to the light). There is a say in Russian which conveys this idea well: "Nothing is sweeter to the Devil than the soul of a saint".

Since during the session you are in a very open state, you are particularly vulnerable to infestation by darker entities. I can always tell when a patient of mine has seen a medium – I can sense it. It would be a good idea, as a protection from these disturbed energy clusters, to practise some of the protection exercises and techniques described in the next chapter. Afterwards, you can use a salt bath (see page 54).

Siberian method for removing entities

If you really do believe you have discarn-ate entities attached to you, I suggest you use this ancient, very powerful Siberian method for removing entities. It uses flame, a burning candle, because no entities can survive in the burning flame. Wax is a material capable of absorbing energy information. So the wax absorbs the negative energy while the candle flame burns it.

You will need three pure beeswax candles and three holders (traditionally malachite was used for holders but any holder will do).

☆ Sit on the floor with your legs as widely open as is comfortable; make sure that you are barefoot.

☆ Place one candle just between your legs, close to your pubic bone.

☆ Place the second behind your back, close to your coccyx.

☆ Place the third opposite the sole of your right foot.

☆ Imagine yourself to be a vibrant burning flame. The base of the flame is deep in the earth and your body is like a wick. You have fire all around you. Violet or golden flame is around you. Imagine that all bad thoughts and feelings are being burned in that. It burns very brightly and powerfully. No bad emotions are allowed to penetrate through that flame.

☆ After about seven or eight minutes, move the third candle so that now it is opposite the sole of your left foot.

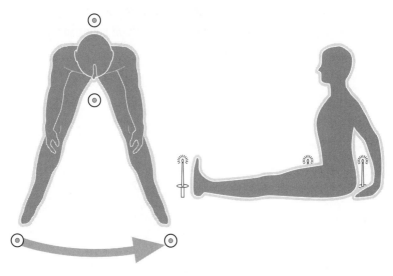

Frontal view　　　*Side view (the legs are widely open)*

☆ Continue with your flame meditation for another seven to eight minutes.

Energy shower

You can also use the shower I first described in Chapter 5 to help with this problem. Salt helps to absorb and neutralise any negative energy you might be carrying in your aura that day.

☆ Prepare a salt rub. You need to add a little sweet almond oil to a handful of sea salt – just enough to make a thick paste. Add two or three drops of either sandalwood, sage or juniper essential oil.

! Avoid sage oil during pregnancy.

☆ Standing in the shower, smear the mixture all over your body (you can avoid your head and face if you wish).

☆ Shower (you can pick your choice of water temperature). While you shower, sincerely and confidently ask the water to wash away anything negative that you may have accumulated during the day. It is important, as the shower rinses the salt off your body, that the water runs over the top of your head.

CHAPTER NINETEEN

Protection

Now you are aware of the problem, I think it's vital you know how to protect yourself. We should all master certain protective practices to protect ourselves against negative external influences, such as those I described in Chapter 18.

The most important thing I can tell you about this subject is always to remember that nobody *ever* has the power to influence you negatively if you keep your aura strong and if you refuse to allow other people to gain power over you. This motto has been imprinted on my psyche by my mother since I was a little girl.

We always have a choice – whether to engage in energy exchange or not. Just because another person is standing next to you does not mean that their energy should cross or interact with yours. We all have a final outer layer of protective energy in our auras. This energy is almost like a thin membrane that protectively wraps our auric egg. When you are healthy and balanced, this protective layer is elastic and tight. But when you are thrown out of kilter, it becomes weak and porous. In a balanced state, any negative energy channelled at you will bounce off that shell. In a weak state negative energy will filter through and cause damage to all the layers of your aura.

If at any time you feel threatened, know you are under attack, or have the sensation that somebody is invading your space, the best option is to get up and leave. However, when people do not have that option, they will tend to cross their arms instinctively over their solar plexus. Unfortunately this will not help in any meaningful way, so I would like to teach you a technique I think you should know which will close your energy circuit, making it difficult for people to enter your personal energy space.

Diamond protection

☆ Place your hands in front of you, comfortably on your thighs.

☆ The index fingers and thumbs of opposite hands meet at the tips, forming a diamond or teardrop shape.

☆ The remaining fingers of your right hand curl up and rest on top of the fingers of the left hand.

By placing your hands in this way you form a protective "diamond" in front of your body, because it will close your energy circuit. The beauty of this exercise is that it is subtle and nobody need know what you are doing, or why.

Stronger protection

You can also build up a stronger protection, just before important meetings and job interviews so you will not be intimidated, by placing your left hand on top of your right hand, and then placing the palm of your right hand on top of your solar plexus. At the same time, tell yourself very clearly and firmly:

"My energy will go nowhere. My energy is always with me."

Try to work on yourself, imprinting the deeply seated knowledge that nobody can ever influence you. If you practise this energy exercise often, you will never feel intimidated or crumble under somebody else's presence. You will always keep your energy balanced and grounded.

White rose protection

In the next part of the book I will be talking about the protective properties of salt and water, but there is another beautiful weapon for protection – the white rose. If you know you are going to have to take part in a difficult, possibly aggressive, meeting you should place a vase with white roses in-between you and the other person or people. This will significantly neutralise all the negative energy exchange. I recommend that a vase of white roses be kept in the meeting rooms of all offices, and in personal offices too.

Core self-protection

If you feel you have been subjected to a psychic attack, or if somebody is trying to play havoc with your mental energy by planting seeds of fear, anxiety and helplessness, you should immediately reconnect with your core self. I advise you to stand straight, with your head up, looking straight ahead so your gaze is just above the top of the head of the person who has been attacking you. As you look above their head, you should very clearly and firmly say to yourself:

*"I reject all harmful influences of all people and all circumstances.
I pronounce my supremacy to these influences."*

I also advise you to try to establish in your mind why, for whatever personal reason, the invading person has the need to attack you with fear, anxiety, constriction or whatever. Becoming aware in this way is the first step to preventing such attacks affecting you.

Mental screen protection

As soon as you realise you have been attacked by another in an attempt to purposely irritate you and force you to experience negative emotions and thoughts, try this. Place a mental screen – a strong tough wall – between you and the other person. Or you could have more fun and imagine this person underneath a big glass cup. When you look at them through the thick glass, their words seem distant and muffled.

If you can see a person in this way, you won't fall victim to his or her space invasion. When you can laugh at the attacking person, or see them in a humorous way, you will never become their victim. Humour is one of the biggest protections one can have. So go on and "cup" all your aggressors and "vampires"!

Resolving arguments

Another tip I can give, which will save you a lot of energy and protect you, is this. Never go to bed with your partner if you have had an argument that has not been resolved. In fact, I would suggest you have a rule in your home that you put closure on all conflicts before bedtime. There is a saying in England, "Never go to bed on an argument" and this is the reason. If you go to bed angry, all the hostile energy you feel towards each other will pollute you both, as energy is able to move more freely when you are asleep. So, when there is another person lying next to you, this energy will most definitely cross over.

One of the simplest ways of resolving arguments is to forgive and embrace that person (even if it's only in your mind).

Bedtime protection

However, if for some reason you are unable to make up and still have to sleep in the same bed, you should perform the following visualisation for protection.

☆ Imagine that there is a screen hanging between you and the other person. It is important that you visualise this screen hanging right from the ceiling down to the floor.

☆ Every time you exhale, imagine that each exhaled breath channels more energy into the protective screen. With each breath it becomes thicker and thicker.

☆ You can increase the effect by using your imagination still further. You could, for example, imagine your screen is made from really tough materials, such as steel, lead, solid brick etc.

Forgiveness ritual

If you carry non-forgiving, aggressive energy during your sleep, you are in danger of self-destruction. This hostile energy will eat you up during your sleep and will prevent your positive energy from regenerating. I therefore suggest that, even if you find it difficult to express forgiveness to a person, that you do the following:

☆ Place your right palm on the left joint between your neck and your shoulder (on your collarbone). Ask the universal energies to cleanse you.

☆ Then move your right palm and place it on your forehead, just over your sixth (third eye) chakra.

☆ Bow slightly and say clearly in your mind: "I forgive myself. I forgive everybody. I forgive myself, I forgive myself, I forgive myself."

Protection from psychic attack

If you feel you are in danger from "energy vampires" or from any form of psychic attack, immediately imagine that you are in the centre of a spinning sphere, similar to that of a child's spinning top. Imagine that it is spinning around you, in a clockwise direction, faster and faster. While doing this, it is also good to visualise that you find yourself in a milky-coloured energy cocoon, within the sphere. If, however, you feel you are under severe pressure you should imagine the cocoon is black in colour.

Cutting energy cords

You might also feel that certain people have connected themselves to you through unwanted energy cords (as described in Chapter 18). You will probably be able to figure out who the person is who is draining your energy or trying to change it according to their will. You will need to cut this cord. Here's how.

☆ Imagine the person in your head. If you find this difficult, look at a photo of them.

☆ Now shut your eyes and try to remember everything about this person – their voice, their eyes, the way they walk, their facial expression. These will all help to reproduce a solid, vivid image of the person.

☆ Now open your eyes and imagine that the person is next to you. Feel their presence, using all your senses.

☆ Close your eyes, holding a strong image of this person in front of you.

☆ As you are visualising him or her, imagine the image of this person getting smaller and smaller in size.

☆ After a short time you will see them diminish to a dot. Then this dot eventually melts into eternity.

☆ Once this has been done, try to visualise and sense this person again, one more time. However, this time, imagine that you stretch energy strings from your heart chakra and your solar plexus chakra to that other person.

☆ Again, imagine that person diminishing while they are hanging from the projected energy string – as a puppet would. Stay with this feeling.

☆ Then visualise that you are cutting the energy strings with a big pair of sharp scissors. Again, the dot to which that person has been reduced will disappear into eternity.

☆ As the dot disappears into nowhere, it forms a figure of eight.

You can repeat this exercise again and again, until you feel that you are completely free from the overpowering energy of that person, and no longer feeling any negative feelings towards them.

You should not perform this energy meditation if that other person is phy-sically near you.

To maximise the effect of this liberating cutting of the energy cords, you can combine the exercise with the ritual walnut bath I described on page 214.

Another good way to shake off someone else's command from you is to practise the exercise "Reprogramming the subconscious mind" that I gave in Chapter 17 (page 192).

CHAPTER TWENTY

Energy Preservation

People with balanced energy have a healthy instinct for self-preservation. When this instinct is strong, we basically keep ourselves well. We never feel tempted to eat food that could damage (and eventually kill) us. We never connect to people who disturb us. We never live in places with negative energy.

However, most of us are so blocked that our intuition simply does not function. We no longer listen to or follow our instinct for self-preservation. As a result, we allow other people to destroy us mentally and emotionally; we let ourselves eat a diet that kills us physically. I hate to demonise food as I do believe in the maxim "everything in moderation", but when we are disconnected from our intuition, we no longer know what moderation means for us personally. Consequently we eat and drink to excess. We stop being selective about the food we choose to put in our stomachs, just as we stop being selective of the people we allow near to us.

First of all, I suggest that you economise on your energy expenditure, by avoiding unnecessary events. If you were to measure how much of your life force has been used attending needless parties and enduring empty conversations, you would wonder, "Why do I do this?" We willingly spread our energy on vacuous, empty things when, instead, this energy could be used to have a one-to-one conversation with a close friend or to enjoy reading a good book, or walking out in nature.

To preserve your energy, avoid interaction with crowds of people and try instead to get together with smaller groups of people instead. So many people go off to party after party, not really knowing why they are going. People tend to spend most of their free time chatting about nothing. They meet with people who don't really interest them; they waste a phenomenal amount of their precious energy, reducing their level of consciousness.

You should start avoiding crowds and, instead, spend more time with a group of like-minded people who are on the same "wavelength". By doing this, you will not only preserve your energy, but also enrich it. Remember that the Universe does not always send people to us for our lifetime. Some people might beautifully enter your life for one day; some may stay a little bit longer. If you are lucky, a special few will maintain a true connection with you throughout your life journey. Please do not expect the same people to follow you through all the cycles of your life, and do not spend emotional energy trying to connect with them if you are no longer in tune with each other. You can either accept the differences, and stop hoping for an old connection, or just move on.

Look around you, look through your address book, and try to distinguish those who enrich your life and those who bring burdens and who drain your energy. Once it is clear to you from whom you should distance yourself, you should do so by sending them a lot of love. Thank them in your mind for being in your life (for however long it has been) and then let go. Of course, there are certain people in your life to whom you have a certain duty – your parents for example. While it may be difficult, it is vitally important to practise unconditional love for your parents, refraining from making judgements on their past actions or their particular ways. Remember that they are still on their learning curve as well. I also believe that the soul chooses its parents according to the life lessons it wants to learn.

Finding out the most important thing in your life

Once you learn to view your every action through a prism of energy expenditure, you will realise just how much energy you have, in the past, wasted for nothing. It will also help you to establish what is most important in your life and what is secondary. This level of awareness will also make you more grounded.

To help you connect and establish what the most important thing in your life is, you can practise the following breathing meditation.

☆ Find somewhere quiet and calm. Sit down comfortably and allow your breathing to become calm and relaxed.

☆ Breathe in and ask yourself: "What is the most important thing in my life?"

☆ Breathe out and ask yourself: "What is the most important thing in my life?"

☆ Breathe simply like this, asking the question on both the inhale and the exhale, for about three minutes. You will find that everything will become very clear and ordered.

Full yogic breath

Yoga teaches us certain breathing exercises that can help to preserve our energy. This one is called the full yogic breath. It will give you a sense of lightness and vitality. It can also stimulate secretion of all your glands, and can especially stimulate the digestive system. You may feel dizzy when you first practise this, but this will soon pass.

☆ Lie on the floor or on a firm bed. Keep your body as straight as possible.

☆ Rest one hand on your navel and the other on your chest.

☆   Close your eyes and inhale deeply and slowly. You will feel your chest is expanding upwards and your abdomen should naturally expand and push upwards. You will know you have it right when you feel the movement in your hands.

☆   Do not force the breath.

☆   Exhale slowly, applying a light pressure on your abdomen with your hands, so your navel is almost drawn towards your spine. You will have the sensation that you are squeezing the air from your abdomen towards your chest. Then your rib cage helps to squeeze the air up and out through your nose.

☆   Practise this exercise between ten and fifteen times.

☆   Resume normal breathing and rest for at least a minute after completing the exercise. Stay flat and don't try to get up too soon.

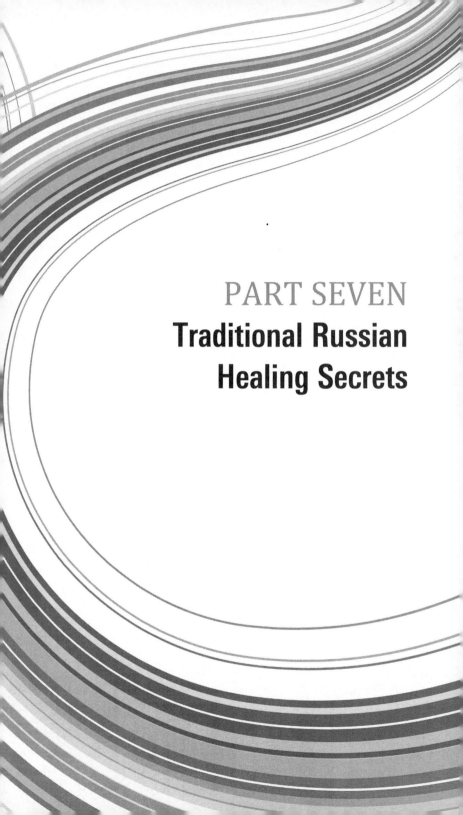

PART SEVEN
Traditional Russian
Healing Secrets

CHAPTER TWENTY-ONE

Healing with Water

In this part of my book I'm going to share with you some of the most wonderful, magical techniques and tools of the ancient Russian healers. These are the procedures, the powerful energy exercises with which I grew up. We're going to talk about the magical healing properties of salt, water, eggs and mirrors. These follow on from the work we have already done in Part 6. They are yet more wonderful ways of releasing negative energy and bringing balance and harmony to your energy bodies.

The exercises may seem strange to you and, to be honest, a lot of them seem strange to me, as I cannot rationally explain how they work. But, nevertheless, they really do work. They have travelled through many centuries and have been a part of the Russian healing tradition for many many generations. Once again, I'd ask you to approach this with an open mind. As I have told you already, I never suggest anything that does not work. By now your intuition should be functioning clearly and well, so I probably won't need to work too hard on persuading you!

Water as an energy stabiliser and cleanser

For many centuries people washed themselves not only for physical cleanliness, but also for psychological and spiritual cleansing. The healing, energising action of water has been known for many thousands of years. For this reason it often crops up as a vital part of many cult, magical and healing procedures. Dipping a body into water is a common and deep part of the ritual of baptism, symbolising the removal of Adam's sin. In Islam the act of washing before prayer demonstrates the believers' desire to appear pure before God. In Russia, many temples and monasteries have been built next to rivers. Lakes, rivers and springs have the unique ability to take away the pain, sorrow and fear of people with their water.

It is not for nothing that there has been this long-term interest in water, nor that nowadays the properties of water are once again under scrutiny. Water truly has many unique properties. The most important quality of water is its ability to keep and maintain infrastructural changes for a certain time. That sounds complicated, but it really just means that water has a memory. Although it is still subject of scientific debate, this is the theory behind homeopathy in which remedies contain not one molecule of the original substance, but instead carry the "memory", the energetic imprint of the substance. Flower and gem remedies follow the same principle.

It is a very important fact that water "memorises" the effects of electromagnetic radiation. Back in the 1930s an Italian researcher, J. Piccardi, established a connection between the activity of the sun and some parameters of water quality. As the water was exposed to the sun, it vibrated differently and became more energised. Soon it became clear that water "remembers" not only the effects of all electromagnetic radiation, but also the actions of technical vibrations, ultrasound and weak electrical currents, and so on. For centuries, Russian healers have chanted over water to energise it and to use the water for healing.

Yogis also give insights into the magical properties of water. According to yogis, water contains large amounts of the energy of space, *prana*, part of which is absorbed by our bodies when we drink or bathe in it – especially if our bodies are in need of extra energy. That's why, when you feel thirsty, you're probably not just needing the physical liquid as such, but also desperate to absorb the energy component of water. A glass of water, drunk at the appropriate time, will give fresh powers to your body and stimulate its efficiency. It's worth remembering this when you feel weak – a glass of water will give you an instant energy boost. To achieve this, you need to drink the water slowly, with small sips, keeping the water in your mouth for a few seconds before swallowing it.

We subconsciously use the energy-balancing properties of water throughout our lives, without consciously acknowledging it. For example, if someone suddenly feels weak or ill, our first instinct is to bring them a glass of water and to help them take a few sips slowly. It's widely known that if someone has been sexually abused or regrets having been physically intimate with someone, they have a strong urge to spend a considerable amount of time – almost in a meditative and entranced state – under the shower in an attempt to flush away the energy of the person who invaded their space.

Many of us spend a lot of money buying crystals in an attempt to purify and balance our energy, but we forget that the most powerful and readily available crystal of all is water. Water a crystal? Surprisingly, yes it is. A single water molecule, seen through a microscope, looks like a large circle (oxygen) with two smaller circles (hydrogen), almost like the ears on Mickey Mouse. All the water molecules want to link up with other water molecules (and create so-called hydrogen bridges) and so water is made up of billions of tiny crystal-like structures. In fact, the more crystalline the structure, the healthier and more energetic the water. Cluster formations enable water to store information. Scientists say there are at least thirty-six different "types" of water, with varying combinations of hydrogen and oxygen – in actual fact it is overly simplistic to describe water as H_2O.

If you learn how to use water for your energy balancing on a daily basis, you will both purify your energy and boost your energy levels.

Flowing water constantly absorbs energy from the cosmos and, in turn, re-releases it back into the surrounding environment. The faster the stream of water flows, the higher the energy field that surrounds it.

There are water reservoirs which have a draining effect on our energy – such as ponds and lakes, especially those which are contaminated with old leaves, sticks and other debris. These act like vampires, draining our energy. This is why, when you are choosing a place for resting, meditation or recharging, I strongly recommend that you do not pick a place next to still water. I also recommend that you avoid pictures, paintings or images of still water, or water with overgrown vegetation, as these will have quite a draining effect on your aura.

Of course, it's not always possible to find water streams that are gushing and energetic in everyday life. However, you can still find a way to benefit from the power of water. I would like to suggest you use the following energy exercise that uses water as its main tool. This exercise is very good for removing negative energy.

Water exercise to balance energy

☆ Begin with a large glass of natural spring water. Sit quietly while you slowly drink it.

☆ Feel the water pouring down inside you.

☆ Feel the coolness and wetness of the water – especially when it hits your stomach.

☆ Imagine the feeling as it passes through your body.

☆ Now turn on the cold-water tap in a sink. Stand in front of it with your back straight.

☆ Stretch out your arms and hands towards the cold-water stream, turning your palms so they are facing each other around the cold-water stream. Ensure that the water flows down in-between your palms without touching them. All the time, very slowly.

☆ The sense of coolness soon changes to a sense of rejuvenation and empowerment that spreads through your body, starting from your hands.

☆ Once you have experienced this increased sense of vitality and purity, stop the exercise. In your mind, thank the water for the power it has given you.

Waterfall meditation

This meditation combines the physical and metaphysical aspects of water.

Natural waterfalls are fantastic for clearing negative energies, but unfortunately most of us don't live near a handy waterfall! However, you can follow the Russian method of purifying energy by throwing a large amount of water over your head. In Russia people would literally pour buckets of water over their heads, but you can improvise by using a shower. In Russian villages people would stand barefoot so that the water would run straight into the earth, so they connected with the ground. If you have a garden, or can go to a natural environment to do this cleansing, do take advantage of that. It will be much more effective than doing it in your bathroom. Don't be tempted to skip your head and let the water merely hit your shoulders – make sure it runs right over the top of your head, from your crown chakra down.

Sometimes, after healing patients with disturbed energy, and particularly those whose energy is disturbed by entities, I have to go and do this exercise straight away.

If you go with the shower option (and, I admit, it is the easiest way of doing this) please make sure the water pressure is not too strong and that you are standing directly under the showerhead. Make sure the water temperature is comfortable. Place a clean shower robe ready for use after the shower. You should use the following "waterfall" meditation at the same time.

Waterfall shower and meditation

☆   Focus on your breathing, taking deep easy breaths. Step into the shower cabinet and gently close your eyes. You must stay close to the running shower.

☆   Imagine, or get a sense of, a beautiful crystal-clear waterfall splashing down nearby. The water has a diamond-like quality to it.

☆   Now step under the shower and imagine you are standing underneath this waterfall. It is going right through your auric field, taking with it any slow-frequency or sluggish energy, any blocks of static you have picked up or accumulated during the day.

☆   Its clarity and refreshing coolness feel invigorating and refreshing.

☆   Now place your head under the running water and imagine that the water is entering in through the very top of your head, through your crown chakra.

☆   It goes right through your body and comes out at the tips of your fingers and toes.

☆   Notice that the water coming out of your fingers and toes might seem cloudy and dark.

☆   Allow the water to continue to move through you until the colour coming out of your fingers and toes is as clear as the waterfall itself.

☆   Once this happens, imagine you are filling your inner space with the water – clean and clear, invigorating and revitalising.

☆   Now step out of the "waterfall" (and out of the actual shower too). Put on the white cloth or shower robe that you had prepared. As you wrap it around you, imagine that you are wrapping yourself in a protective layer, ensuring that your physical space is totally safe from invasion.

☆   Take a deep breath; wriggle your fingers and toes, and give yourself a good smile.

Magical properties of water

I would also like to give you a few final tips for using the magical properties of water.

☆ When you have a meeting with people, always place a glass of water between you and the other person or people. Do not drink this water and, at the end of the day, flush this water down the toilet. This is a nice, subtle way of protecting your energy from that of other people.

☆ Be careful when you are preparing food, drinking tea, water or wine that you do not have any bad thoughts in your mind. Water (even in the form of tea or alcohol or cooking water) will remember all the words of anger and aggression. When we pronounce a toast with a drink we are subconsciously performing a ritual, without realising that what we are doing is energising the drink with the power of our positive words.

☆ Don't share your bath water or leave it for someone else – energetically this is not good practice. The other person could pick up negative energy sloughed off in the water. Flush away used water.

Water as protection while sleeping

While you sleep you can be exposed to any number of different forms of negative energy, because your defences are down. Water, however, offers great protection. Our energy systems release a lot of negative energy during the night and it is very good to neutralise it before it pollutes the energy of our space. This ceremony to protect our energy during sleep is known as "Sleep with the water". I'm sure many people already do this ritual unconsciously, never thinking about its true purpose.

Sleep with the water

☆   Before you go to sleep, take a glass of water and place it next to the headboard. It should be at the same level as your head while you are sleeping. A bedside table is ideal for this. Never drink from the glass. Just leave it there.

☆   In the morning, pour the contents of the glass down the toilet, using your non-dominant hand, rinsing the glass three times under running tap water and each time throwing the water down the toilet (this is more symbolic than merely using the sink). Flushing away the water will wash away all that has been accumulated in the glass during the night.

If you have very disturbing dreams or if you are scared of entities around you while you are sleeping, add a few drops of camphor to the glass. You need only a tiny bit of camphor – about the size of a match head.

It is important always to use your weaker hand (not the one you use for writing) for flushing away the water. By using this hand to empty the glass, you symbolically refuse to take back all that was released in the glass.

CHAPTER TWENTY-TWO

The Power of Salt and Eggs

Salt and eggs have been used in Russian folk healing for many centuries. Let's start by looking at the role of salt. Salt in Russia symbolises eternity and living forever, as it never goes off nor does it rot. Russian healers praise salt for its magical qualities, believing that it possesses a supernatural ability to absorb all our energy impurities. Consequently salt is used in many healing ceremonies as a tool to ward off negative energies and entities. I have already discussed the use of salt for balancing energy in the home in Part 2. Now I'd like to look a little deeper at this wonderful crystal and its quite magical properties.

Salt crystals: history and traditions

Salt as a crystal has the ability to absorb all energy information from a very wide spectrum of frequencies: both negative and positive. Salt crystals are very powerful carriers of information. All the information that is channelled into the crystal will be recorded in the salt's crystal grid. Salt not only receives incredibly well, but also transmits energy information and, because of these qualities, salt crystals have often been used in technical equipment to transmit signals.

The Celts used salt to treat many problems. Interestingly the Celtic word for salt is *hall,* which comes from the word *heil*, meaning whole. Pure crystal salt is still geologically defined as "halite", which comes from the Celtic word *hall* for salt and *lit* for light. So, translated figurately, it means "light vibrations". Salt has its individual crystalline structure. The cubic structure of salt is constructed from light quanta, also called photons, which are pure light energy. The English word salt is based on the Latin word *sol*, for sun and the Celtic word *hall*. The Celtic word *hall* also means the same as the German word *seele*, or soul in English. The Celtic people believed the soul originated from the ocean, hence the word saline.

If you are using salt to work with energy, make sure you use coarse crystalline sea salt. This is because the crystals have not been crushed and so remain more vibrant in their energy.

An old tradition in Russian families was always to put a salt cellar in the middle of the table. Before each meal, people would read their prayers and, by doing this in front of the salt, the salt would become charged with positive energy. It was also thought that the salt would cleanse and balance the atmosphere around the table, and that it would absorb any negative emissions. Even in Britain, when we are laying the table, one of the first things we place in the middle of the table is salt.

In many traditions spilt salt signifies bad luck – this is probably due to its ability to connect with energy.

In the Russian tradition, salt would often symbolise the purifying light force of the earth. In Russia there was one day of the week that was dedicated to cleansing: Thursday. The synonym for Thursday was "Purifying Day" and salt used for cleansing purposes was called "Thursday's Salt". When I talk to you about taking showers and baths with salt, I would also like to point out that the best time to do a salt cleanse is during a full moon. This is because we believe that all negative energies and entities concentrate themselves on the surface of the skin at this time and therefore the salt can absorb these energies and entities much more easily. Again remember only to use coarse salt for this purpose.

Charging salt

Salt that you use for energy cleansing will be even more effective if you charge it with positive energy beforehand. In Russia, it is believed that the hollow of a tree possesses magical power, as the tree sends all its healing energy towards the hollow. Sometimes sick children would be placed in the hollow of the tree, in order to be charged with the healing energy of the tree. A similar kind of power can be found between two trees that have split from the same root.

It is believed that, out of all the trees, the oak has the most powerful ability to recharge our energy. I think this is why, when we are choosing flooring or furniture for our homes, so many of us like using oak. If you are lucky enough to have oak flooring, make sure you walk barefooted on its surface as much as possible. Oak is a common tree, especially in Europe. Before Christianity became the official religion of Russia, Russians used to worship the oak tree and often created altars in oak wood.

When choosing a place for your meditation or a place in which to recharge salt, use – if you can – the places described above. To charge salt with the energy of the tree, place the salt in a bag made of natural fibres and put it inside the hollow of the tree or hang it from the branch of a split tree. Leave the salt there for twenty-four hours and your wonderfully charged salt will be ready for your use.

Of course, not everyone has ready access to a tree, or the privacy needed for this exercise. So the alternative is to place your salt in a clear glass jar, along with a rose quartz crystal. Put it on the window ledge so it catches the sunlight and leave it there for twenty-four hours. It needs to see the early morning sun on two mornings, so put it there in the morning and leave it there until the next morning.

You can reuse the salt many times, but remember to neutralise its negative emissions first. To do this, simply place the salt in a hot oven for ten minutes. A high heat will destroy energy emissions of all kinds.

Baths for removing negative energy

There are two types of bath I would like to describe to you. Both of them help to remove negative energies from your subtle energy bodies. They are wonderful for purifying the aura. You can choose whatever temperature water you find most comfortable.

Method one

☆ Take a 1 litre jar, and mix in it one cup of water, one cup of ammonia and one teaspoon of sea salt.

☆ Add one more glass of water.

☆ Pour the contents of the jar into a full bath and get in for five minutes.

☆ Submerge yourself fully three times, ensuring your whole body and head are fully immersed.

☆ Imagine each time you submerge that the negative energy is being washed away.

! Do not take this bath if you have sensitive skin.

Method two

☆ Add one-quarter of a cup of bicarbonate of soda and one tablespoon of sea salt to a full bath.

☆ As with method one, submerge your body into the water three times. Once again, ensure your whole body is submerged and that you consciously imagine the negativity being washed away.

! You should always take a shower after the baths described above.

End of the day footbath

There is a certain footbath I recommend for the end of the day. This helps you to unload pathological energies that you may have accumulated throughout the day. Water can pull down many energetic impurities through the soles of your feet. It is very important, for this reason, to keep the heels of your feet clean and clear of any hard skin. Always make sure the skin of your heels is soft, elastic and a little moist, by massaging them with oil or moisturiser. This will help your system to discharge all energy impurities through your heels. Every morning and night, wash your feet under cold running water. This not only purifies your energy, but also stimulates biologically active points on the soles of your feet – you might be familiar with this idea through reflexology.

I recommend that my patients have pedicures for this reason. Dead skin carries information about death. Apart from this, remember that earth energy enters through your feet. So your feet should be beautiful gates of terrestrial energy! It's a great excuse for treating yourself to a little pampering.

How to neutralise the energy of jewellery and paintings

With the help of salt, you can cleanse, not only yourself and your house, but also your jewellery and pictures. This is very important, particularly if you have bought second-hand jewellery or if some-one has passed his or her jewellery on to you. You need to clean and neutralise the energy of the previous owner – you don't want to be wearing their aura along with their jewellery!

☆ Add one tablespoon of coarse salt to a glass of cold water.
☆ Place your jewellery in the glass.
☆ Put the glass in the fridge, as this will maximise the energy of the water. Leave it there for twenty-four hours.
☆ Remove the glass from the fridge, take your jewellery out of the glass and rinse it under cold tap water.

You can clean the energy of photographs or paintings in the following manner.

☆　Put the photograph or painting on a flat surface, so that the picture is facing upwards.

☆　Place a piece of paper on top of the photograph or painting and evenly sprinkle salt on top of the paper. Leave it like this for ten to fifteen minutes.

☆　Afterwards, either throw away the salt and paper outside or burn it.

The power of eggs

In Russia, eggs are held in deep esteem and they have always carried a huge magical importance in traditional healing. Virtually every Russian household would have a wooden egg or painted egg on display as a kind of amulet. Eggs are believed to symbolise newborn life, development and growth. They also stand for a state of purity; buried within the egg lies the potential for true divine power. The egg further symbolises conception, the start of life.

As well as having symbolic meaning, eggs are one of the most effective tools for absorbing spiritual and psychic negativity. The energy field around eggs is very strong, as the energy of life itself is concentrated inside it. This energy combined with the energy of growth creates very powerful, light frequencies around the egg. These frequencies help to disperse negative energy. Very often, houses would be cleansed by putting an egg in each corner of the house. It was strongly believed that the eggs would absorb all the negative energy. They would be left in the corners for seven days, after which they would be thrown away without being broken. However, eggs work only in the immediate area in which they are placed, as opposed to other substances used for cleansing energies in the home (such as salt, frankincense, candles) that can absorb energy from a wider area. So eggs are excellent for precise, localised cleansing.

Eggs, like salt, have been used in Russia for many generations – the methods are passed from one family to another. There are many, many wonderful and strange methods involving eggs, but most are extremely complicated and need a lot of expertise. However, this effective ritual is simplicity itself.

Egg bedtime ritual

If you have frequently disturbed sleep, or you see the same person again and again in your dreams, try this very old Russian ritual, using an egg.

☆　Take an egg and write your name on it with a pencil or pen.

☆　Place this egg on your bedside table, at the same level as your head.

☆　Allow it to stay there for seven days. If the egg cracks, which it will do if it absorbs too much negative energy, throw it away and replace it with a new one.

☆　When the seven days are up, throw the egg away without breaking it.

Important note: only ever use organic eggs for energy work.

CHAPTER TWENTY-THREE

Mirror Meditations

Mirrors provoke deep thought. When we look at our reflection in a mirror, it's almost as if we were submerging ourselves in our inner world. Looking at yourself in a mirror can be a meditation in its own right. It's as though we try to understand our true essence, our inner being, by looking deeply at our external self. Do we truthfully project our inner reality? Or, when we see our reflection in the mirror, do we see a completely different person, one we do not know, possibly even one who scares us? Looking into the mirror gives you the chance to ask yourself questions, to try to understand yourself, your actions and your decisions. You can ask yourself: how pure is my consciousness? How honest am I with myself? How honest am I with the people around me? Do you become the image you want to create for yourself, or the image you would like the people around you to see? It's as if you were looking into the very depths of your real self through the pupils of your eyes, trying to understand your true core. It gives a feeling of cleansing yourself and also of discovering your real truth.

Looking at yourself in a mirror and looking directly into your eyes is almost like confessing to yourself. A mirror is a window into another reality, one that is not fully controlled by our consciousness, but which is capable of influencing our lives. Women, in particular, often do this when they sit at their dressing tables – it's not vanity, it's soul-seeking in a very real sense.

Ancient wisdom states that a mirror reflects your soul. In Russia, there is one widely known superstition that says you should not look into a broken mirror, as this can provoke a break in your aura and life force.

I would like to describe a few effective methods of working with mirrors. These will supplement the work we have already done at balancing your astral body and, hence, your entire aura.

The choice and care of mirrors

Choose the mirrors with which you intend to work with care. Ideally they should be clean and new. Do not use old, antique and particularly not tarnished or cracked mirrors.

Mirrors are believed to absorb information from the environment, both positive and negative energy. For this reason, it was always the tradition to cover the mirrors in the house when somebody died – to prevent the mirrors absorbing the energy of death. So you must always clean your mirrors carefully before each use because, if you don't, they will act like a negative energy generator. Use a cloth made from natural materials, not synthetic and wipe in a clockwise direction. If you like, you can use a tiny bit of ammonia on the cloth to deepen the cleaning.

End of the day mirror exercise

This exercise helps to remove negative influences to the aura. It will help to overcome any sense of discomfort and unbalance you may have felt during the day. It will also lighten up any stress and purify your soul.

You should perform it at the end of each day and it should take about five minutes.

☆ Make sure your mirror is clean, then stand or sit in front of it.

☆ Now analyse your day while gazing into your eyes and

watching your facial expressions. Recall both the positive and negative emotions that arose during the day.

☆   You need to explore your reactions to certain situations, and discover if they were accurate or not. It's a way of putting closure on the day.

Mirror exercise to lighten your astral body

Once you are used to doing the preceding exercise, you can progress to a more advanced level of work with your mirror. This method will very powerfully clean your aura and lighten up and feed your "astral body".

You can use any mirror, either one hanging on the wall or one on a stand in front of you. Remember to clean it before use. Repeat this meditation over two days. If possible you should carry it out at 1 pm.

☆   Move towards the mirror, and stop when you reach a distance of approximately 30 cm.

☆   Look directly into the mirror, as far as possible without blinking, for ten minutes. Look into your eyes, deep inside them.

☆   Throughout this time, it is very important that you keep positive thoughts in your head (beautiful memories, heart-warming moments) or you can simply repeat your name over and over again.

☆   You can also listen to your favourite music, or any music that takes you back to pleasant events in your life. I personally find that music by Mozart has very positive effects during this meditation.

Flowers of love mirror meditation for attracting love

When we have love in our life, it neutralises all the negative emotions and energies inside and around us. Love gives a deep cleansing to all layers of our aura. Love is the most powerful nourishment and protection our bodies can have. There is a wonderful meditation, which comes from the ancient Russian tradition, that will help to attract love into your life.

If you feel sad or are lonely, or if you feel you simply cannot live one more day without love, you should practise this meditation. You will need two things for it: a medium-sized mirror and nine fresh flowers. These can be any type of flower (with the exception of lilies) although red roses are the best. If you do use roses, ensure you remove all the thorns from the stems. You can either pick them from your garden or buy them from a shop. Nature, in the form of flowers, is a huge source of love energy. Roses, as you probably know, symbolise love.

This meditation should be performed when you are completely alone. Switch off your telephone and do not answer the doorbell. Wear a loose robe so you can have easy access to your bare skin.

☆ Put the flowers in a big vase, placing the mirror next to them at a level so that you can see your face.

☆ Sit comfortably, or kneel, in front of the vase.

☆ Take one flower from the vase and start stroking your hair, forehead and ears with its petals. Then move down your cheeks to your chin.

☆ Allow yourself to open to the energy of love, which radiates from the flower.

☆ Close your eyes and stroke your eyelids with the petals, while saying out loud: "I can see love."

☆ Move the flower lower to the level of your nose and inhale the flower's aroma, allowing it to feed your soul. In a whisper, say: "I inhale love."

☆ Open your eyes and lift the flower above your head and pronounce: "Love is in my hands."

☆ Press the flower to your heart, so the petals are forced to open against your skin. Feel how the love that is locked in the flower flows into you. Then say clearly: "I feel love."

☆ Lightly touch your solar plexus (again, against your bare skin) and say: "I absorb love."

☆ Now, holding the flower in front of you, look at your reflection in the mirror, focusing directly on your eyes, ensuring that your attention does not waver. Now say the following words out loud: "In front of me, love. Behind me, love. Love is next to me. Love is above me. Love is under me. Love is inside me. I radiate love and love is coming my way. I glow with love."

☆ After you have finished this meditation, put the vase with the flowers in a place where you will see them always and pass by them frequently.

☆ If you like, you can carry the flower you used during the meditation with you until it dries. Then bury it in the ground, thanking it for its energy.

It is very important that, when you say these affirmations, your tone is strong and your words are definite.

PART EIGHT
**Rejuvenation
Secrets**

CHAPTER TWENTY-FOUR

The Rejuvenation Diet

People are always seeking to look younger, to live longer and better. The market for beauty creams and treatments promising fewer lines, fewer wrinkles and a taut body is immense. However, if you really want to rejuvenate yourself you need to look further than skin-deep. The good news is that, if you have followed the programmes I have given, for detoxing your home, body, mind and emotions, you will already be well on the way to rejuvenating yourself on all levels. In this section I'm going to give you more tools that will boost the work you have already done and pave the way for true rejuvenation.

In the next few chapters I'm going to look a little more deeply at diet. Let's hope that, with your intuition firing beautifully, you will no longer be making bad choices in your food. You will no longer be tempted to eat food that carries negative, or deathly, energy; food that pollutes and deadens your cells. Instead your diet should be giving you wonderful, life-enhancing energy.

We all know food is fuel – without food we have no physical energy and, left without food, we eventually die. But few of us really take the time to give our bodies the food they really need. If you want to cleanse your body and clear your mind, you have to pay attention to the food you put into your body, not just when you're detoxing, but on a regular basis. Remember too, that subtle energy is in everything.

So it goes without saying that your food should have the best possible vibrations. It should be living food packed with energy.

My firm belief is that we should be very careful about the food we eat. Much of the food that is available today is polluted food, dead food that emits no energy or, even worse, sick or damaging energy. Fortunately, it really isn't that difficult to eat well. All you need do is follow very simple rules.

Basic guidelines for healthy eating

I am going to give you a template for healthy eating. If you can shift your diet into this pattern, you will be giving your body the best possible nutrition and the best possible energy.

Ease yourself into these good eating guidelines. Don't demand too much of your body and your willpower by shifting everything at once. Make small changes and notice how much better your body feels with each one. This makes it easier to keep on fine-tuning your diet.

What to eat and drink

Wherever you possibly can, seek out the freshest, purest food – organic food if you can afford it as it is grown without damaging pesticides, fungicides and excess nitrates. Good food is fresh food, local food, seasonal food and safe food. Work with nature: food that grows in the season in which it was intended to grow is ideal for our health. Nature is clever: cooling salad crops in summer; hearty root vegetables in winter when we need warmth and bulk. I know it's tempting to buy strawberries in winter – but your body would be far happier with apples and pears!

☆ Make the most of fresh organic vegetables and fruits. Base your meals around these.

☆　Add in whole grains. Any whole grain is superb. I will explain later how best to cook grains for optimum nutrition.

☆　Beans and pulses are excellent – and even better when sprouted. I'll discuss sprouting in greater depth a little later.

☆　Nuts and seeds provide much-needed protein and are a great source of micronutrients.

☆　A little lean organic meat and game is fine in moderation, when you are not detoxing. Don't overload your system with meat, however.

☆　Fish is an excellent source of vital vitamins and minerals. Make sure it comes from non-polluted waters and is not an endangered variety. Seafood, unfortunately, can often be polluted.

☆　Plenty of fresh water – around 2 litres a day. Use a filter if you drink tap water. Buy mineral water in glass bottles, not plastic, to prevent bacteria.

☆　Alcohol should be taken strictly in moderation. Cut down on your alcohol intake as far as possible. Remember there is no alcohol at all on the detox programmes.

☆　Use cold-pressed olive oil for cooking. I particularly like Udo's Choice™ (which contains the Omega 3, 6 and 9 varieties of essential fatty acid sources), cold-pressed walnut oil and linseed oil for dressings or to add to grains.

☆　Fermented soya products, such as tofu or tempeh.

☆　Almond or rice milk and products (good alternatives to dairy and non-fermented soya products).

☆　Herbal and fruit teas. *Sbitin*, which I will discuss later, is a wonderful alternative – a warming spicy Russian drink.

☆　A little of what you fancy. I don't believe in demonising food so once in a while a little chocolate, or coffee, or whatever is fine. Just choose the best quality and purest you can – i.e. "real" potato crisps or "real" (not decaff) coffee.

You may think this sounds tough. Where are those nice convenience meals you pop in the microwave? How can you manage without a pitstop at McDonald's? Truly, it's easy. If you follow my plan and eat as much raw food as possible, you will spend barely any time in food preparation – a salad takes just minutes to prepare. Soups and juices are swift cooking too. Even traditional "slow-cook" foods such as grains and pulses can be made labour non-intensive, as I will show you.

What not to eat and drink

As I have said, I don't like to demonise food, or anything. I hope that now you have worked through my programme and rediscovered your powers of intuition, it's very unlikely that you will be tempted to eat dead or damaging food. It just won't be conceivable. But, I would like to give you some guidance, just in case. Remember, these are not "forbidden" foods, just foods and drinks that will not support your body or balance your energy.

☆ Caffeine: cut down and eventually cut out coffee, tea, sodas and chocolate. Caffeine stresses the adrenal glands and makes you tense and anxious.

☆ Processed food, "fast" food, convenience food and junk food: all these are "dead" foods, packed with toxic additives. Beware of E numbers! Also, remember that manufacturers now often use the whole name of an additive, to avoid using an E number. A rule of thumb is that, if the name is long and chemical, it's probably an additive.

☆ Fatty foods, such as sausages and pies: saturated fat clogs the arteries, and these foods are also usually packed with additives.

☆ Burned or barbecued foods: cooking food this way makes the food potentially carcinogenic – causing cancer.

☆   Salt: raises blood pressure, stresses the kidneys, encourages bloating.

☆   Processed "white" grains – white bread, pasta and rice: empty food that causes spikes in blood sugar levels.

☆   Dairy food – especially cow's milk products: dairy is highly mucus-forming.

☆   Soya milk products: again, soya products (apart from the fermented varieties) are very mucus-forming.

☆   Sugar and foods containing sugar: sugar provides empty calories and upsets blood sugar balance.

☆   Excessive alcohol.

Food as an energy carrier and sustainer

Food affects not only our physical health, but also our emotional and mental well-being. As I have already explained, you can be drained by other people's energy as well as by stressful external events. However, what most people don't realise is that you can also be drained and affected by food. It's not just a question of the nutritional content (or lack of it), but also a matter of the energy of the food you eat. Even if you use products that are enriched with vitamins, enzymes and have a good energy around them, you can still destroy all the goodness by incorrect preparation. Excessive heating can destroy the energy of food, as well as its nutritional content. I suggest you always try to avoid using high temperatures when preparing food. The only exception is pulses, which should be soaked overnight and then boiled swiftly. Grains can be cooked with the Russian oven method I give below. Eat as much as you can of your fruit and vegetables raw. If you must cook vegetables, lightly steam them.

Russian oven method for cooking grain

In Russia, grain symbolises life and we recognise that it is full of valuable vitamins and enzymes. It needs careful handling so we tend to cook our grains following this method.

When you are consuming grains, I would like you not only to absorb their nutritional goodness but also to be able to recharge from their energy. Over the centuries, grain (especially whole wheat grain and buckwheat products) have been praised throughout Russia and awarded a cult-like status. Up to now bread has been treated with huge respect and every Russian would cringe before throwing away bread.

I do not want to start going into the nutritional value of different grains, as I am sure you can find that in other books. I would like to focus on the energy of the food, and how to preserve it so you enrich yourself with it. Here is how to cook grain the Russian way.

☆　Before cooking any grain, soak it in plenty of fresh water for two hours.

☆　Discard the water and bring the grain to the boil in fresh water.

☆　Simmer for 5–7 minutes and then remove it from the stove, cover it with a tight lid and place in a pre-heated warm oven (150°C) for about 10–15 minutes.

☆　Add a little cold-pressed oil of your choice and it is ready for use.

It is especially beneficial to eat grains that have been sprouted. This is because a sprouted grain becomes a protein rather than a carbohydrate and so the energy of sprouted grains is much higher than ordinary grain. So I strongly suggest you add sprouted grains and seeds to your diet on a regular basis. They are an invaluable source of vitamins, minerals and universal life force. Sprouted seeds and grains are also less mucus-forming. Whenever you can, add uncooked sprouted seeds to your salads. I will talk about sprouting in Chapter 26.

Nowadays we tend to be obsessed with the nutritional value of food, and especially its calorific value. The energy qualities of food are kept in shadow. Food can have either a heavy or a light energy about it. It can carry information about life or about death. Food with bad energy can directly affect our own energy with its damaged vibrations. All refined preserved foods, with E numbers and additives, have a very heavy, empty energy about them. Then there are manufactured products, which claim to mimic the taste of the original natural products: the dense energy of these products can significantly clutter ours.

But don't become obsessive about your diet. As I have already said, I do believe it is okay to have junk food once in a while, providing it is the best quality junk food available. I know that sounds funny but what I mean is that, if for example you wanted a bag of crisps, make sure they are high-quality oven-baked crisps, made from potatoes, rather than some strange composite. If you would like chocolate, make it the dark organic choc-olate with the best, purest ingredients and no additives. If you crave butter, get the real full-fat butter. If you have to have a coffee, get a true caffeine coffee, as opposed to the decaffeinated variety. Always bear in mind that the technology used to restructure food can have harmful effects on the body, both physically and energetically.

I very strongly believe that everything is good in moderation. Just make sure you are always in touch with your intuition and let it act as your guide in knowing what to pick and what not to pick; when to eat and when to stop.

CHAPTER TWENTY-FIVE

Further Secrets of the Rejuvenation Diet

In this chapter I'm going to share some more useful information on how to ensure your diet is the very best it can be.

Cutting out pollution in our food

In an ideal world our food would all be pure, free from pollution, pesticides and other toxins. Sadly we don't live in an ideal world. Organic food seems to be the answer – on the whole it is produced without toxins but it is very expensive and not always readily available. So, if we want to live long and healthy lives, we have to be pragmatic and look at ways we can reduce our toxic load.

There are many kinds of toxins in our food: pesticides, herbicides, fungicides; excess nitrates; heavy metals (such as mercury and lead); antibiotics and hormones in meat – the list, sadly, goes on and on.

I don't want to alarm you but I do feel it's essential you know what goes into the food you most commonly eat.

Let's take, as just one example, the nitrate content in the foods we consume. Nitrate compounds consist of salts of nitric acid, which are major sources for plant growth and development. Nitrates have always been present in soil and have always been consumed by plants. However, alas, in the modern urge to increase soil productivity, we have over-fertilised the soil.

Plants are only able to process the absolutely necessary amount of fertiliser, so any excess ends up on our tables and inside our bodies. Unfortunately attempts to give up nitric fertilisers have been unsuccessful since the productivity and quality of vegetables would be greatly reduced.

Should we be worried about nitrate levels in our food? Yes, most certainly. Increased amounts of nitric acid in the human body have been suspected of having a carcinogenic (cancer-promoting) effect. In the digestive system of the human body, nitrates are transformed into nitrites, which are substances thirty times more toxic than nitrates.

Nitrites are also known to contribute to metahaemoglobin formation. This is a special form of haemoglobin, which is unable to supply body tissues with blood, thus distorting the metabolism and suppressing the immune system.

The food we eat can also be affected by the salts of heavy metals such as lead and mercury, carried into the earth by water containing the highly toxic wastes of industrial plants, car exhausts or poisonous chemicals used in agricultural processes. These and other impurities in our food, such as pesticides, have carcino-genic and mutagenic (affecting our genes) effects upon the human body. They can, in addition, cause allergies and generally weaken the immune system.

What can be done to reduce our intake of these numerous toxic substances? We are unable to determine or change the fertilising process in which our fruit and vegetables are grown. We cannot force farmers to stop using hormones and antibiotics in rearing animals for meat consumption. Buying organic is an obvious answer. However, if you can't buy organic food, don't panic. It is still better to eat non-organic fruit and vegetables than not to eat vegetables or fruit at all. Plus there are ways that you can significantly reduce the pollution.

☆   Soak all non-organic fruit and vegetables in water to which you have added a little salt. Then discard the water and rinse them under running water.

☆   Peeling vegetables and fruit will shed up to half the nitrates, pesticides, herbicides, lead and mercury.

☆   If you are cooking vegetables, cook them whole. Then slice or chop once cooked.

☆   Take off the outer leaves of cabbages, lettuces etc. Don't eat damaged greens – jettison any cut, broken or torn leaves.

☆   Choose fruit and vegetables that are fully ripe – fully ripened fruit and vegetables contain fewer nitrates than those picked before their natural time.

☆   Soured, pickled and marinated vegetables and fruits are practically void of nitrates, so make the most of these.

☆   Eat as little non-organic meat as possible. If you do eat non-organic meat, eat it alongside fresh green vegetables – the vitamin C will help offset any chemicals.

☆   Choose your fish carefully. Sadly a lot of fish is now polluted with heavy metals, such as mercury and lead. Eat less tuna for this reason. I no longer recommend fish oil to my patients and instead suggest they use Udo's Choice™ (readily available from health stores, or see the Resources section for online ordering).

The pH equation

There is one further tweak we can make to give us the optimum diet for health and rejuvenation – and that is paying attention to the pH of our food. This really is at the cutting edge of nutrition and I guarantee that the new buzz in eating will no longer be a debate about whether you eat carbs or not, or what the GI (glycaemic index) of your food is – instead everyone will be asking what pH your food is!

The pH of a substance is a measure of its relative acidity or alkalinity and is measured on a scale from 0 to 14. Anything above 7 is alkaline and anything below 7 is acid. For optimal health, the pH of your blood should be 7.4, in other words, alkaline.

When the pH of your body shifts too far to the acidic side, you tend to become ill, as all pathogens are bred in an acid environment. Excess acid accumulates in your bones and joints. One of the biggest problems with our bodies is the depletion of calcium and over-acidity. Sadly supplements won't help. It doesn't matter how much calcium you take in, if your body is still acidic the calcium will be used to try to stabilise the acid/alkaline equilibrium. It has been said, "You are not what you eat, but what you absorb". A stable pH helps you absorb food, vitamins and minerals in an optimum manner. It also will stabilise your emotions and reactions, as proven by much research.

In order to return to this balance and to maintain it, we need to watch our diet. Ideally the food that we eat every day should be 80 per cent alkaline and 20 per cent acidic. If you tend to exercise a lot, you can afford to increase the consumption of acidic foods – but don't overdo it. Almost all impurities and toxins in the body have an acidic nature to them. Therefore it is very important to counterbalance this with alkaline foods, fruits and vegetables. You may be surprised by some of the foods in the table below. Many people make the assumption that citrus fruits (for example) would be acidic because of their taste. You need to know that it is not the taste of the food that counts, but its effect on the body.

! Pregnant women should not consume unpasteurised milk products.

Herbs

Some herbs are known to be strongly acidifying or alkalinising. Obviously it makes sense to boost your diet with the alkalising herbs. You can add them freely to your cooking. However, should you wish to take any herbs in a concentrated supplement form, I would urge you to check with a health practitioner as some of them do have contraindications.

Acid, Alkaline and Neutral Foods

Acid Foods	Mild or Neutral Foods	Alkaline Foods
	Meat and Protein Substitutes	
Chicken	Fish	Tofu
Eggs		
Red meat (beef, pork)		
Seafood (lobster, oyster)		
	Vegetables	
Concentrated,	Acorn squash	Artichoke
cooked tomato	Butternut squash	Asparagus
sauce (pizza sauce)	Dried beans (kidney, lima,	Avocado
	mung, navy, pinto, soy,	Beet and
	white)	beet greens
	Aubergine	Cabbage
	Lentil	Carrot
	Potato	Cauliflower
	Pumpkin	Celery
	Sweet potato	Chard
	Yam	Cilantro
		Courgette
		Cucumber
		Garlic
		Grasses (such
		as wheat grass)
		Green beans
		Kohlrabi
		Leek
		Lettuce
		Lotus root
		Okra
		Onion

Acid, Alkaline and Neutral Foods

Acid Foods	Mild or Neutral Foods	Alkaline Foods
	Vegetables	
		Parsley
		Peas
		Pepper
		Radish
		Spinach
		Sprouts
		Taro root
		Tomato
		Turnip
		Watercress
	Fruit	
	Apple	Banana
	Apricot	Coconut
	Cranberry	Fig
	Grape	Grapefruit
	Mango	Lemon
	Melon	Lime
	Orange	Nectarine
	Papaya	Persimmon
	Peach	Sweet berries
	Pear	
	Pineapple	
	Plum	
	Sour berries	
	Tangerine	

Acid, Alkaline and Neutral Foods

Acid Foods	Mild or Neutral Foods	Alkaline Foods
	Grains	
White flour	Amaranth	Brown rice
White rice	Kamut	Buckwheat
	Oat	Millet
	Quinoa	Spelt
	Whole wheat	
	Milk Products	
Cheese	Butter	
Yogurt	Ghee	
	Milk	
	Nuts, Seeds and Legumes	
Peanut	Sesame seed	Almond
		Brazil nut
		Cashew
		Pumpkin seed
	Condiments	
Jam	Honey	Apple cider vinegar
Lard	Most oils (avocado, coconut olive, pumpkin seed)	Ginger root
	Rice syrup	Miso
	Sea salt	Molasses
		Seaweeds
		Soy sauce
	Beverages	
Carbonated drinks	Green tea	Mineral water
Fruit juices		Vegetable juices
	Miscellaneous	
		Baking soda

Strongly acidifying herbs

Cayenne pepper
Hawthorn berry
Pond lily bulb
Strawberry leaf

Strongly alkalising herbs

Alfalfa
Amla fruit
Black pepper
Gotu kola
Licorice
Nettle
Pau d'arco bark
Thyme leaf
Turmeric
Yucca root

Testing your pH

It is easy to check your pH level at home. Then you can monitor your acid:alkaline balance on a regular basis and be warned if you are slipping out of equilibrium. You will need to buy some pH testing strips (available from most chemists). You can use either saliva or urine for testing.

☆ Saliva: always check your saliva pH before breakfast. The normal range is a pH of between 6.8 and 7.5.

☆ Urine: dip the strip into mid-flow urine any time during the day except first thing in the morning. In other words, you should not test your first urination of the day.

How to test

☆ Take one strip and wet it with saliva or urine.

☆ Blue indicates alkalinity.

☆ Pink indicates acidity.

☆ There will be a colour strip given with your kit to gauge your precise score.

I recommend that you test the pH of your body once a week while you are trying to balance your pH. Once you have it at the right balance, you should test it once a month thereafter.

Egg alkaliniser

If you establish that you are too acidic, you should try this Russian method to help you become more alkaline.

☆ Take an organic egg and thoroughly wash it in water.

☆ Cook it for six or seven minutes.

☆ Peel the egg and put aside: it's the shell you need. Crush the shell until it becomes a fine powder.

☆ Every morning take 0.5–3 g (depending on how acidic you are) of this powder together with a few drops of lemon juice as calcium is absorbed much better with vitamin C.

Note: remember that although you might think lemon juice would be acidic, it actually has an alkalising effect on the body.

Kitchenware

Stainless steel or enamel pans are best for cooking. I personally never use aluminium pans in my kitchen.

Breathing yourself to balance

Not only do certain foods affect your pH, but also the emotions of anger, stress and anxiety tend to provoke the release of stress hormones, which shift your body's pH towards the acidic. When you feel calm and relaxed, it helps to stabilise the pH of the body. Obviously the exercises we have already discussed, such as the middle state of attention (pages 149–50), will help here. But I would also like to introduce you to a breathing technique – called the cleansing breath – that can help to balance the pH of the body, by reducing acidity and balancing the adrenal glands.

☆ Kneel down, resting your buttocks on your heels.

☆ Make sure your back is straight (but not rigid) and that your hands are resting gently on your knees.

☆ If you have back problems or this feels uncomfortable, you can place a small cushion under your buttocks.

☆ Breathe in deeply through the mouth, your lips formed in the shape of a tube.

☆ Then blast out your breath through the mouth, in brief exhalations, placing your tongue at the back of your teeth, producing the sound "th-th-th".

☆ While exhaling, slowly bend forwards until your forehead touches the floor just in front of your knees. You may find this hard. If so, just go as far as you comfortably can without straining.

☆ While breathing in through your nose, bring yourself slowly back into an upright sitting position.

Try to practise this cleansing breath about six times a day. It is also a very good exercise before and after any physical exercise.

CHAPTER TWENTY-SIX

Super-foods and Supplements

I do not tend to recommend that my patients take loads of supplements. Once you have cleansed your body so it can absorb nutrients in the optimum way, and providing you are eating a good, healthy, balanced diet, there should be no need. However, there are a few herbs I do recommend and also some very special foods – what I would call "super-foods".

The power of honey

First of all I would like to introduce you to one of the most wonderful secrets of Russian health – honey. In Russia we have a long tradition of using bee products for health and I would suggest you follow the example and start including these "super-foods" as part of your regular diet.

Beekeeping dates back to very ancient times. The knowledge was passed on, not only from generation to generation but also from state to state. In one of the birthplaces of civilisation, ancient Egypt, the bee was a symbol of the first dynasty of pharaohs and stood for submission and obedience to the will of the ruler. The Egyptians considered the beehive to be a model of a slave-holding state centred upon the rule of a pharaoh. "Nomadic" beekeeping was also first recorded here. Because flowers blossomed earlier in the south of Egypt, beehives were moved from Lower to Upper Egypt. No wonder the people of Lower Egypt chose the bee for their emblem.

Bee products (honey, propolis, royal jelly etc.) have been used by priests in their rituals virtually throughout the world. For example, in classical Rome honey was generously poured over offerings to the gods Bacchus and Asclepius. While Egyptians mummified the bodies of deceased rulers, the Assyrians waxed their bodies and immersed them in honey for preservation.

A bee faithfully accompanied many gods too, such as the Indian Krishna and the Greek goddess Artemis whose temple at Ephesus was considered one of the Seven Wonders of the ancient World. The priestesses in Artemis' temple were known as "Melissas", meaning bees. Not surprisingly the Ephesian coat of arms was adorned with the winged worker bee.

This insect was revered in ancient Indian mythology too. The supreme god Vishnu was often portrayed in the form of a bee.

The peoples of the Caucasus region were no strangers to beekeeping. In fact the members of Armenian communities living in the state of Uratu were accomplished beekeepers, making artificial hives from clay and twigs. The neighbouring peoples of Kara Bakh meanwhile fenced hollows in woodland to harvest honey and wax. According to an early written account, the mountains of Georgia were rich in hives. The Scythians, who inhabited Russia in the third and fourth centuries BCE, were famous for their trade in bee products.

In Kievan Rus (what is now Ukraine) special laws about beekeeping were recorded in early written annals entitled "Russian Truth". Honey was a popular product, not just on the domestic market, but also for export, to the northern Scandinavian countries and Britain, to the southern developed world of Greece and Rome, and even as far as Jerusalem where Russian honey had a far greater value than the locally produced variety.

Russian honey production reached its zenith in the latter part of the sixteenth and early seventeenth centuries, when the populations of whole villages were engaged in honey production and an individual beekeeper would keep from one hundred to one thousand hives.

Honey was a particular favourite of the Russian royal family and, indeed, in 1698 Peter the Great established his own beehives at Strelna, a small hamlet outside what was going to be become St Petersburg, the new capital. Peter's plan was that his new city would become the world capital for honey. He issued a decree that a lime tree should be planted in every courtyard within the new city of St Petersburg, in order to ensure continued honey production. The northern capital was soon producing a wide variety of rare honeys from an unusual array of flowers, such as lily of the valley, mignonette, lilac, and chrysanthemum, while honeys such as wild raspberry, strawberry and cherry were considered commonplace. Undoubt-edly the most sought-after were lime, maple and raspberry.

Use honey freely – to sweeten drinks, to add to salad dressings, as a glaze for vegetables and meats, or spread over bread or toast. Or simply stick your spoon in the jar! Just remember however that too much of a good thing can be bad for you.

! Use honey in minimum quantities if you are allergic to pollen, if you retain water or if you have high blood pressure.

Sbitin

One of the most delicious ways of using honey is in *sbitin*. There are many ancient recipes for this famous Russian drink, which is over a thousand years old. *Sbitin* (translated from Russian, it means "to whip" as in whipping cream or eggs) is a delicious, sweet and spicy drink consisting of water, honey, herbs and spices. This is a non-alcoholic drink, which for many years (up to the end of the nineteenth century), was a substitute for tea and coffee in Russia. Russian people drank *sbitin* throughout the day, but especially in the morning. It is not only refreshing but also hugely nourishing and invigorating; yet it does not include any artificial stimulants. I find it incredibly useful when suggesting people go on a detox, because so many people can't imagine life without hot drinks, such as tea and coffee. *Sbitin* is the answer – a hot, warming, comforting drink that also does you good. What more could you want?

Here's how to prepare the most common *sbitin.*

☆ Bring 1 litre of water to the boil.

☆ Add 100 g of honey, plus cinnamon, cloves, cardamom and ginger to your taste. You may, if you like, also add one peppercorn and three tablespoons of dried mint leaves. Boil these all together for thirty minutes.

☆ Sieve the infusion and serve. You can drink *sbitin* hot or cold.

If you do not have time to prepare fresh *sbitin* often, you can prepare a large amount of concentrated *sbitin* in advance and then dilute a couple of teaspoons (according to taste) with hot boiled water. This is a great way to use *sbitin* during the day at work.

Concentrated sbitin

☆ Bring 300 ml of water to the boil.

☆ Add one tablespoon of cloves, one tablespoon of cinnamon, one tablespoon of ginger, one tablespoon of cardamom, one tablespoon of nutmeg and two bay leaves.

☆ Bring this mixture back to the boil and take off the stove once it starts to bubble.

☆ Keep a lid on and leave for one hour.

☆ Sieve the infusion.

☆ Add 200 g of black treacle and boil the mixture again until it becomes dark red in colour.

☆ Let it cool so it's about 40 degrees (lukewarm).

☆   Add 500 g of honey and stir the mixture thoroughly.

☆   Pour into a sterilised jar and close the lid tightly. Keep the mixture in a dark cool place.

Every time you want to enjoy Russian *sbitin,* just add a teaspoon of this mixture to a cup of boiled water. For a richer or more concentrated flavour, just add a few more teaspoons – try it out and decide for yourself.

Dried sbitin

☆   Take one tablespoon each of the following: ground red pepper, ground black pepper, ground ginger, cardamom, cloves, nutmeg and cinnamon. Plus one bay leaf.

☆   Chop all the ingredients together, mixing well.

☆   Pour into a dry glass jar and close the lid tightly. Keep in a cool, dry place.

Now when you want to drink *sbitin,* bring water to the boil, add a teaspoon or so of the dried spice mixture and bring the water to the boil again. Let the drink cool for fifteen minutes before adding honey to taste. Once again, it's up to you just how spicy and concentrated you want the mix to be.

Sbitin is a useful ally in detoxing as it helps to warm and loosen all the mucus and toxins in the body. It is also a fantastic drink for the cold winter months in general. If you're feeling low due to a lack of sun, you can add one teaspoon of the herb St John's Wort to your spice mix.

! If you are on any medication check with your doctor before taking St John's Wort. It is not recommended, for example, if you are on orthodox antidepressants or the birth control pill, etc.

Or, simply do as we in Russia do, enjoy *sbitin* all the time!

Supplements for energy

In Russia we use certain herbs and fruits as vital tools for enhancing our energy. I often recommend these to my patients as part of their rejuvenation programme.

Tea

In Russia, tea was discovered not that long ago and was originally introduced as a present from the Mongolian Khan and praised as a treasure. Later, it was brought to Russia from China. From the nineteenth century, tea has been grown in Georgia and Azerbaijan. Since tea contains caffeine, I like to offer people alternatives. What has been used in the past as a warm alternative to tea (and which is still used by some Russians) is the zest of lemons and oranges infused in hot water. It's incredibly simple, yet very tasty and refreshing. Also, many Russians grow mint in their kitchens or gardens, which they also infuse in boiled water. These Russian alternatives to tea also work quite well to boost your energy.

Siberian ginseng

Ginseng has been known as a true tonic for thousands of years. In Russia, this magical root has mostly been grown in Siberia and is used a lot to boost the performance of sportspeople and to elevate the physical and mental energy of cosmonauts. If you need to reduce your stress and improve your ability to handle a busy lifestyle, ginseng supplements can offer a real helping hand.

Russian scientists have carried out numerous studies on the powers of ginseng supplements and have concluded that Siberian ginseng is an adaptogen, an ideal herb for all kinds of stress, due to its balancing affect on the adrenal glands. It is also widely known in Russia that Siberian ginseng increases the oxygen supply to cells and as a result, gives you more energy and a higher level of alertness. If you are going through a stressful period and need a good boost, I recommend that you take 200 mg of dried root ginseng once or twice daily. Please remember however, that you should never take ginseng on a continuous basis for more than three months in a row.

Make sure you buy Siberian ginseng (Eleutherococcus) – it is a completely different plant from Chinese or Korean ginseng, or American ginseng.

Rhodiola

Sometimes known as "Arctic root", rhodiola grows in the Arctic region of Siberia. It has been known in Russia for hundreds of years as an energy booster. As with Siberian ginseng, rhodiola is an adaptogen. I recommend that you take rhodiola supplements when you are feeling low (it's a wonderful natural antidepressant) and when you need to increase the sharpness of the mind. It has also been noticed that rhodiola boosts the immune system and has anti-carcinogenic properties as it is rich in antioxidants. Rhodiola is absolutely packed with vitamins; 200 mg of rhodiola rosea should be taken three times a day with meals.

Walnuts

In Russia, walnuts have been cultivated in monastery gardens for centuries. Nuts are highly effective as a fuel for the body because they are naturally rich in many nutrients as well the live energy of the sun. Walnuts, in particular, are one of the few plant sources of Omega 3 fatty acids (which help keep your heart healthy); they are also rich in plant sterols (which can help lower serum cholesterol levels), and a good source of fibre and protein. Plus they pack a hefty vitamin and mineral punch: vitamin E, copper, folic acid and magnesium. They also have very high antioxidant qualities. The walnut truly is the king of the nuts. In Russia, quite a few recipes exist that teach how to use nuts as a booster for the immune system and vitality. There are even rumours that Russian cosmonauts used to take a walnut paste and cream into space with them. I would like to describe a recipe, which I believe helps to improve the immune system of the body as well as rejuvenating and restoring energy.

☆ Mix together 500 g of finely chopped walnuts with 300 g of Manuka honey and 100 g of aloe vera juice.

☆ Once mixed, store in a tightly sealed glass jar in a cool dark space.

☆ Take one tablespoon, three times a day before your meal.

Sprouting

Sprouted seeds are a rich source of vitamins, minerals and phytonutrients. Soaking and germination release otherwise dormant enzymes and dramatically increase the micronutrient content of seeds. For example, vitamin C levels multiply five times in the three days following germination. Also sprouts are almost beaming with the energy of life itself. The seeds use this energy to grow and, when you eat the sprouts, you also absorb their unique and vibrant energy.

Sprouts are powerful rejuvenators primarily because of their high levels of antioxidants (which neutralise the free radicals responsible for much of the ageing process). I am a fierce advocate for all forms of sprouted seeds, beans and grains – alfalfa, radish, mustard, aduki, mung, quinoa, red clover, fenugreek, chickpeas, lentils and so on.

However, above all, I recommend broccoli seeds. Research into their amazing properties was carried out at the Johns Hopkins University Medical School in Baltimore, Maryland, (and published in the *Proceedings of the National Academy of Sciences*). This found that broccoli is rich in sulforaphane glucosinolate (SGS™), a precursor to sulforaphane. Sulforaphane is an extremely powerful antioxidant that triggers the production of an army of powerful antioxidants that can neutralise free radicals and help to detoxify cancer-causing chemicals. SGS™ was found to be twenty times more concentrated in young, three-day-old broccoli sprouts than it is in more mature broccoli plants. The effects are not only powerful, but also long lasting.

Sprouts are not just good for you, they taste great too. Add them to salads to provide a pleasant "crunch" – or just nibble on them as a snack.

How to sprout

You can buy sprouts from most good health stores or even order by Internet (see the Resources section). However, the best sprouts are those you grow and harvest yourself at home – because you can guarantee their total freshness.

Choose organic seeds and buy them in small quantities to ensure their freshness.

You can buy fancy equipment (web-sites selling kits are also listed in the Resources section), but this is not really necessary. All you need are a few large jars. You simply put a couple of table-spoons of dry seeds in each jar and cover the jars with mesh so water can drain out and air can circulate. You can use garden mesh or nylon net, secured with a rubber band. The aim is to grow them fast and eat them while they are young, fresh, with all their micronutrients intact. You will need to soak your seeds, pulses or grains for several hours to start the process – the amount of time will vary according to the sprout – for example, alfalfa, radish, mustard, fenugreek, red clover and quinoa need five to seven hours; lentils, aduki, mung beans and broccoli seeds need eight to twelve hours; chickpeas require about fifteen hours.

The jars should then be allowed to drain by keeping the jars tilted downwards at a 45-degree angle, so water can drain out and air can circulate. You can prop them on a dish-rack or similar. Sprouts are pretty tolerant and easy to grow but they do need warmth (though not direct heat) and to be protected from direct light while germinating (so don't keep them on windowsills or above radiators). If you have one, you can start them off in an airing cupboard. Rinse them twice a day (three times a day if the temperature is high which will make them grow faster). Always handle sprouts gently and be careful not to damage the growing shoots and leaves.

! Some people are allergic to sprouted grains and seeds. They should be avoided if you have lupus. If you are on the birth control pill or taking hormone replacement therapy, you should eat alfalfa sprouts in moderation due to their phytoestrogenic effects – if in doubt, check with a nutritional therapist.

Wheat grass

Wheat grass is another super-food and one I heartily recommend. Why? Because it is high in beta-carotene, vitamin K, vitamin B6 (pyridoxine) and calcium. Wheat grass is also a wonderful source of protein – it contains all the essential amino acids, in the right amounts needed by the body. It is also thought the chlorophyll in wheat grass may – in some way not yet understood – provide protection against DNA mutations.

Again, you can buy wheat grass from health stores or grow your own. Many people like to add it to smoothies, particularly at breakfast, when it gives you a healthy start to the day.

CHAPTER TWENTY-SEVEN

Ice and Cold for Energy

It may come as a surprise to you but cold and ice can be perhaps the most powerful way of rejuvenating your body and mind. In this chapter, I'm going to share with you the Russian secrets of rejuvenation using cold water and ice cubes.

Balancing using cold temperatures

In Russia, as much as we love the heat of the *banya*, we also love the cold! Our country can be cold, very cold, but we do not avoid this extreme of temperature, but rather revel in its health-giving benefits.

Mentions of the therapeutic use of cold temperatures have been found in Hippocrates, Avicenna and other early medical works. At the beginning of the seventeenth century, foreign ambassadors to Russia reported that Russian people would throw cold water on their naked bodies during the winter just after they come out of the *banya* or would even jump into a pile of snow and rub the snow into their bodies, as if it were soap. When Peter the Great visited Paris, Russian cadets demonstrated their hardiness to the Parisians, by swimming in ice water after *banya*. The French were amazed and came in droves to see the display. They were stunned to find that this seemingly crazy activity did not result in death or illness but, rather, increased the stamina and boosted the health of the cadets.

It's not just Russians either. Ancient religions in many parts of the world quite apart from Russia have recommended tempering the body with cold water. In Russia we have a specific word that translates as "tempering" – it means to toughen and strengthen your body through the use of cold and ice. There is simply no equivalent in English! Many temples would intentionally be built next to the vivifying waters of mountain or forest springs and rivers.

The famous philosopher, Plato, as well as Hippocrates, recommended cold water treatment as a vital part of medicine. Both strongly recommended it in their teaching.

A famous Russian commander, A. B. Suvorov (1730–1800) suffered from poor health from birth. However, he managed to live a full and effective life. He swore this was due to his habit of using cold water, habitually throwing a bucket of cold water over his body.

Many other Russians were fans of this treatment. Leo Tolstoy, the famous Russian author, was a big fan. In his house, in Ysnya Polyna, he had two special baths built for him. By the nineteenth century, the famous Russian physician G. A. Zaharyn became one of the first Russian doctors to teach his students the health benefits of cold water treatments. He believed that, no matter where you were in the world, you would always have access to water and that even the simplest use could do more for your health than any modern drugs. Modern naturopaths would agree.

So what happens during cold water treatment, or as we say in Russia, *morzevanye* (Russian slang for "walrus-like winter bathing")?

During exposure to cooling temperatures, the body responds with a series of consecutive reactions. In the beginning, we experience anxiety and the emotion of fear (a natural emotion with which we are born). This causes our adrenal glands to release the stress hormone, adrenalin, into our blood stream. This, in turn, makes our skin and blood vessels contract, while the blood vessels of the heart, brain and lungs open up. All these reactions are due to our body's attempt to prevent a change of temperature in our internal organs and to prevent them cooling. As a direct result, heart activity is activated. Blood pressure rises, supplying blood and nutrients to our muscular tissue and brain. All this assists the rising temperature of the body, optimising the flow of biochemical reactions, which gives additional energy to our body. At the same time, we experience an emotional burst because our blood receives increased levels of endorphins.

All this gives us a sense of perkiness and a new vitality. In addition, it repels toxic matter and even prevents the desire to overeat. It is also known to improve memory and concentration.

I recommend that, when showering or bathing, you always end up with a splash of cold water – even if it's only for a second. Start short and sharp, and gradually build up over time. It is very effective to combine cold water with gentle massage. I would like to describe to you how to take a cold steam bath – massaging with a cold patting technique.

! The following is not suitable for anyone with heart or circulation problems. If in any doubt, please consult your physician.

Cold water patting

This combination of water and gentle massage of the body has a very positive effect on the entire body and all its systems.

☆ Stand naked in your bathroom.

☆ Put one hand under running cold water and energetically pat the cold wet palm against your other dry palm, until both palms become slightly pink in colour.

☆ With one hand (up to you which one) continue to wet it under the tap and rhythmically and energetically pat your chest, arms and legs all the way down to the soles of your feet.

Salt water shower

This is another method which is very effective. This procedure, using cold salt water, not only helps with the "tempering" but also stimulates both physical and auric detox – it helps to clear the aura. Use this method either in the morning or evening.

☆　Prepare a bowl of water, slightly cooler than room temperature, and dissolve a tablespoon of sea salt in it.

☆　Dip your hands into the water and gently rub the salt water all over your body.

☆　Now rhythmically pat your skin all over, from top to bottom, always moving in the direction of your heart – i.e. from fingers to armpits; from feet to groin.

☆　Now take a shower. Women should take a quick shot of cool water and then a warm shower to enhance feminine energy. Men should take a warm shower first, and then follow with a quick shot of cool water to enhance masculine energy.

Working with ice

I would now like to describe one of my favourite and very effective ways of working with ice. This therapy has the power to strengthen the body and it also stimulates your endorphins (feel-good chemicals).

Endorphins are nature's universal painkillers and antidepressants. They calm you when you are over-excited and give you a boost when you're feeling emotionally depressed. Unlike drugs, however, they never disturb your perception of reality. They bring you into emotional balance. When you have enough endorphins, you do not expect anything bad to happen and, even if it does happen, you don't brood over it.

This course works wonders on hormonal problems and overeating. It also has fantastic results on depression and can be of enormous help to anyone suffering from addictions or who is in recovery.

I recommend you use this therapy with ice over a period of twenty-eight days. During this time, you should not take the following:

☆ Any stimulants such as coffee, tea, sodas.
☆ Heavy fatty foods, spicy foods, any excessive eating.
☆ Alcohol, narcotics.

If you take sleeping pills, try to wean yourself off them before going onto this programme. If you take antidepressants, again it is beneficial if you can finish your course and slowly come off them (under the guidance of your physician). Obviously this is something you will need to discuss with your doctor and it may be that it is not advisable to stop taking them at this time. If so, you can still complete the course but it will be less effective.

You should not interrupt the therapeutic course for longer than three days; if you do, then start again from the beginning.

! If you suffer from asthma or epilepsy or have any medical condition, please consult your physician before embarking on this programme. You will most probably be able to do it, but may need medical supervision.

Ice cube therapy

During this procedure you will be working with two points. One is on the coccyx, at the base of the spine. The other is at the Chinese acupuncture point known as *Fan Fu* (see the diagram overleaf). This point is the only point on the human body where it is possible to work directly with the brain. Directly underneath this point is the position of the medulla oblongata, which is responsible

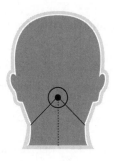

for the centres of breathing and blood circulation. Just above that area, deeper into the brain, lie the hypothalamus and pituitary glands. These centres of the brain are responsible for a huge number of functions in the body, energy metabolism controls, the immune system, the centres for pleasure and over-indulgence. Chinese doctors have, for the past two thousand years, stimulated this point using burning herbs (*moxa*). However, I think a stronger effect can be achieved using ice, as we do in Russia.

Week One

Repeat this procedure twice a day, in the morning and the evening. Two to four hours before you start the ice cube therapy, you need to fast – so no food at all, but you can drink water freely. Make sure the room in which you practise it is airy. Your sessions should last for about twenty-five minutes each. You will be lying on your stomach and concentrate on the therapy. Breathe slowly and do not be tempted to read or watch TV.

☆ Take an elasticated headband, bandage or tight hair ribbon and put it on your head, making sure that the lower part of the back of your head down to the top of your neck (where your neck joins your head) is covered.
☆ Gently pulling your hair up, lift your hair from the area described above.

☆ Lie on your stomach. Feel for the groove at the back of your neck with your fingertips. You will find it in the area where the neck leads to the head.

☆ Place an ice cube underneath the headband in the groove, sliding it up to the point where you can feel your skull. It will be in the region of the first neck vertebra. The ice cube should be in direct contact with the skin (with the exception of hair).

☆ Put a towel around your neck to prevent cold water from trickling down your neck.

☆ In the beginning, you will feel a very strong, uncomfortable and aching sensation. Bear with it because, after this initial discomfort, the aching will disappear and the ice will melt without further discomfort.

☆ Place a second ice cube on your coccyx (right at the very base of your spine, the tailbone down in the cleft of your buttocks). Fix it with an elasticated belt or piece of cloth. Put a towel underneath the coccyx, again to prevent water from dripping down.

Week Two

Repeat the morning procedure as for Week One.

In the evening, instead of using the ice cube on your coccyx, substitute a mustard plaster (or any plaster you can find at your local pharmacy which has been designed to warm up the skin). The area covered by the plaster should be approximately 2 cm x 2 cm. Alternatively you can use a hot water bottle. This temperature contrast between the upper and lower spine will greatly help the therapeutic effect.

! The skin on the coccyx is very delicate and cannot bear hot temperatures for a long time, so you can put some fabric or a towel between the skin and a hot water bottle. If this becomes uncomfortable, remove the hot

water bottle or the plaster – leaving just the ice cube in place for the duration of treatment.

Weeks Three and Four

Apply the ice cube only at the neck point, and only once a day, ideally in the morning.

Russian garlic infusion

While you are undergoing this powerful ice cube therapy, you can boost the effects by combining it with a Russian garlic infusion. This has been used for many hundreds of years by Russian healers to purify the blood vessels. It makes the blood vessels very elastic and flexible. Our bodies become rejuvenated and younger.

☆ Fill one-third of a 0.5 litre glass jar (only use glass containers) with 350 g of peeled and chopped garlic.

☆ Top it up with organic vodka.

☆ Cover and keep in a dark place for two weeks, shaking the bottle daily.

☆ After two weeks, the infusion is ready to consume. Take it every day during the twenty-eight-day ice cube therapy course. Dosage is five drops of the infusion diluted in a teaspoon of cold water, three times a day before each meal.

If you are worried about your breath smelling with so much garlic, you can chew a little fresh parsley to take away the odour.

You can also augment the effects of ice cube therapy by combining it with the "Inner Smile" exercise you will remember from the detox programmes (see pages 103–5).

Ice cube therapy creates a very strong, steady and habitual flow of blood to the brain, deeply nourishing the brain and all its functions long after you have finished the course. After your ice cube therapy course comes to an end, you can still apply ice to the neck area any time you need a boost, or simply want to enhance your positive emotions.

Energy exercises for rejuvenation

I will end with a few additional exercises that are very useful for recharging energy and enhancing rejuvenation.

The "Breath of Life"

P. K. Ivanov (1898–1983) was one of the most famous Russian proponents of healthy living. He was an incredible cult figure who taught the importance of good food, exercise and breathing. He was also a huge fan of cold and ice therapy: he used to walk barefoot in the snow! He taught his students the following breathing exercise, which he called "The Breath of Life".

☆ Go outside. Stretch your head gently upwards, looking up to the sky (don't overstrain your neck).

☆ Open your mouth and slowly inhale through your nose (it is important you inhale through the nose). Imagine you are drawing in air from the sky above.

☆ At the natural end of the inhale, instead of exhaling, swallow. This can take some practice so don't worry if you don't get it right straight away. As you swallow, visualise life energy of the inhaled air spreading right through your body.

☆ Exhale through the nose and repeat from the beginning.

This is a very powerful exercise and you should not perform it more than three or four times consecutively. However, it's perfectly safe (and very good for you) to come back to it at various times during the day. Not only does this exercise strengthen your aura, but also it can help you moderate your food intake! Simply practise it before each meal.

Recharging your energy using a candle

I would like to share with you two excellent exercises using candles. The first is a potent pick-me-up. I advise you use it on a regular basis and particularly if you are feeling tired or need some energy.

☆ Light a beeswax candle and sit next to it.

☆ Place your right palm above the flame so you can feel the heat but not burn yourself.

☆ Now move your hand above the flame as if you were trying to gather the flame into your hand – it's a scooping, gathering movement, as if you were scooping water up into your hand.

☆ When you feel you have absorbed enough energy into your palm, close your fingers, as if you were grasping the flame close.

☆ Twist your hand so your palm is facing upwards and then open your fingers. Imagine the energy of the heat you have taken from the ball; try to feel it in your palm.

☆ Imagine this ball as vividly and brightly as you possibly can. Then very delicately move your hand behind your back (still holding the image in your head and in your hand) down to the base of your spine.

☆ Now imagine that you bounce the ball and release it into your coccyx.

☆ The ball goes into your spine and unrolls itself up along your spine, like a carpet being rolled out or a ball of wool unravelling. As it moves up your spine it becomes a bright golden cord, like a ray of light. It shares its light with your spine and radiates energy out from your spine into the rest of your body.

☆ As it moves up your spine, the ball becomes smaller and smaller. When it reaches the top of your head (the crown chakra) it has become a golden dot. This dot is released through the top of your head.

The second exercise is useful if you feel weak or if you need to boost your immune system. Use it every day for seven days to empower your internal energy.

☆ Light the candle and place your palms either side of the flame, about 10–15 cm from the flame on each side. Your palms should be facing the flame.

☆ Breathe slowly, in a calm and relaxed way. Gradually let your breathing become deeper and deeper.

☆ With each inhale, imagine the energy of the flame enters your palms. With each exhale, the energy travels down to your solar plexus.

☆ Keep up this breathing and intake of energy for no more than five minutes.

Conclusion

My sincere hope is that, having worked through my programme, you will have discovered your unique energy identity. Your personality should never get lost and should never be melted into other personalities. Each and every one of you should treasure your self and maintain what you have. A choir sings harmoniously and beautifully because each and every member of that choir has his or her own part, his or her own voice. When you join your voice with the bigger choir, never forget that your voice is unique and always try to maintain your own inner heart-felt sound. That way you maintain your identity as a vital part of the whole.

To protect your individual vibration, you need to pay careful attention to your energy, listening to what it requires for its own natural harmonious development. Maintaining your own vibration is a vital prerequisite for a balanced life. It is also totally necessary for your health – remember that healthy energy equals a healthy body. Illnesses and diseases always have their roots in your submersion into alien, different, destructive vibrations.

Everyone has a life task, which has been selected individually, just for them. This task may be difficult but it won't be impossible – nobody is given more than they can handle. However it will push you, and the way you deal with your life, your task, will push your soul to grow further.

Remember, too, that nothing unfair will be given to you. If you find problems or difficulties arising in front of you, they are there to be overcome, and rest assured that you have the means of overcoming them. Ask yourself: what can I learn from this? Never give up. Never submit to the problem.

In Russia there is a joke about two frogs that fall into a jug of milk. The first frog swiftly gives up hope and allows itself to drown. The second frog, however, starts paddling its legs furiously, and keeps going on and on, even though the situation seems quite hopeless. After a while the frog feels something hard underneath its legs and quite soon it is able to jump out from the jar. What had the frog done? It had whipped the milk and created butter!

Of course there are some times when it's sensible to be submissive and surrender, but there are also times when we need to take action to change things. You need to follow your intuition to find out when patience is the only solution and when you should not waste time but rather get cracking and act as fast as possible.

There is no universal recipe and there never will be one. The only helping voice is the voice of your consciousness and your deep intuitive feelings. Submissiveness and activity are two different polarities of our behaviour, just as rest and movement are. Never undermine either of them, as they are both equally important. On the whole, personal freedom is locked in a discovery of the unique way you solve your life tasks. For each person, his or her life is like a creation of art. It can be created in different styles and genres but you must have the freedom to create it for yourself. You should never copy or mimic others, but instead listen to the gentle sounds of your own soul. Only then will this art have its value. By harmoniously express-ing yourself in your own life, you contribute to the world, so it can blossom and evolve.

Now you have reached the end of this book. In Russian, we have an interesting word root: *iskhod*. One of its meanings is "the final";

however, in the phrase *iskhodnaya tochka*, it also means "the point of a new beginning". So, although you have reached the end of this book, I hope that this will also signify a new beginning for you – *iskhodnaya tochka!*

Finally, I would like to share with you the best definition of a teacher that I have ever come across. Imagine that you have lost your way in the woods and that you meet a teacher. You say: "I'm lost, please show me the way." The teacher guides you in the right direction; so you follow that direction and the teacher goes off on his/her way. I hope that the knowledge I have shared with you will be that sort of guide for you, as it was – and still is – for me. May it help you in your own homecoming and encourage you to step onto your unique path.

Good luck on your journey.

Appendix: Two Tunings

I will describe two tunings. The first is called *Healthy Spirit*; the second is called *Healthy Way of Life*. As far as I am aware, this is the first time G. N. Sytin's tunings have been translated into English.

How to use tunings

These tunings have been carefully translated from the Russian. They may sound strange to you on first hearing but they are not intended to be poetry! The repetitions and hyphenated words are intentional. So too are some sentences that are extremely long. Tunings are not spoken in a normal way but chanted, in a monotonous tone and rhythm, rather like monks intoning a prayer – they are a form of meditation. Practise until you find yourself almost falling into a hypnotic state when you say them.

You will use one or other of these tunings throughout the cleansing programmes in Part Four. However, you can read them to yourself on a daily basis at any time – whether you're sitting on a bus or lying in bed just before going to sleep. The very best of all would be to read them out aloud to your family. Try to memorise the tunings so that you can boost your energy and re-attune your thought processes whenever you feel the need, simply by saying one to yourself. Alternatively, a good idea is to tape yourself saying them so you can play them to yourself anywhere – on the way to work, or at any quiet period during the day.

Tuning 1: *Healthy spirit*

This is an excellent tuning for general strength and health. It is used in the colon, liver and kidney phases of the cleansing programme.

*New healthy newborn life is pouring into me and I am being filled
with new-new healthy newborn life.
Enormously strong newborn life is pouring into my head.
An enormously strong young soul is being born in me.
An enormously strong healthy spirit is being born within me.
An immense enormously strong healthy spirit
is being born within me.
An invincible healthy spirit is being born within me.
I am trying to understand it as deeply as I can.
An invincible healthy spirit is being born within me.
The healthy spirit brings forth healthy-healthy thoughts.
The healthy spirit brings forth healthy-healthy thoughts.*

*An enormously strong life-creating newborn life
is pouring into my head.
An enormously strong young soul is being born within me.
An invincible healthy spirit is being born within me.
The healthy spirit creates life: the healthy spirit
gives birth to healthy-healthy-cheerful thoughts.
The healthy spirit brings forth healthy-healthy-cheerful thoughts.
The healthy spirit gives birth to new-renewed-
healthy-cheerful-happy thoughts.*

*An enormously strong life-creating newborn life
is pouring into my head.
An enormously strong newborn young innocent soul is being born
within me.*

A healthy-healthy-cheerful-innocent soul is being born within me.
A cheerful-happy young soul is being born within me.

The newborn-young soul brings forth a
young healthy strong head.
The young soul gives birth to a healthy-strong head.
The invincible healthy young soul gives birth to a strong-healthy
head, gives birth to new-healthy-happy thoughts, new
young-youthful thoughts, new young-youthful thoughts.

The whole soul is filled with bright healthy-cheerful thoughts.
The whole soul is filled with bright healthy-happy thoughts.

An enormously strong youthful soul fills my
head with colossal life energy.
Huge colossal life energy is pouring into
all the brain mechanisms.
Huge colossal life force is pouring into all the brain mechanisms.
Huge colossal life force is pouring into all the brain mechanisms.

All the brain mechanisms are born healthy and strong.
The young soul produces healthy brain mechanisms.
The healthy spirit gives birth to healthy-healthy brain mechanisms.
The healthy spirit gives birth to strong-healthy nerves.
The healthy spirit gives birth to a healthy-
strong nervous system.
The healthy spirit gives birth to a healthy-
strong robust nervous system.

A colossal strength of spirit is being born within me.
A colossal strength of spirit is being born within me.
An invincible healthy spirit is being born within me.

The healthy spirit gives birth to a healthy-strong body.
The healthy spirit gives birth to a healthy-strong stout head.

An enormously strong young soul is being born within me.
An invincible strong young soul is being born within me.
A playful-cheerful young soul is being born within me.
A playful newborn young happy soul is being born within me.
Total dominance of spirit over body is being born.
The healthy spirit gives birth to a strong healthy head.
The healthy spirit gives birth to healthy-cheerful-happy thoughts.
The healthy spirit gives birth to
cheerful-cheerful-healthy-happy thoughts.
An immense, colossal life-creating newborn life
permeates my head.

A colossal energy of life permeates my head.
My head is permeated with colossal and
irrepressible energy of youth.
The healthy spirit gives birth to young
healthy happy thoughts.
A healthy, young, playful soul is being born within me.
A cheerful-happy playful soul is being born within me.
A newborn-youthful innocent soul is being born within me.

A newborn-youthful irrepressibly healthy soul is
being born within me.
An irrepressible healthy spirit is being born within me.
The healthy spirit gives birth to a healthy-strong head.
An enormously strong young soul gives birth to
energetic-strong brain mechanisms, gives birth to energetic
strong brain mechanisms, gives birth to energetic-strong healthy
brain and spinal cord.

The healthy young soul gives birth to a healthy strong-robust
nervous system, gives birth to a healthy-strong head.
My head is filled with colossal irrepressible energy of youth.
An energetic-strong head is being born.
An energetic-strong head is being born.

An immensely strong life-creating newborn life
permeates my head.
A newborn young courageous-strong-willed-daring
soul is being born within me.
A strong-willed-daring soul is being born within me.
I am born a daring, assertive, confident person.
I am born a daring, assertive, confident person.
I am bold and I can do anything.
I can control my thoughts and my feelings.
I know firmly for a fact that I can control my thoughts,
I can control my feelings.
Total dominance of the spirit over thoughts is being born.
Total dominance of the spirit over feelings is being born.

An immensely strong young soul is being born within me.
An invincible healthy young soul is being born in me.
A cheerful-playful-cheerful-playful young soul is
being born in me.
A newborn youthful innocent cheerful-happy-playful
soul is being born within me.

A merry twinkle shines in my eyes; a sunny, bright,
spring-like smile is on my face.
The youthful soul gives birth to a young
handsome and innocent face.
The young soul gives birth to a young handsome innocent face.

The young soul gives birth to young, innocent, beautiful eyes,
strong-willed and intelligent eyes.
An enormous strength of spirit shines in my eyes.

Total dominance of the spirit over thoughts is being born.
I have total control over my thoughts and my feelings.
I have total control over my state.
I am a person with a strong will, an all-conquering strong will.

Strong will shines in my eyes, an immense strength of spirit shines
in my eyes, and all the people who deal with me are aware of the
strength in me.
A strong-willed and bold soul is being born within me.
A courageous-bold soul is being within me.
I am born a bold, self-assured person.
I dare to do anything and I can do anything.
Total dominance of spirit over body, total dominance
of spirit over thoughts is being born.

The healthy spirit gives birth to a healthy strong, robust body.
The healthy spirit gives birth to a strong,
healthy, Herculean body.
I am filled with mighty, healthy Herculean strength.
An immensely strong young soul turns me into
a born-again young person possessed of immense strength.
Herculean strength is being born within me at this moment.
Panache is being born within my soul.
Herculean strength is being born within me.

An immense life-giving newborn life is pouring into my head.
An invincible healthy spirit is being born within me.
The healthy spirit creates life: the healthy spirit gives birth to

young-youthful cheerful thoughts, cheerful-happy-healthy thoughts.
All my soul is filled with healthy-cheerful-happy thoughts.
I am being born cheerful-energetic-cheerful.
A cheerful fire flickers in my eyes.
A sunny bright spring-like smile is on my face.
The soul is singing from happiness and the joy of life.
All the internal organs become more cheerful, more joyful,
and more cheerful-energetic.
Joy and good cheer fill my heart.
Joy and good cheer fill my heart.
The young soul gives birth to a cheerful-cheerful-happy heart.
A cheerful-cheerful-laughing heart.
A cheerful-cheerful heart roaring with laughter.

The healthy spirit gives birth to a strong
and healthy young heart.
The healthy spirit gives birth to a Herculean healthy heart.
A hugely strong, Herculean heart is being born.
The heart is keenly aware of its Herculean strength.

I am running, I am flying like a bird, my breath is light and
free, I am running, I am flying on wings like a bird: I am keenly
aware of my youthful elan, I am keenly aware of
my Herculean strength.
A newborn youthful innocent soul is being born within me.
An immensely strong youthful soul is being born within me.
An invincible healthy youthful soul is being born within me.
An invincible healthy young soul is being born within me.
The healthy spirit creates life: the healthy spirit gives birth to
youthful, healthy, cheerful-happy thoughts.
The soul is filled with cheerful-happy youthful thoughts.
I am keenly and clearly aware of myself as newborn-young

cheerful-happy.

The soul is filled with bright dreams of future happiness.
An invincible strong spirit is being born within me.
An immense strength of spirit is being born within me.
Total dominance of spirit over body, total dominance of spirit over thoughts is born within me.
The healthy spirit gives birth to healthy-cheerful-cheerful thoughts.
The healthy spirit gives birth to healthy-healthy-cheerful thoughts.
I am young-cheerful invincibly healthy thirty years on and beyond.
Fifty years on and beyond I will be young-cheerful, invincibly healthy.
In a hundred years time and beyond I will be a young, young-cheerful invincibly healthy Hercules with a powerful physique.
With my inner vision I see ever more clearly and vividly myself in thirty years time, in fifty years time and further on as young-cheerful, young-cheerful invincibly healthy person
and it fills me with the joy of life.
My life is ever more cheerful-cheerful-joyful, a merry twinkle shines in my eyes, my whole body exudes colossal energy, I am filled with colossal inexhaustible energy of youth.

Tuning 2: *Healthy Way of Life*

This is the tuning we use in the preparation phase of the cleansing programme. It is wonderful for boosting your willpower and determination to succeed in starting to create a healthy life and overcome any unhealthy habits. It will help you to alter your eating habits and to start the new programme. You might be surprised at how vehemently it decries the use of alcohol. However, I have found that many of my clients really do find the idea of giving up alcohol – even for a few weeks – totally daunting. I am very strict when it comes to alcohol on my programme because it really does affect the treatment. If you know you have any other addiction – sugar, drugs, caffeine etc. – you can carefully reword the tuning to reflect this. However, for your first use of this tuning, I would recommend that you try it just as it is.

Steely strength, steely strength, steely strength is pouring into my psyche, in all my nerves.
Strong steely strength is pouring into my personality.
Invincible spiritual strength is pouring into me.
I am a person of invincible steely will.
Invincible steely will shines in my eyes and all the people who deal with me feel it.
I am a bold and self-assured person, I dare to do anything and I can do anything and I am not afraid of anything.
I stand like a rock in the midst of all the hurricanes and storms of life, which break against me.
I firmly know that if all the problems come down on me suddenly and at once, they will still be unable to crush my powerful will.

So, I look the world in the face without being afraid of anything and I stand for a healthy way of life amid all the adverse forces.
Every day I stubbornly tune myself in to a healthy way of life, I constantly overcome all the forces that stand in the way and that are trying to upset my healthy way of life, I create a powerful support to my healthy way of life, I create powerful protection for my healthy way of life.
I have bitter and ferocious hatred of everything that hinders my healthy way of life.
I am ever ready to fight and overcome all the harmful influences that are trying to push me into the abyss of alcoholism.
Alcohol is my most dangerous and treacherous enemy that is destroying my health, paralysing my will, depriving

*me of my human dignity and turning me
into a creature despised by people.
I firmly know that I remain a person and keep my will only as long as
not a single drop of alcohol has got into my body.
So, I will not drink a single drop of alcohol and no cajoling on the
part of drunkards will divert me from my sober way of life.
I know firmly that a person inspired by the idea of recovery is more
powerful than all the natural elements, all the adverse forces, and
a person who in defiance of the adverse influences sticks to the
healthy way of life.*

*I look forward to an energetic, healthy young life now, in ten years
time, in thirty years time and in fifty years time.
I am committed to constantly building up the effort of my will in
fighting for a healthy way of life and thus constantly increase the
strength margin of a sober way of life.
I am growing stronger than all the counteracting forces, which are
destroying my commitment to a sober way of life.
I am constantly strengthening my commitment to a sober way of life
and no harmful influences can destroy my commitment
to the sober way of life.*

*I feel that I am growing healthier and stronger and it fills my whole
being with the joy of life.
I have many years of a happy young life before me and it fills me
with triumphant strength of youth.
An irrepressible cheerful fire always shines in my eyes, the sunny joy
of life shines in my eyes.
My whole body exudes powerful energy; all my internal organs
are working energetically and cheerfully, all my internal organs are
working with great panache.*

My walk is springy, cheerful and brisk, I walk as if I were a flying bird, I am keenly aware of my youthful elan.

In the face of adversity I steadily preserve my well-being and my cheerful and optimistic mood.
I become more cheerful, more cheerful-optimistic with every passing day.
There is always a cheerful smile on my face, spring is always blossoming in me and a sunny joy of life fills my soul and body.
There is always an irrepressible cheerful fire burning in my eyes.
Irrepressible steely will is shining in my eyes.

I am a bold person, assured of myself, there is nothing I do not dare to do and I can do anything and I am not afraid of anything.
I can lead a healthy and sober way of l ife contrary to all the adverse forces.
I feel that I am immeasurably stronger than all the harmful influences.
All my life is filled with the joy of constant triumphs over all the obstacles.
I become more cheerful and optimistic every day.

Further Reading

Anatomy of the Spirit: The seven stages of power and healing by Caroline Myss (published by Bantam)

Balancing Your Chakras: How to balance your seven energy centres for health and wellbeing by Sonia Choquette (published by Piatkus Books)

Body Balance: Vitalize your health with pH power by Karta Purkh S. Khalsa (published by Twin Streams Health)

Chakras: Balance your energy flow for health and harmony by Patricia Mercier (published by Godsfield Press)

Colour Power by Philippa Merivale (published by Vega Books) (www.color4power.com)

Hands of Light: Guide to healing through the human energy field by Barbara Ann Brennan (published by Bantam)

Light Emerging: The journey of personal healing by Barbara Ann Brennan (published by Bantam)

Spiritual Nutrition: The Rainbow diet by Gabriel Cousens (published by Cassandra Press)

Water and Salt: The essence of life – The healing power of nature by Barbara Hendel & Peter Ferreira (published by Natural Resources Inc.)

Wheels of Life: A user's guide to the chakra system by Anodea Judith, (published by Llewellyn)

Yoga in Practice: A complete system to tone the body, bring emotional balance and promote good health by Katy Appleton (published by Macmillan)

Zest for Life by Dawn Breslin (published by Hay House)

In addition to the resources listed above, there are some amazing Russian naturopaths and healers whose work is not known in the West. Throughout the book I have tried my best to introduce you to their techniques and wisdom; if you are a speaker of Russian you could also look out for the published works of N. Semyonova, A. Balaz, Y. Ivanov, G. Malahov, S. Jacovlev, V. Lobodin, S. Rozov, P. Uspenskiy, S. B. Nikitin, A. Levshinov (www.levshinov.ru)

Resources

You can find more details of my work, talks and retreats on my website (www.allasvirinskaya.com)

If you would like to work with a healer on a one-to-one basis, I suggest you get in touch with the National Federation of Spiritual Healers (www.nfsh.org.uk) who can put you in touch with healers in your area or arrange distant healing. The College of Psychic Studies (www.collegeofpsychicstudies.co.uk) also offer a wealth of resources and courses.

The following websites might prove of interest.

Promoting health

Dr Nikolay M. Amosov's website www.icfcst.kiev.ua/Amosov has fascinating information on ways to promote health.

Bells (*kolokol*)

www.russianbells.com is informative and interesting; it also has information on how to buy bells – but these are the large ones for church use.

www.easternchristiansupply.biz sells Russian bells, censors, incense, charcoal and egg decorating kits.

Enemas and pH strips

You can buy enema kits from chemists or order online from websites such as www.e-enema.co.uk.

pH strips are available from chemists – or you can order online at websites such as www.ph-ion.com.

Clay

Eytons' Earth is a great source of information on clay: www.eytonsearth.org.

Phybiosis is another informative website on clay: www.phybiosis.com.

Banya

The nearest you can get to Russian *banya* in the United Kingdom are Victorian Turkish baths: see www.victorianturkishbath.org for a list of baths around the country.

www.living-foods.com, which has useful information on raw and living foods, also includes a section on Russian *banya*.

If you fancy trying to build your own *banya*, see www.rusbanya.com.

Eggs and Russian artefacts

www.therussianstore.com has a large selection of decorated eggs.

www.therussianshop.com has many Russian artefacts.

Beekeeping and honey

www.beedata.com gives information on beekeeping and books on the history of beekeeping.

www.apitherapy.com is also a good resource on all aspects of apitherapy (the therapeutic use of bee products).

Sprouting

For more information on the science behind broccoli sprouts see www.broccosprouts.com and its links to Johns Hopkins University.

www.wholisticresearch.com provides sprouting equipment in the United Kingdom.

www.sproutpeople.com is a US website with a wide variety of seeds and equipment.

Udo's Choice™ oil

This is available from most health stores. For more information and details on ordering it online, see www.udoerasmus.com.